THE
INVESTMENT
TRUSTS
HANDBOOK

2023

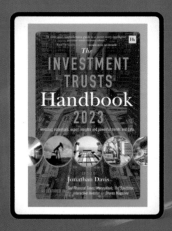

THE
INVESTMENT
TRUSTS
HANDBOOK

2023

*Investing essentials, expert insights
and powerful trends and data*

EDITED BY
JONATHAN DAVIS

**Harriman
House**

www.ITHB.co.uk

HARRIMAN HOUSE LTD
3 Viceroy Court
Bedford Road
Petersfield
Hampshire
GU32 3LJ
GREAT BRITAIN
Tel: +44 (0)1730 233870

Email: enquiries@harriman-house.com
Website: harriman.house

First published in 2022.

Hardback ISBN: 978-1-80409-036-7
eBook ISBN: 978-1-80409-037-4

British Library Cataloguing in Publication Data
A CIP catalogue record for this book can be obtained from the British Library.

www.ITHB.co.uk

CONTENTS

INTRODUCTION

Another year of great drama

AFTER THE EUPHORIA that gripped many investors as the Covid virus receded in 2021, it has been back to earth with a bump in 2022. Instead of a global pandemic to contend with, the financial markets have instead had to come to terms with two phenomena which many of us had hoped we would not see again in our lifetimes – inflation spiralling out of control and the desperate sight of Russian tanks rolling uninvited into a neighbouring country's territory.

The Russian invasion of Ukraine is a shocking reminder that peace in Europe can never be taken for granted. President Putin's calculated decision to weaponise his country's oil and natural gas resources at the same time, sending the price of oil and gas to unprecedented levels and triggering a likely recession, is a painful reminder that the West's whole way of life remains dangerously dependent on the availability of affordable energy. The inflationary shock that the Russian leader inflicted on Europe unfortunately only compounded what was already becoming a serious failure by complacent governments and central banks to head off an incipient inflation crisis of their own making. This latest edition of *The Investment Trusts Handbook*, now in its sixth year, chronicles the dramatic impact of these two developments on investors' experiences:

- sharp falls at the same time in both equity and bond markets;
- dramatic increases in bond yields and interest rates, reversing a trend that has endured for 40 years;
- a notable widening of investment trust discounts across most sectors of the investment trust universe;
- continued rotation in investment styles and a reversal in fortunes for many of the previous biggest winners winners;
- the effective closure of the trust IPO market; and
- political drama in the UK with the departure of Boris Johnson, the British prime minister, followed shortly by that of his successor Liz Truss, and a subsequent crisis of confidence for the pound and gilts.

As we have noted in previous editions, one of the great strengths of the investment trust sector is its ability to adapt to a changing environment, but this year's unique and ugly combination of events undoubtedly represents the biggest set of challenges

abrdn

To invest with confidence, seek out experience.

abrdn Investment Trusts

Now more than ever, investors want to know exactly what they're investing in.

abrdn investment trusts give you a range of 21 carefully crafted investment portfolios – each built on getting to know our investment universe through intensive first-hand research and engagement.

Across public companies, private equity, real estate and more, we deploy over 800 professionals globally to seek out opportunities that we think are truly world-class – from their financial potential to their environmental credentials.

Allowing us to build strategies we believe in. So you can build a portfolio you can rely on.

Please remember, the value of shares and the income from them can go down as well as up and you may get back less than the amount invested.

Request a brochure: 0808 500 4000
invtrusts.co.uk

the sector has faced since the global financial crisis. While I have no doubt that investment trusts will once again rise to the occasion, it will require patience and fortitude from shareholders and resolute action from boards of directors.

Spreading the word

The Investment Trusts Handbook is an independent editorial publication in which we look to pull together all the most important developments of the past 12 months into a single, handy reference volume. It has already been bought or downloaded more than 45,000 times, and the publishers and I remain grateful for your continued support.

The 2023 edition follows a now-familiar pattern:

- a detailed review of the last 12 months by our resident experts;

- a look ahead to an unusually uncertain future and what it may bring;

- Q&As and conversations with a selection of analysts and fund managers;

- my own thoughts on the year just gone and the one that lies ahead;

- reviews of the model portfolios I monitor for readers; and

- a detailed how-to/data section at the end of the book.

This year's *Handbook* includes articles by the usual mixture of new and regular contributors, as well as features about a number of individual trusts. The forum features five of the best-known professionals who analyse or invest directly in investment trusts. As always, the data and analysis sections have been completely revised and updated.

I am happy to report that many of the readers of the *Handbook* now also listen to the free *Money Makers* investment trust podcast that I record each week. We have now clocked up more than 150 episodes. Simon Elliott, the knowledgeable and articulate head of investment trust research at Winterflood Securities, has moved on to an important new job elsewhere and is no longer able to share his expertise each week, but I have been fortunate to introduce some brilliant replacements and listener numbers continue to rise.

Several hundred of you also now subscribe to the *Money Makers Circle*, a subscription service which, for a modest monthly or annual fee (equivalent to £2 a week), gives you access to a range of content relevant to an investment trust investor. These include in-depth profiles of more than 50 trusts, regular summaries of the latest results and market movements, interviews with fund managers and analysts, portfolio updates and commentary by myself and others.

You can find out more about both the podcast and the subscription service from the *Money Makers* website (www.money-makers.co). Thanks also to the many subscribers who have come up to introduce themselves at events where I have been a speaker, including the annual Master Investor show and the Mello trust and fund seminars.

Still the connoisseur's choice

For reasons that have been well rehearsed here and elsewhere, investment trusts remain the connoisseur's choice when it comes to selecting investment funds. There are good ones and bad ones, just as in any field of activity, and turbulent periods like the last 12 months pose specific difficulties because of the way that discounts can widen dramatically in times of market weakness, as they have done so far this year.

The risk of discount volatility has been regularly flagged in past editions of the *Handbook* and those who have followed my thoughts in the *Money Makers Circle* will know that I have been advocating a much more defensive posture since the end of last year, given the excesses of monetary policy and the unsustainably strong performance of almost every kind of asset over the past low interest rate decade. In my view that remains the correct stance going into the first half of 2023.

It is important to remember however that periods like the first nine months of 2022, while painful, are also great opportunities to invest in good trusts at discounted prices. And even if markets remain volatile and difficult for a little longer they will revive at some point in the near future, and investors who have the patience to sit out this difficult phase will in due course reap the rewards in superior performance over time. It has always happened in the past – 2009, the year in which the markets finally started to recover from the global financial crisis was one of the greatest money-making opportunities in my lifetime. And it will happen again.

In my judgement, for reasons that I lay out in the Editor's Notes, a careful selection of the best trusts in their field will continue to serve you well whatever the future brings, through both good times and bad. Investment trusts are excellent options for the more sophisticated investor, one who values good corporate governance, understands the role of discounts, can resist the temptation to panic and has a sensible medium- to longer-term horizon.

JONATHAN DAVIS

JONATHAN DAVIS *is one of the UK's leading stock market authors and commentators. A qualified professional investor with 40 years of experience as a financial journalist and investment strategist, his books include* Money Makers, Investing with Anthony Bolton *and* Templeton's Way with Money. *After writing columns for* The Independent *and* Financial Times *for many years, he now writes a private circulation newsletter. Find out more from the* Money Makers *website: www.money-makers.co.*

STAY INFORMED

For portfolio updates, market commentary, interviews with top professional investors, performance data and links to topical research, Jonathan Davis now writes a regular subscription newsletter for *Money Makers* (See www.money-makers.co for how to subscribe).

ACKNOWLEDGEMENTS

Producing *The Investment Trusts Handbook 2023* is, as it has been for the last six years, an intensive and collective effort. Thanks to all of those who have helped to bring it to fruition, whether as contributors or handmaidens to the production process.

At Harriman House: Myles Hunt, Sally Tickner, Nick Fletcher, Tracy Bundey, Victoria Lawson-McKittrick, Christopher Parker. Thank you also to Chris Wild.

Our publishing partners: abrdn, Alliance Trust, Allianz Global Investors, Baillie Gifford, BlackRock, Fidelity, and Schroders.

Contributors: Emma Bird, John Baron, Annabel Brodie-Smith, James Carthew, Richard Curling, Alex Davies, Nick Greenwood, Peter Hewitt, Max King, Alastair Laing, Ewan Lovett-Turner and Stuart Watson.

Research: Ewan Lovett-Turner and Colette Ord (Numis), Simon Elliott, Kieran Drake and Emma Bird (Winterflood Securities), Christopher Brown (J.P. Morgan Cazenove), Alan Brierley (Investec), Annabel Brodie-Smith (the AIC), Richard Pavry (Devon Equity Management), William Heathcoat Amory (Kepler Intelligence), Ed Marten and James Carthew (QuotedData).

Statistics: big thanks again this year to David Michael and Sophie Driscoll at the Association of Investment Companies (AIC) for all their help in providing the performance statistics and a lot of other data.

Financial well-being.

Investment trusts have offered access to successful investment strategies for decades, helping generations of private investors build wealth and experience financial well-being. See how BlackRock's range of Trusts might help you do the same.

blackrock.com/its

BlackRock.

Cut through with conviction

FIDELITY INVESTMENT TRUSTS

Truly global and award-winning, the range is supported by expert portfolio managers, regional research teams and on-the-ground professionals with local connections.

With 400 investment professionals across the globe, we believe this gives us stronger insights across the markets in which we invest. This is key in helping each trust identify local trends and invest with the conviction needed to generate long-term outperformance.

Fidelity's range of investment trusts:

- Fidelity Asian Values PLC
- Fidelity China Special Situations PLC
- Fidelity Emerging Markets Limited
- Fidelity European Trust PLC
- Fidelity Japan Trust PLC
- Fidelity Special Values PLC

Past performance is not a reliable indicator of future returns. The value of investments can go down as well as up and you may not get back the amount you invested. Overseas investments are subject to currency fluctuations. The shares in the investment trusts are listed on the London Stock Exchange and their price is affected by supply and demand.

The investment trusts can gain additional exposure to the market, known as gearing, potentially increasing volatility. Some of the trusts invest more heavily than others in smaller companies, which can carry a higher risk because their share prices may be more volatile than those of larger companies and their securities are often less liquid.

The investment trusts use financial derivative instruments for investment purposes, which may expose them to a higher degree of risk and can cause investments to experience larger than average price fluctuations. Some of the trusts invest in emerging markets which can be more volatile than other more developed markets.

To find out more, scan the QR code, go to fidelity.co.uk/its or speak to your adviser.

EDITOR'S NOTES

Reality bites

I T HASN'T BEEN quite a case of the four horsemen of the apocalypse arriving, but the year that's elapsed since the last edition of *The Investment Trusts Handbook* has been one to forget for the great majority of investors. A combination of surging inflation, higher interest rates, a sickening war in Ukraine, and oil and gas prices reaching record highs has contributed to one of the worst years on record for anyone with money to invest or wealth to protect.

Unusually, in the unrelenting market sell-off that began in January there have been very few of the normal places in which to hide. Bonds, which traditionally are negatively correlated with equities (meaning they tend to do well when share prices are falling and vice versa) have declined almost in lockstep with the value of shares. Commercial property has slumped alarmingly in the face of rising interest rates, while the price of gold, seen by many as the safest of havens in inflationary times, has disappointed (in dollar terms, though not in sterling). Index-linked bonds have seen the most dramatic price declines and volatility in their history.

As a result, anyone with anything approaching the simplest classic, balanced, private-client portfolio (made up of 40% bonds and 60% equities) has been feeling real pain. Professional wealth managers have been unable to save their clients from losses. According to Asset Risk Consultants, a firm which monitors the performance of wealth management firms, even clients with the most cautious portfolios have experienced a fall of 10% in the first nine months of 2022, rising to 15% or more for higher risk portfolios. If yours has done better than that, consider yourself well served.

The performance for diversified UK investors would have been worse had it not been for the weakness of sterling against the persistently strong dollar. This had the effect of increasing the value of holdings in asset classes that are priced in dollars. This includes not just US equities and bonds, but many commodities.

The pain has been particularly keenly felt by investors in investment trusts. The average weighted discount on the trusts which are in the FT All-Share index has widened dramatically from just over 1% at the start of 2022 to around 15% by the end of September, compounding falls in net asset values (NAV) across many sectors. Save only for the brief pandemic sell-off in March 2020, these are the widest average discounts – and certainly the biggest annual derating – we have seen for many years.

Discounts: the big story

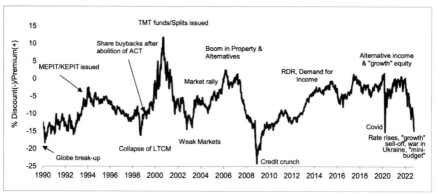

Source: Numis Securities. October 2022

It is the derating that has caused the most damage. NAV data shows, according to Numis Securities, that even in these difficult conditions seven out of the 16 most important trust sectors achieved positive weighted returns in the first nine months of the year. More than 40% of trusts tracked by Numis delivered a positive NAV return between the start of the year and mid-October. The average NAV decline across the whole sector was 4%.

Yet in share price terms, only one of these 16 has produced a positive total return. As many as 10 of the 16 sectors showed mark-to-market losses of more than 20%. The average share price decline was 14%, fully 10% worse than the equivalent NAV performance.

Because of those adverse discount movements, over the past year all-equity investment trusts as a group have for once underperformed comparable open-ended funds (unit trusts and OEICs). Taking the 14 largest equity sectors, all but two were showing lower 12-month total returns at the halfway stage than their open-ended peer group, and the margin was widening going into the fourth quarter. To complete a dismal picture, the average alternative asset trust has also derated sharply in the face of rising bond yields, as the chart indicates.

Alternatives fading

For good reason alternative assets, many paying attractive and seemingly stable yields, have been the fastest growing segment of the investment trust sector in recent years, but their sparkle has faded since mid-2022. Sharply higher government bond yields no longer make their dividend yields look so compelling. Specialist property, renewable energy and infrastructure trusts, while mostly continuing to perform well in NAV terms, have seen their customary premiums reduce or disappear, while many commercial property and private equity trusts now languish at disturbingly wide discounts, up to 40–50% in some cases. September was a particularly brutal month for commercial property.

Ten-year discount history: absolute discounts

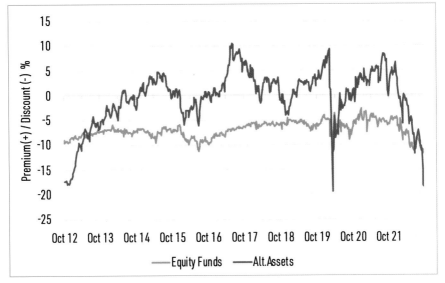

Source: Numis Securities. October 2022

The pain has been felt most keenly by those who have kept their holdings in some of the most popular and fastest growing investment trusts of 2020–21, many of which performed spectacularly well in the aftermath of the pandemic. Scottish Mortgage, the largest trust of all at the start of 2022, is the most notable example; its market capitalisation has fallen from £19 billion at its peak to £14bn now. Memories of its spectacular 100% one-year gains between 2020 and 2021 are receding.

It is a similar story with other big winners of the post-pandemic recovery, such as Chinese, biotech and technology trusts. All of them have seen their shares slump and now trade at discounts compared to the often sizeable premiums which were common earlier. Allianz Technology and Polar Capital Technology, two heavyweight former darlings, have lost about a combined £1bn in market value from their peak. Away from the investment trust sector, the dramatic surge in the prices of bitcoin, meme stocks, SPACs, non-fungible tokens and other exotica that we saw last year can be seen in retrospect as what many of us suspected at the time – symptoms of a mad speculative sugar rush to rival the internet bubble of 2000 and other excesses of the past.

As I write these notes in early October, there is as yet no sign that the market turmoil is easing. Faced with rising interest rates and still high inflation, a recession in many developed countries looks inevitable, while the war in Ukraine carries on, threatening consumers across western Europe with a daunting winter of huge energy bills and potential power cuts. Central bankers are caught between the need to hike interest rates to control inflation and a fear of recession, or even a new financial crisis.

In the UK, a new government headed by Liz Truss failed to survive its poorly handled tax-cutting plans, which sent the pound and gilt prices tumbling. The Bank of England predicted inflation will hit 10% per annum and is officially forecasting a recession. What we are living through, reported a gloomy IMF in October, is "a regime shift from an environment of low inflation and low volatility to an environment where inflation is rising. So markets are fragile and fragility makes financial risk more elevated." Investors the world over are having to live with the consequences.

The sun will come up

So is it all doom and gloom for the investment trust sector? Certainly not. The first law of sound investment practice is to be a realist, not a dreamer. It is impossible to deny that 2022 has been a poor year for the sector, and the outlook remains highly uncertain. That is no reason, however, to abandon one's faith in what we have always confidently dubbed the connoisseur's choice of investment funds. The intrinsic strengths of the investment trust sector – its superior corporate governance, more or less permanent capital, ability to use gearing and greater diversification – remain as compelling as they always have been.

As I have already noted, there have been plenty of parts in the investment trust universe which have continued to deliver positive NAV returns. The volatility in discounts, while alarming for anyone who has not lived through a bear market before, is both a worry and an opportunity. Being able to buy established investment trusts with experienced managers and good long-term track records for 90, 80 or even 50p in the pound is one of the gifts that investment trusts continue to throw up every few years or so.

Discount volatility is the price that investors in investment trusts pay for the privilege of accessing the other advantages. It is the reason why we always make a point of saying that they are ideal vehicles for sophisticated investors with medium- to longer-term time horizons, but not for those looking for short-term speculative gains (although those too are available in certain years and market conditions, as we have seen).

INVESTMENT TRUSTS
PRIVATE EQUITY | REAL ESTATE | UK | ASIA

THE BEST OPPORTUNITIES LIE BENEATH THE SURFACE.

We see opportunity differently. With specialist expertise across UK and Asian Markets, as well as established teams in global private equity and real estate, we can examine markets and company fundamentals in greater depth – helping you find opportunity where others don't.

Search schroders.com/investmenttrusts

Schroders

One of the challenges that the sector undoubtedly faces now stems from the growing popularity of investment trusts among private investors, the great majority of them able to buy and sell holdings with ease as clients of retail investment platforms. While it would be comforting to think that every first-time investor in trusts will have fully understood the nature of what they were buying, including the risk of changes in discounts, such understanding is not going to be universal.

It would be disappointing if this year's sell-off and dramatic discount movements prompt a proportion of the newcomers to retreat, chastened, from the field. As noted already, however, with the experience of professional wealth managers, it is not as if there have been plenty of other places to hide. A survey by Trustnet showed that 90% of all open-ended funds on offer to private investors had lost money in the first nine months of 2022. The combination of factors which have produced the current state of affairs is historically – and one might add, fortunately – rare.

Double-digit returns

It is important to remember too that all this comes at the end of a period in which investors have consistently been able to harvest returns which, for many types of asset, have been well above the long-term historical norm, thanks in part to the exceptionally low interest rates that have, until this year, characterised the period since the global financial crisis. Investment trusts in particular have enjoyed a boom period, with the majority of the important sectors delivering exceptionally strong NAV returns of around 10% per annum or more in the 10 years to the end of 2021, a period during which inflation has averaged little more than 2%.

In fact, despite some memorable bear markets and at least four economic recessions along the way, the favourable tailwinds for invested asset returns stretch all the way back to the 1980s, which was when central banks finally started to purge the developed world of the high inflation that had caused such mayhem in the 1970s. Bond yields have declined steadily since then and for a few years in the last decade have been negative in real (meaning inflation-adjusted) terms, an exceptionally helpful climate for investors.

According to Professors Dimson, Marsh and Staunton, authors of the definitive source book for investment returns since 1900, the real (meaning inflation-adjusted) returns bond investors experienced between 1980 and 2021 were greater than over any other multi-decade period. For equities it has been a similar story. Taking 1980 as the starting point, from 2010 to the end of 2021 the real annualised return on world equities has been nearly 3% per annum greater than the 5.3% long-term average, a record margin. Compounded over a decade or more, that adds up to substantial gains in wealth.

Translated into plainer English, what that means, as Simon Elliott, then head of investment trust research at Winterflood Securities, pointed out a couple of years ago, is that for a long time investors in investment trusts "have never had it so good". This year's unhappy developments need to be seen in that context. The good times, characterised by the double whammy of narrowing discounts and rising NAVs, could never roll on indefinitely.

We were always going to have a moment of reckoning during which prices adjusted to more normal, realistic levels. With the inflation genie out of the bottle once more, and governments and central banks struggling to control the fallout, bond yields have broken out of their long-term downward trend, and that moment has now arrived. It takes time for investors to adjust to a new reality, but that is what we all now have to do.

Just to give one example, instead of earning virtually nothing on your cash for years, you can today earn more than 4% from an online Hargreaves Lansdown cash account and [however briefly – this is the day I am writing] a 5% yield from a two-year government bond. If that persists, it is bound to change the relative attractions of all other types of investment and reverse the decade-long trend of savers being forced into ever-riskier assets just to earn a return.

Prophets with honour

Before commenting further on the outlook for investment returns from here, I cannot resist making the point that the disappointing returns enjoyed by the majority of investors so far in 2022 should not have come as a total surprise to alert investment trust followers. Although the timing and the extent of the declines that we have seen this year were unknowable in advance, the risk of just such an outcome occurring has been well flagged by some wise and experienced professional participants in the trust world.

When the Queen, whose sad loss this year also marks the end of an era, asked pointedly why nobody had foreseen the global financial crisis before it broke, she was raising a valid concern. Yet there were those in the professional investment community, albeit not very many of them, who did predict before it happened in 2008 exactly how the sub-prime mortgage market would implode and trigger a violent threat to the financial system.

Prominent among them was Ian Rushbrook, then manager of Personal Assets (ticker: PNL), who sadly died in 2008, just as his prediction of a systemic financial crisis was in the process of coming true. Another voice crying publicly in the wilderness about the risks was Jonathan Ruffer, founder of the fund management business which bears his name and manages, among many other funds and private client accounts,

RISE
above market uncertainty

with an investment trust that's built for long-term peace of mind

Stock markets can be unpredictable, but Alliance Trust's global equity investment trust is designed and structured to reduce investor anxiety.

Our multi-manager approach provides built-in diversification across regions, sectors and investment styles.

Instead of following market trends, our Stock Pickers focus on finding the best companies for long-term returns.

Allowing you to rise above the noise of an uncertain market.

Rise above with Alliance Trust.

alliancetrust.co.uk/riseabove

the Ruffer Investment Company (ticker: RICA). Yet another warning came from Peter Spiller, the long-serving manager of Capital Gearing Trust (ticker: CGT).

All three of these trusts sailed through the global financial crisis, producing positive returns while almost everyone else was haemorrhaging money. It was the makings of a new sub-sector in the investment trust world, made up of 'all-weather' funds which aim to make positive returns in every year, preserving capital in bad periods and grinding out positive, though not exceptional, returns in the good years. A number of such trusts now sit in the recently created 'flexible investment' sector in the AIC's categorisation.

These types of trusts need to be distinguished from a related breed of 'absolute return' funds, many of them run by hedge funds, which also proliferated in the period running up to the global financial crisis. Most of those, unlike Ruffer and co., promptly blew up when the severe stock market decline that they had been designed to protect against actually occurred. Their use of leveraged derivatives to manage the risk of an equity market decline proved wholly inadequate to the reality of what transpired.

It is no accident however that the managers and boards of Personal Assets, Capital Gearing and Ruffer have also been among those who have been most prominent in highlighting for a long time the elevated levels of risk in today's financial markets, with their concerns principally directed at the shortsightedness (*folly* might be a more appropriate term) of the inherently inflationary easy money, 'lower for longer' interest rate policies that central banks around the world have been pursuing for the past decade.

Those policies, which helped to drive up asset valuations and contributed significantly to the recent surge in inflation, are now reaping their inevitable reward. After years of trying but failing to stimulate inflation, the Federal Reserve, the European Central Bank and the Bank of England have all now had to change tack and are urgently pushing through multiple consecutive interest rate rises in order to try and control an explosion in prices. Vladimir Putin's invasion of Ukraine and his weaponising of Russia's oil and gas resources have further fanned the inflationary flames, sending asset prices into a tailspin. But it is not as if we have not been warned how vulnerable such richly valued asset prices had become to any kind of disruption.

Heeded warnings

The difference this time round, compared to the global financial crisis, is that a great many more investors have been listening to the prophetic warnings emanating from the investment trust world. All three trusts mentioned have been able to issue handsome quantities of new shares in the period since the Covid outbreak in 2020, and the faith of those who bought them to protect themselves against the risk of change in direction have been amply vindicated so far this year. While not immune entirely to the market headwinds, Ruffer, Capital Gearing and Personal Assets have proved to be among the few genuinely defensive havens open to investors this year.

Along with BH Macro, a specialist, hedge fund-managed trust whose methods do actually work when stock markets crack, they are among the few trusts which have preserved the market value of their shareholders' money year-to-date. BH Macro has returned its shareholders more than 25% over 12 months. Ruffer's shareholders are slightly ahead over one year, while the other two are effectively flat after accounting for dividends. Only the remarkable gyrations in the price of index-linked bonds, one of the mainstays of the defensive trusts' portfolios, has prevented them from doing better.

All four of these trusts, I am happy to report, together with holdings of gold ETFs, feature in the *Money Makers* defensives portfolio I created last year in anticipation of just such a year as we have experienced (more on them later). Two other large multi-asset investment trusts in the flexible sector, Caledonia (the present day successor to a shipping dynasty's family office) and Tetragon Financial, also deserve mention for producing positive share price returns in the year to 30 September 2022. The latter was helped particularly by operating in dollars; sterling's weakness translated a fall in NAV in its base currency into a gain in sterling terms.

An honourable mention in this context should also go to two other global trusts. One is the Global Opportunities Trust (ticker: GOT). Its manager, Sandy Nairn, published a book last year, entitled *The End of the Everything Bubble*, in which he explained in detail why the world was facing a severe asset price decline.* This year the board of the trust he manages, formerly a conventional global equity-only vehicle with a value bias, obtained shareholder approval to become a self-managed trust with what is effectively a new 'all-weather' mandate. The portfolio has been repositioned for a bear market and while its shares remain at a wide discount, the NAV per share has risen by more than 10% in the last year, as the world plays out just as he expected.

Another creditable performance to be mentioned in despatches is that of F&C, the oldest investment trust of all, founded in 1868, which after a number of years of steady but uninspiring performance has notably sharpened up its act in the last few years under manager Paul Niven. It too has broadened its reach to include a greater proportion of different types of asset, including private equity and bonds. It has delivered a positive shareholder return so far in 2022, while most other trusts have been drowning in red ink. It is nice to see a good old 'un doing well.

---

* By way of disclosure, I helped him with research and editing of his book.

How long will this bear market last?

This is no doubt the question that every investor will be asking themselves. By the time you read this, we may have the glimpse of an answer, but it seems unlikely to be a conclusive one. In the short term, there are some parallels in previous historical experience that can be called on for comfort. There has never before been a year, for example, in which the US equity market, as represented by the S&P 500 index, and the 10-year US Treasury, the cornerstone of the global financial system, have both fallen by more than 10% at the same time. That was the case at the nine-month stage: surely, one may think, that means the fourth quarter will be better?

Three successive quarters of stock market falls, which we have seen this year, are genuinely rare occurrences. Likewise, in years with midterm elections in the United States, as 2022 is, there is almost always a year-end rally once these elections are out of the way – so why not another? (You can speculate about the reasons for that, but one plausible idea is that the results effectively eliminate the risks of Congress passing some of the candidates' more insane or disruptive ideas.)

Even if we are only halfway through a deeper and more protracted equity market sell-off, experience shows that there will always be a number of so-called 'bear market rallies', in which stock markets perk up for a few weeks before resuming their decline. These rallies prompt many investors to decide that the worst is over, only to be proved wrong later. There is nothing to say that can't or won't happen again before this toughest of years is up.

For much of the last decade, 'buying the dip' has been the right thing for stock market investors to do, given the willingness of central banks to step in with quantitative easing, interest rate cuts and other types of stimulus the moment either the bond market or equity market shows real signs of weakness. The reality, as the former chairman of the Federal Reserve, Ben Bernanke, pointed out after collecting the Nobel Prize for Economics this year, is that in the short term nobody knows what financial markets will do. Anything can happen over a few months.

From a longer term perspective, however, the omens are less promising. Periods in which the Federal Reserve 'tightens' policy by raising interest rates always tend to end in a recession, bear market, or both. The difference between 2022 and recent years is that, with inflation having risen so rapidly, instead of remaining quiescent, none of the most important central banks can really afford to change course on monetary policy until they are able to show that inflation, which they have a mandate to keep to around 2% per annum, has been tamed.

How to respond

We are some way from seeing that at this point. At the same time, because both equities and bonds have become so richly valued, there is no immediately obvious floor at which a sell-off in either asset class should stop. Far more likely, I suspect, is that in the absence of a resolution to the Ukraine war in particular, the bad news for most investors will continue into 2023. At some point bond yields will reach a peak and equity markets will bottom out, but the realist in me thinks it is unlikely that the worst will be over for a while.

The average bear market lasts around 18 to 24 months, which suggests this one may not be over until the second half of 2023. If that is right, it means that anyone investing in investment trusts will need to show the traditional virtues of patience and resilience. The AIC, the industry trade body, correctly points out that money that investors lose during recessions is typically more than recovered within two to three years of the recession starting, rewarding the patience of those who stick them out. Opportunities to take advantage of the big movement in discounts that has marked the year so far will also be coming – some may already be here – and the brave will already be starting to make plans to add to holdings in the most distressed sectors.

Where are the biggest rebounds likely to occur? One obvious example is in the UK smaller companies sector, which has sold off dramatically this year. Discounts are already about as wide as they have ever been and approaching levels last seen in the depths of the global financial crisis, while the share prices of UK companies generally are as cheap compared to similar companies in other leading markets as they have ever been. Because of its distinctive makeup (with a heavy weighting in oil companies, banks, insurance companies and miners), the FTSE 100 Index has been a relative safe haven this year, but mid- and small-cap companies have not.

Net asset values could easily fall further still, but looking through the impending economic slowdown the upside potential is starting to look materially greater than the downside risk. For anyone with a five-year investment horizon, gradually feeding money back into the better, smaller companies trusts (of which there are a fair few) looks sure to be well rewarded. More immediately the prospects for established vehicles in the UK equity income sector, which have been out of favour for a long time, look reasonably positive too.

This is despite the succession of political dramas to which the UK appears to have become addicted in the last few years, the latest of which is playing out as I write this. While still a hugely important financial centre, the UK stock market is now only a small part of the global equity markets. While overseas companies have taken advantage of sterling weakness to buy some of our most promising companies,

Actual investors look to the future. Not the past.

doceo®

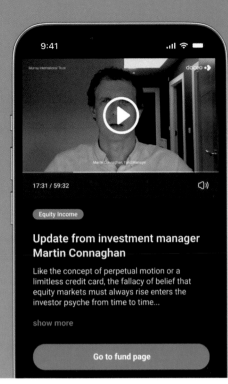

Doceo connects self-directed investors looking for high quality information with investment trust managers

The platform is home to bitesize elevator pitch videos and regular update videos allowing investors to engage more readily with their portfolios, and understand key changes under the bonnet of their investment trust holdings. The advanced filtering and comparison tools help cut through the noise. A selection of the very best articles, podcasts, interviews and webinars explore trends and set out how the top investment thinkers are navigating the current environment. Sign up at **doceo.tv** for free now to stay informed like a professional.

Discover new investments:

      **doceo.tv**

overseas investors have largely shunned the UK market for several years. In due course that will change.

The following chart and table show the total returns from UK gilts (D), the FTSE All-Share index (C) and the FTSE World index (A) in sterling terms over different periods, comparing them to an index of inflation plus 3% per annum (B). Note how the weakness of sterling has shielded UK investors from the full extent of the decline in US/world equities this year. The figures include reinvested dividends and interest payments on gilts. Discount movements have resulted in lower returns than these for investment trust shareholders in 2022, but helped in earlier years.

Five-year total returns

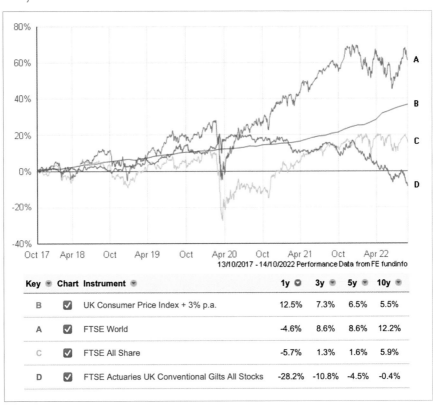

Key	Chart	Instrument	1y	3y	5y	10y
B	✓	UK Consumer Price Index + 3% p.a.	12.5%	7.3%	6.5%	5.5%
A	✓	FTSE World	-4.6%	8.6%	8.6%	12.2%
C	✓	FTSE All Share	-5.7%	1.3%	1.6%	5.9%
D	✓	FTSE Actuaries UK Conventional Gilts All Stocks	-28.2%	-10.8%	-4.5%	-0.4%

Source: Trustnet, 14 October 2022

One important indicator to watch is the price of the dollar. It has been strong against most other currencies for quite a long time now and approaching its highest level since the 1980s, which has far-reaching consequences for other markets. At some point that too will turn and when it does that will be one of the signals that the worst of the current global market sell-off may finally be over. Emerging markets and Japan will come back into favour at that point.

A new investment regime?

If, as many seasoned professional investors believe, we are entering a new investment climate, one characterised by higher interest rates and tighter monetary conditions, it is likely to accelerate the rotation of styles that has already become evident, off and on, over the past couple of years. The most notable shift has been from growth to value, away from trusts that invest in companies with strongly growing revenues and profits, towards duller, more established companies that churn out dividends from more secure cash flow streams. It is a reasonably safe bet that as interest rates rise, value investors are likely to fare somewhat better than growth-oriented competitors.

The growth style is most closely associated at present with the family of trusts managed by Baillie Gifford, with Scottish Mortgage as its flagship, although it does, in SAINTS, manage one trust with a quite different approach (see page 137). The firm has also been prominent in another clearly discernible trend, which is towards owning more unlisted private companies. Many other equity trusts have copied this move to varying degrees, which itself is only part of a wider trend towards bringing the ownership of privately owned or non-tradeable assets into the investment trust universe.

The rise of the alternative asset sector is a big part of that wider trend. Ten years ago there were only a handful of investment companies investing in infrastructure, renewable energy and energy transition. Today there are 30. Private equity itself remains one of the largest sectors in the universe. Commercial property is another sector which by definition embraces only illiquid physical assets that no ordinary investor can buy or sell themselves. Investment trusts have turned out to be the best vehicle through which private investors can now own this kind of business.

This theme of increasing investment opportunities for private assets is evident in several of the trust interviews we feature in this year's *Handbook*. Schroders, for example, has made 'democratising' the ownership of private assets one of its core strategic targets (see page 155). Three factors have helped to drive this trend. One is the fact that the number of companies which opt for being listed on stock markets has been falling for more than a decade, limiting the range of opportunities.

The second is the belief that privately owned assets offer potentially higher, or at least less volatile, returns than publicly owned stocks and shares. And the third is that owning private assets opens up the potential for broader diversification, one of the few proven ways that investors can control risk. The ever-expanding range of assets into which trust investors can now put money, a list that has grown to include space exploration, music royalties, data towers, social housing, shipping and battery storage, is evidence of how useful the investment trust structure has become in opening up these areas to private investor participation.

Private assets to be tested

Like so many trends in investment, the validity of the theoretical superiority of being able to access privately owned assets is being tested in this year's changing market conditions. As publicly quoted companies, investment trusts promise shareholders the ability to buy and sell their holdings every day, should they so wish. The drawback is that the prices on offer will adjust to supply and demand, and when sentiment deteriorates the strain is taken by the discount widening. You are free to sell, but you may not get a price that is close to net asset value, and the amount you can sell will, in practice, often be limited to lots of just a few thousand pounds.

That, pretty much, is what we have been seeing this year in the alternative asset space. Having been much in demand for a long time, many alternative asset trusts have gone from trading at a premium to trading at a discount. Instead of a flood of new trusts coming to the market and existing companies issuing a steady stream of new shares in order to meet demand, the reverse is now happening. There were 15 IPOs in 2021, virtually all in the alternative asset space, and so far this year, not a single one, while secondary issuance has also fallen away sharply.

It is true that another factor may also be at work here. By their nature, many types of alternative asset take time to value. In the case of private equity, there are often long lags between the end of a reporting period and publication of the latest net asset value. By the time the new figure appears it may be several months out of date. For infrastructure and renewable energy trusts, the NAVs depend on complex models which attempt to discount their expected future cash flows up to 20 years ahead. Even small changes to the model inputs can result in larger changes in valuations.

Both these factors help to explain why ratings have changed so sharply this year. In the case of private equity, among other concerns investors seem to have decided that reported NAVs are overstated, given the extent to which shares in similar publicly traded companies have declined. For infrastructure and renewable energy trusts, the damage has been done by the sharp rise in bond yields, which increases the rate at which future cash flows must be discounted, combined with a threat by the UK Government to tax renewable generators more harshly.

Commercial property has suffered even more as the gap between the yields from government bonds and commercial property has narrowed in favour of the former. More broadly, if interest rates are to remain for some time at much higher levels than those we have seen in the last few years, it will be a headwind for alternative assets generally. Since they sell mainly on the strength of their yields, those cash and two-year gilt yields have become more credible competitors for income-seeking investors. Within that space, however, there will be good opportunities: when any market reprices suddenly (as the gilts market has done this autumn), share prices often adjust indiscriminately, creating more bargains. The worse the discounts get, the quicker and sharper they will rebound, underlining the need for patience through the storm. Specialist property trusts with long index-linked lease income, for example, have sold off but are likely to remain attractive once their capital values have adjusted.

Highs and lows

The best and worst experiences of the past year are well covered in the professional investor forum and review articles that follow, so I won't belabour the highs and lows at any great length here. My investment trust of the year would be BH Macro, the defensive hedge fund, for doing its job so well in rough markets. Turkey of the year, I fear, has to go to Chrysalis, whose shockingly poor performance has been compounded by the extremely large performance fee that its managers were able to extract in recognition of performance that has now comprehensively disappeared. Any repeat of this unhappy episode risks bringing investment trusts into disrepute and highlights the drawbacks of performance fees, badly formulated ones in particular.

On a more positive note, it has been good to see a number of boards taking decisive action to bring the lives of trusts that are underperforming and are too small to be sustainable to a close. Jupiter Emerging & Frontier Income is one example. I cannot resist observing that, just as I suggested might be the case a year ago, after several years of underperformance the venerable Scottish Investment Trust disappeared into the arms of JPMorgan Global Growth & Income just as the deep value style of investment which 'the Scottish' had championed in vain for so long, turned out to be the right approach for the very different market conditions we have seen this year.

A significant number of investment trusts have adopted zero or fixed discount control targets – there is a list on page 258 in the Analysis section – and many of them have duly bought back shares to help try and control their discounts as markets derated. Some boards, however, have failed to follow through as they promised, in some cases relying on the let-out clause that their discount control objectives are conditional and can be ignored in exceptional market conditions.

While that may be justifiable in very extreme circumstances, like the pandemic sell-off in March 2020, it is not consistent with best practice. Trusts that happily issue shares at a premium, but are slow to buy back when discounts appear, should be treated warily. If you own one of these trusts, don't hesitate to get in touch with the board or vote at the AGM. The big retail investment platforms are making it much easier to vote at AGMs and one, Interactive Investor, says it will now automatically submit votes for your holdings in future by default, a positive development.

INVESTMENT TRUST CHAMPIONS
FOR GENERATIONS

Allianz Global Investors and its predecessors have been managing investment trusts since 1889. Our trusts span investor needs – from income, to growth, to the specialist sector of technology – and offer a path to investment opportunities around the world. So whatever your investment goals, please take a closer look and discover what our investment trusts could bring to your portfolio.

Please note: investment trusts are listed companies, traded on the London Stock Exchange. Their share prices are determined by factors including demand, so shares may trade at a discount or premium to the net asset value. Past performance does not predict future returns. Some trusts seek to enhance returns through gearing (borrowing money to invest). This can boost a trust's returns when investments perform well, though losses can be magnified when investments lose value.

0800 389 4696   uk.allianzgi.com/investment-trusts

Trusted counsel, pragmatic implementation, measured results.

Quill is a leading UK financial services media relations agency. Creative yet pragmatic, Quill delivers effective public relations campaigns tailored to meet each client's specific communications objectives.

Our team's many years' industry experience means that we are an invaluable adviser, guiding our clients through today's fast-moving media environment.

Quill is a trusted business partner combining senior level service with original strategic thinking to achieve high quality, targeted media relations.

Call us – +44 (0)20 7466 5050

Email us – info@quillpr.com

Drop in – 107 Cheapside, London, EC2V 6DN

www.quillpr.com

Portfolio updates

I am not sure whether it is gratifying or disappointing to be able to report that the model portfolios I monitor for *Money Makers* subscribers have performed pretty much as expected. There are four in total, one of which I have tracked since the launch of the *Handbook*, and three more I have added since to reflect my concerns that different tactics would be required in the changing market environment. The original *Handbook* portfolio, an illustrative diversified multi-asset portfolio, is down around 15% this year, somewhat less than the average investment trust, having delivered a total return of 60% since launch in January 2017.

The growth portfolio, whose origins date back to 2010, is down 20%, having produced much higher annualised returns than the others until this year. The income portfolio has fallen a little over 5% in price terms, but that is before accounting for the dividend income, which has fully compensated for the decline in capital value. It currently yields more than 5%. Finally the defensive asset portfolio, which I mentioned earlier, has done its job well, gaining more than 10% in the last 12 months. All four portfolios have delivered good positive returns since the January 2017 start date. You can find more about them on the *Money Makers* website.

The caution I have urged since the end of last year, which has driven me to put my own money mostly into the defensive and income portfolios, has turned out to be well rewarded. I am sticking with that approach for the moment, while waiting for evidence that the tide has turned. I should emphasise that my approach, which is based on 40 years of professional involvement in tracking financial markets, may well not be appropriate for most private investors.

Not knowing the extent of readers' knowledge and risk profiles, it would be impossible, as well as wrong, for me to suggest a specific course of action. For a long-term investor, there is much to commend a policy of building and then holding through thick and thin a broadly diversified portfolio of investment trusts that cover all the major asset classes, and continuing to add savings on a regular basis through tough markets, riding out the inevitable volatility.

Still kidding us

In these notes a year ago, I highlighted the fact that the Financial Conduct Authority was close to publishing the results of its long-awaited review into the infamous KIDs (Key Information Documents) that the AIC has been campaigning against for years. KIDs are short three-page documents that investment trusts were originally required to publish under EU regulations. After the Brexit vote, and despite their many obvious flaws, the KID rules were copied and then adopted by the UK, and they remain obligatory.

The results of the FCA's review which did appear in early 2022 have been underwhelming, although not completely without merit. The most idiotic requirement, the need for trusts to publish a future performance scenario under different market conditions, has been dropped. The results that emerged from the formula laid down in the regulations were so absurd, inconsistent and removed from reality that they prompted the distinguished academic Sir John Kay to issue this withering assessment about KIDs: "burn before reading".

Instead trusts now have to make do with a general description of the performance history of the trust, and there is no pre-ordained requirement for how they should do this. Another much-derided element in the KID – a particular formula for calculating a trust's ongoing costs – remains, however, despite much criticism of its arbitrariness (it is, to be fair, a surprisingly complicated subject). So too does the need to include in the document a risk rating, on a scale from one to seven. This single number is intended to provide the reader with a simple all-embracing measure of a trust's riskiness, which is sadly an impossibility.

The AIC continues to campaign against these aspects of the KID, but progress remains slow. The Treasury, which oversees the FCA, has promised a review of the broader topic of how financial consumer information is provided, but no date for its completion has been released. Behind this whole saga lies the universal wish of regulators the world over to standardise disclosure rules – often with good intentions, but not always with common sense – and the universal fact of life that bureaucrats almost invariably take a long time before coming to conclusions.

It irritates the AIC, with some reason, that the providers of open-ended funds, their main competitors in the fund world, were given a five-year exemption from having to apply similar EU regulations. That exemption won't expire until 2025. The good news is that in the meantime the practical impact of the KID regulations has largely shrivelled into irrelevance.

Even the FCA's own research now shows that hardly any investor in investment trusts ever looks at the KIDs, even assuming they can find them on a trust's website. The irony is that the EU regulations were largely drafted by the UK in the first place, which may explain why there is so much reluctance to junk them or amend them into something more practical and sensible. Don't get me wrong. Disclosure of costs and risks is an important topic, and one that investors should take very seriously, but doing it badly is often worse than doing nothing at all. In this case ridicule has proved the most potent weapon in the AIC's campaign.

Looking ahead

If 2022 has been a year to forget, will 2023 be a year to remember? By this time next year, it could well be. One of the consequences of *The Investment Trusts Handbook* publishing timetable is perhaps worth mentioning. We go to print in mid-October and publish in the first part of December. As luck would have it, for each of the last two years, the intervening period has proved to be a turning point in the direction of financial markets.

In 2020 the announcement of a successful Covid vaccine trial was the trigger for equity markets to take off on their wild ride into exuberance, but came too late for inclusion in that year's edition. November last year then marked the point at which investors started to come to the conclusion that the complacent belief of central bankers that inflation would be 'transitory' was wrong, a view that was already pretty clear to me, as subscribers to *Money Makers* will know.

The invasion of Ukraine in February not only confirmed that view, but added a new and powerful negative factor, intensifying the slide in market values which by then had already begun. What will this November bring? You will of course know by the time you read this…my guess is we may well have had a relief rally of some sort, but don't count on it persisting. An end to the Ukraine war would be a huge bonus in 2022, but that still looks unlikely, despite some recent Ukrainian success on the battlefield.

Now, next November – well, that could be a very different thing. A great buying opportunity for investment trust enthusiasts is coming in due course and the worse things get, the better that opportunity will be. Markets look forward, so the time to buy is typically when sentiment is at its worst, what Sir John Templeton called the point of maximum pessimism. It will be disappointing if we aren't able to report that the moment has arrived by the time we return this time next year. You won't want to miss it when it does. Investment trusts have weathered storms many times before, and you can be sure that this time will be no exception.

YEAR IN REVIEW

MONTH BY MONTH IN 2021/22

W E SUMMARISE HERE some of the main events of the past 12 months in the investment trust world.

OCTOBER 2021

Sector performance

The UK market delivered a positive return in October 2021, with the FTSE All-Share Index rising 1.8%. The investment trust sector outperformed the UK market for the third time in five months, with a rise of 2.7% for the FTSE All-Share Closed End Investments Index. Over the first 10 months of 2021, however, the sector lagged the FTSE All-Share Index, with a rise of 11.7% compared with 15.6% for the index.

Corporate activity

Alliance Trust announced a 33% increase in its dividend level in an attempt to increase the attractiveness of its shares. Asia Dragon proposed a five-yearly conditional 25% tender offer to dovetail with its continuation votes. The board of EP Global Opportunities revealed plans to adopt a self-managed investment approach and hold a 20% tender offer. The Chair of Gresham House Strategic resigned after the fund's board acquiesced to Gresham House plc's plans for a managed wind-down. Scottish Investment Trust and JPMorgan Global Growth & Income agreed to a proposed combination, subject to approval from their respective shareholders. Despite more public criticism from a number of its shareholders, the board of Third Point Investors continued to pursue its own strategy to narrow the fund's discount.

Share issuance

October was another strong month for issuance across the investment companies sector, with £1,658m raised. In the first 10 months of 2021, £11,933m was raised, 107% higher than the equivalent period in 2020 and 55% up on the first 10 months of 2019. October also saw the ninth IPO of 2021, with the launch of Castelnau Group (£178m). The largest fundraising of October was for Tritax Big Box REIT (£300m), while other fundraisings in the property sector included Supermarket Income REIT (£200m), Aberdeen Standard European Logistics Income (£125m) and PRS REIT (£56m). Infrastructure also remained in demand, with issuance from Digital 9 Infrastructure (£275m), Greencoat Renewables (€165m), Gore Street Energy Storage (£74m) and Downing Renewables & Infrastructure (£15m). In addition, Harmony Energy Income announced that it had raised £210m through its IPO earlier in the month. The sector continued to see healthy levels of regular share issuance. In October, this included Scottish Mortgage (£111m), Capital Gearing Trust (£31m), Smithson IT (£28m), Ashoka India Equity (£18m), Polar Capital Global Financials (£16m), Pacific Horizon (£13m), Personal Assets (£13m) and Ruffer Investment Company (£10m).

NOVEMBER 2021

Sector performance

November saw the third month of negative returns in 2021, with the FTSE All-Share Index closing down 2.2%. The investment trust sector outperformed the UK market for the fourth time in six months, with a decline of 0.3% for the FTSE All-Share Closed End Investments Index. However, over the first 11 months of 2021 the sector lagged the FTSE All-Share Index, with a rise of 11.4% compared with 13.0% for the index.

Corporate activity

Aberdeen Standard Asia Focus announced a series of proposals that included the removal of the policy that only permitted investment in companies with market caps of US$1.5bn or below. Scottish Oriental Smaller Companies Trust introduced conditional five-yearly tender offers triggered by underperformance over a five-year period.

Share issuance

November saw £2.3bn raised across the sector, the highest monthly total seen in 14 years. As well as five IPOs (Pantheon Infrastructure (£400m), Life Science REIT (£350m), Harmony Energy Income (£210m), Atrato Onsite Energy (£150m) and Foresight Sustainable Forestry (£130m)), issuance included Greencoat UK Wind (£450m), Urban Logistics REIT (£250m), Octopus Renewables Infrastructure (£74m), VH Global Sustainable Energy Opportunities (£70m), Ruffer Investment Company (£41m), Tufton Oceanic Assets (£29m), Nippon Active Value Fund (£14m) and Schroder BSC Social Impact Trust (£11m).

Regular share issuance saw £610m raised including Scottish Mortgage (£369m), Smithson IT (£46m), Capital Gearing Trust (£37m) and Personal Assets (£26m).

DECEMBER 2021

Sector performance

The investment trust sector underperformed in the final month of 2021, with the FTSE All-Share Closed End Investments Index up 1.3%. The sector underperformed in seven of the previous 12 months and three of the previous four quarters. This includes the last quarter of 2021, with a gain of 3.7% compared with an increase of 4.2% for the FTSE All-Share. In 2021, the trust sector was up 12.8% compared with a rise of 18.3% for the FTSE All-Share.

Corporate activity

Schroders agreed to acquire a 75% stake in Greencoat Capital, the manager of Greencoat Renewables and Greencoat UK Wind. Odyssean Investment Trust approached the board of Strategic Equity Capital with proposals for a combination. The chairman of Third Point Investors resigned after 'personal threats' from an activist shareholder.

Share issuance

December was a quieter month for issuance, with £863m raised across the sector. This was down 63% from November, when £2,360m was raised, and 28% lower than the same month in 2020. The final IPO of the year was ThomasLloyd Energy Impact Trust (US$115m), while the largest fundraising in December was for Urban Logistics REIT (£250m). Other placings came from Octopus Renewables Infrastructure (£74m), VH Global Sustainable Energy Opportunities (£70m), Chrysalis Investments (£60m) and Ruffer Investment Company (£41m).

JANUARY 2022

Sector performance

The UK market started the year on a small down note, with the FTSE All-Share Index falling 0.3% in January. The investment trust sector struggled, with a decline of 7.7% for the FTSE All-Share Closed End Investments Index. Over the 12 months to 31 January, the sector lagged the FTSE All-Share Index, with a rise of 5.0% compared with 18.9% for the index.

Corporate activity

Aquila Energy Efficiency Trust opted to hold a review after two of its four non-executive directors resigned over the speed of deployment. The board of Chrysalis Investments committed to review its performance fee arrangements after a £112m fee was triggered. Hipgnosis Songs Fund saw its share price weaken after Neil Young withdrew from Spotify. AVI and three other shareholders proposed the appointment of Richard Boléat to the board of Third Point Investors. TwentyFour Income Fund and UK Mortgages announced merger proposals, with the former to be the ongoing vehicle.

Share issuance

January saw £601m raised across the sector, the highest level seen in any January for 14 years. Infrastructure remained popular, with fundraising from Cordiant Digital Infrastructure (£200m), Digital 9 Infrastructure (£95m) and JLEN Environmental Assets (£61m). Other issuance came from abrdn European Logistics Income (£38m), BH Macro (£34m), Polar Capital Global Financials (£29m) and Residential Secure Income (£15m).

Regular issuance saw £272m raised, including Smithson IT (£68m), Ruffer Investment Company (£29m), Capital Gearing Trust (£25m), Polar Capital Global Financials (£24m), BB Healthcare (£19m), Fidelity Special Values (£19m), Impax Environmental Markets (£17m), Personal Assets (£11m) and Mid Wynd International (£8m).

FEBRUARY 2022

Sector performance

The UK market fell for a second consecutive month in February, with the FTSE All-Share Index ending down 0.5%. The investment trust sector underperformed the UK market for the fourth time in six months, with a decline of 3.4% for the FTSE All-Share Closed End Investments Index. In the first two months of 2022, the sector lagged the FTSE All-Share Index, with a fall of 10.9% compared with -0.8% for the index.

Corporate activity

Honeycomb Investment Trust announced plans to merge with Pollen Street Capital, its investment manager. The board of Jupiter Emerging & Frontier Income proposed liquidating the fund after shareholders reacted negatively to its plans to change its annual redemption facility. The board of Strategic Equity Capital rejected a plan to merge with Odyssean Investment Trust and outlined proposals designed to narrow its discount. Richard Boléat and Vivien Gould joined the board of Third Point Investors resulting in the withdrawal of a requisition from activist shareholders.

Share issuance

February was a steady month for fundraising, with £571m raised, down 5% from January and 65% lower than the equivalent month in 2021. In the first two months of 2022, £1,172m was raised across the sector, down 45% year-on-year.

The largest fundraising was for LXi REIT (£250m) through an oversubscribed placing. A number of other property funds managed to raise new capital, including Impact Healthcare REIT (£40m), abrdn European Logistics Income (£38m) and Residential Secure Income (£15m). February also saw JLEN Environmental Assets raise £61m, while Polar Capital Global Financials Trust held two placings raising £46m in aggregate.

MARCH 2022

Sector performance

After two consecutive negative months, the UK market recorded a positive return in March, with the FTSE All-Share Index ending up 1.3%. The investment trust sector outperformed for the first time in four months, with a rise of 2.7% for the FTSE All-Share Closed End Investments Index. Despite this, the sector lagged the FTSE All-Share Index in the first quarter of 2022, with a fall of 8.5% compared with a rise of 0.5% for the index.

Share issuance

March was another steady month for fundraising, with £621m raised, up 9% from February but 68% lower than the equivalent month in 2021. Fundraising continued to be dominated by infrastructure funds and March saw oversubscribed issuance from Renewables Infrastructure Group (£273m) and SDCL Energy Efficiency Income (£100m), while Greencoat Renewables raised €282m earlier in the month. Other issuance included Polar Capital Global Financials (£17m) and BH Macro (£10m). The sector continued to see healthy levels of regular share issuance at premium ratings to NAV, with £217m raised through smaller, secondary issuance in March. This included Ruffer Investment Company (£56m), Capital Gearing Trust (£43m), Personal Assets (£28m), City of London IT (£15m), HgCapital Trust (£12m), BlackRock World Mining (£8m), JPMorgan Global Growth & Income (£8m) and Ashoka India Equity (£7m).

APRIL 2022

Sector performance

The UK market recorded a second consecutive positive monthly return in April, albeit the FTSE All-Share Index ended up just 0.3%. The investment trust sector underperformed the UK market for the fourth time in five months, with a decline of 3.2% for the FTSE All-Share Closed End Investments Index. In the first four months of 2022, the sector lagged the FTSE All-Share Index, with a fall of 11.5% compared with a rise of 0.8% for the index.

Share issuance

April was a stronger month for fundraising, with £887m raised, up 43% from March. The largest fundraising came from Supermarket Income REIT (£307m), while demand for Renewable Energy Infrastructure remained strong. Greencoat Renewables raised €282m while Gore Street Energy Storage Fund and HydrogenOne Capital Growth raised £150m and £22m respectively. Other issuance came from International Public Partnerships (£325m) and Geiger Counter (£7m). Despite volatile market conditions, the sector continued to see healthy levels of regular share issuance at premium ratings to NAV. An estimated £174m was raised through smaller, secondary issuance in April. This included Capital Gearing Trust (£42m), Ruffer Investment Company (£32m), Personal Assets (£29m), City of London IT (£14m), Merchants Trust (£13m), JPMorgan Global Growth & Income (£12m), Impax Environmental Markets (£6m) and Law Debenture (£5m).

MAY 2022

Sector performance

The UK market recorded a third consecutive positive monthly return in May, with the FTSE All-Share Index ending up 0.7%. However, the investment trust sector underperformed the UK market for the fifth time in six months, with a decline of 3.2% for the FTSE All-Share Closed End Investments Index. In the first five months of 2022, the sector lagged the FTSE All-Share Index, with a fall of 14.3% compared with a rise of 1.5% for the index.

Corporate activity

LXi REIT and Secure Income REIT announced proposals for a merger, with the former acquiring the latter. A period of underperformance meant that BMO UK High Income would face a continuation vote at its AGM in late July. The board of Majedie Investments determined to review the fund's investment objective following the sale of Majedie AM to Liontrust. Jupiter was chosen to take on the responsibility for Rights & Issues after the retirement of its longstanding manager Simon Knott in September.

Share issuance

May was a stronger month for fundraising, with £1bn raised across the sector. In the first five months of 2022, £3.7bn was raised, compared with £5.8bn in the same period in 2021, a decline of 37%. Despite the pick-up over the last few months, by May conditions for fundraising remained mixed and the sector had still not seen its first IPO of the year.

There were a number of oversubscribed fundraisings during May, including International Public Partnerships (£325m), Home REIT (£263m) and Gresham House Energy Storage (£150m). There was also fundraising from BH Macro (£68m), EJF Investments, for its 2025 ZDPs (£13m), and Ecofin US Renewables Infrastructure (US$13m).

The sector continued to see healthy levels of regular share issuance at premium ratings to NAV. An estimated £194m was raised through smaller, secondary issuance in May. This included Capital Gearing Trust (£51m), Ruffer Investment Company (£40m), Personal Assets (£29m), Merchants Trust (£11m), BlackRock World Mining (£11m), Bellevue Healthcare (£10m), City of London IT (£8m) and JPMorgan Global Growth & Income (£8m).

JUNE 2022

Sector performance

The UK market recorded a negative return in June, with the FTSE All-Share Index ending down 6.0%. This followed a rise of 0.7% in May and a rise of 0.2% in the same month in 2021. The index was down 4.6% in the first half of 2022. The (economic) storm clouds continued to gather in June, as fears of recessions in the US and Europe grew. Jamie Dimon of JPMorgan warned of the potential of an economic hurricane hitting the US, while the World Bank suggested that a 1970s stagflation trap was a possibility. The S&P 500 Index was down 20% in dollar terms in the first half of the year, its worst first half return since 1970. The oil price was down 6.0% in dollar terms in June. Prime Minister Boris Johnson survived a confidence vote amongst his fellow MPs in June but would be forced to resign as leader of the Conservative Party in early July after his Government was hit by multiple resignations. In June the investment trust sector outperformed for only the second time in six months, with a decline of 5.4% for the FTSE All-Share Closed End Investments Index compared with a fall of 6.0% for the FTSE All-Share.

Share issuance

June was a quieter month for fundraising, with £462m raised across the sector, down 55% from May and 51% lower than the equivalent month in 2021, which saw £950m raised. In the first half of 2022, £4,165m was raised across the sector, compared with £6,795m in the same period in 2021, a decline of 39%. Conditions for fundraising remained mixed and 2022 had still not seen its first IPO of the year. The sector continued to see healthy levels of regular share issuance at premium ratings to NAV. An estimated £188m was raised through smaller, secondary issuance in June, compared with £194m in May. This included Ruffer Investment Company (£58m), Capital Gearing Trust (£44m), Personal Assets (£19m), City of London IT (£16m), BlackRock World Mining (£11m), Odyssean Investment Trust (£7m), BlackRock Energy & Resources Income (£6m), Law Debenture (£6m) and Henderson Far East Income (£5m).

JULY 2022

Sector performance

The UK market recorded a positive monthly return in July, with the FTSE All-Share Index ending up 4.4%. The investment trust sector outperformed the UK market for the second month in a row, with a return of +6.9% for the FTSE All-Share Closed End Investments Index. In the first seven months of 2022, the sector lagged the FTSE All-Share Index, with a fall of 13.4% compared with a decline of 0.1% for the index.

Corporate activity

All three lead managers of Ecofin US Renewables Infrastructure announced their departure. Jerry Polacek, Matthew Ordway and Prashanth Prakash decided to pursue a new venture and therefore resigned from their roles at Ecofin. While a new lead portfolio manager was sought, the broader 17-person investment team and senior Ecofin leadership oversaw the management of the fund. July also saw the announcement of a number of other management team changes, at Allianz Technology Trust, Brunner Investment Trust, JPMorgan American and Ruffer Investment Company.

Share issuance

July was another reasonably quiet month for fundraising, with £523m raised across the sector. In the first seven months of 2022, £4.7bn was raised, compared with £8.4bn in the same period in 2021, a decline of 44%. Conditions for fundraising remained mixed and the sector had still not seen its first IPO of the year. The largest fundraising in July came from HICL Infrastructure, which raised £160m through an oversubscribed issue. In addition, Pantheon Infrastructure raised £13m through the conversion of subscription shares. The sector continued to see healthy levels of regular share issuance at premium ratings to NAV. An estimated £146m was raised through smaller, secondary issuance in July. This included Capital Gearing Trust (£36m), Ruffer Investment Company (£28m), Personal Assets (£12m), City of London IT (£11m) and JPMorgan Global Growth & Income (£6m).

AUGUST 2022

Sector performance

The investment trust sector recorded a negative monthly return in August, with the FTSE All-Share Closed End Investments Index falling 1.5%. However, this represented an outperformance of the UK market, with the FTSE All-Share Index down 1.7% over the month. In the first eight months of 2022, the sector lagged the FTSE All-Share Index, with a fall of 14.6% compared with a decline of 2.1% for the index.

Share issuance

August was a very quiet month for fundraising, with only £180m raised across the sector. This was down 66% from July and was 25% lower than the equivalent month in 2021, which saw £241m raised. The largest fundraising in August came from BH Macro, which raised a total of £22m through the issue of sterling and US dollar shares. Pantheon Infrastructure raised £13m via the issue of shares relating to the exercise of subscription rights. An estimated £144m was raised through smaller, secondary issuance in August, including by Capital Gearing Trust (£51m), Personal Assets Trust (£30m) and Ruffer Investment Company (£21m).

SEPTEMBER 2022

Sector performance

The UK market recorded another negative monthly return in September, with the FTSE All-Share Index ending down 5.9%. This followed a fall of 1.7% in August and a decline of 1.0% in September 2021. The investment trust sector underperformed the UK market for the sixth time in 12 months, with a decline of 6.2% for the FTSE All-Share Closed End Investments Index. The FTSE All-Share Index was down 7.9% over the first nine months of 2022, with the investment trust sector notably lagging the UK market, with a fall of 20.0%. Negative share price returns were delivered by 86% of investment trusts in September, with nine of the 10 worst performers being property names. NAV moves were much less extreme. Year to date, 79% of investment trusts are in negative territory.

Share issuance

£170m was raised in September, the weakest month for investment trust fundraising since August 2018. £5.1bn was raised in the first nine months of 2022, down 51% from the equivalent period last year. Still no IPOs have been completed so far this year, with two new launches cancelled in recent weeks.

These month-by-month summaries are extracted from the excellent monthly investment trust reports prepared by the Winterflood investment trusts research team and are reproduced here with their kind permission.

The following charts are drawn from the invaluable monthly and quarterly round-ups of investment trust news produced by research firm QuotedData. In addition to these regular charts, the round-ups also provide news and commentary on recent trends in the investment sector and are free for private investors who sign up at www.quoteddata.com.

2021 TOTAL

Figure 1: Best performing funds in NAV terms in 2021

	%
Geiger Counter	81.9
Riverstone Energy	78.7
VietNam Holding	65.6
Tufton Oceanic Assets	51.3
HarbourVest Global Private Equity	49.3
Electra Private Equity	48.8
NB Private Equity Partners Class A	48.8
Ashoka India	48.5
Vietnam Enterprise	48.3
CQS Natural Resources Growth & Income	43.8

Figure 2: Best performing funds in price terms in 2021

	%
Schiehallion	103.3
Geiger Counter	91.3
VietNam Holding	81.8
BMO Private Equity	66.2
NB Private Equity Partners Class A	65.0
Tufton Oceanic Assets	59.7
AEW UK REIT	57.8
Riverstone Energy	56.6
Warehouse REIT	53.6
Tritax Big Box	53.1

Source: Morningstar, Marten & Co. Note: excludes trusts with market caps below £15m at 31/12/21

Figure 3: Worst performing funds in NAV terms in 2021

	%
Amedeo Air Four Plus	(37.2)
Biotech Growth	(23.2)
JPMorgan China Growth & Income	(21.0)
Golden Prospect Precious Metals	(19.2)
Edinburgh Worldwide	(17.4)
Fidelity China Special Situations	(16.3)
Aberdeen Latin American Income	(15.4)
Syncona	(15.4)
Doric Nimrod Air Three	(14.2)
RTW Venture	(14.0)

Figure 4: Worst performing funds in price terms in 2021

	%
Aseana Properties	(33.8)
Macau Property Opportunities	(31.7)
Baillie Gifford China Growth	(28.6)
JPMorgan China Growth & Income	(25.2)
Biotech Growth	(24.6)
Ceiba Investments	(24.3)
Life Settlement Assets A	(21.9)
Edinburgh Worldwide	(20.9)
Golden Prospect Precious Metals	(20.6)
Globalworth Real Estate Investments	(18.9)

Source: Morningstar, Marten & Co. Note: excludes trusts with market caps below £15m at 31/12/21

Figure 5: Money returned in 2021

	£m
Fidelity Emerging Markets	(249.3)
Witan	(160.6)
Alliance Trust	(139.1)
Polar Capital Technology	(80.4)
SME Credit Realisation	(78.8)
BlackRock Frontiers	(68.4)
Third Point Investors USD	(64.3)
Gulf Investment Fund	(59.4)
CVC Credit Partners European Opportunities	(53.9)
BMO Commercial Property	(48.6)

Figure 6: Money raised in 2021

	£m
Greencoat UK Wind	693.1
Smithson	611.6
Renewables Infrastructure Group	489.0
Tritax EuroBox	446.2
SDCL Energy Efficiency Income	443.2
Chrysalis	420.3
Home REIT	417.4
Urban Logistics REIT	405.7
Supermarket Income REIT	389.8
Tritax Big Box	370.1

Source: Morningstar, Marten & Co. Note: based on approximate value of shares at 31/12/21

FIRST QUARTER 2022

Figure 7: Best performing sectors by total price return over Q1

	Median share price TR (%)	Median NAV TR (%)	Median discount 31/03/22 (%)	Median sector market cap 31/03/22 (£m)	No. of companies in the sector
Latin America	23.2	29.1	(12.4)	102.5	2
Commodities and natural resources	17.9	11.3	(3.2)	77.2	9
Leasing	11.6	3.8	(45.4)	99.0	8
Insurance and reinsurance strategies	11.0	1.9	(13.0)	47.7	2
Propetry – UK commercial	6.8	1.1	(9.9)	341.4	15

Figure 8: Worst performing sectors by total price return over Q1

	Median share price TR (%)	Median NAV TR (%)	Median discount 31/03/22 (%)	Median sector market cap 31/03/22 (£m)	No. of companies in the sector
Growth capital	(21.7)	0.0	(25.6)	251.4	7
Japanese smaller companies	(19.5)	(17.2)	(4.2)	160.5	5
Global smaller companies	(18.8)	(14.0)	(10.8)	901.9	5
Biotechnology and healthcare	(18.7)	(5.2)	(6.8)	714.7	6
China/Greater China	(18.2)	(16.1)	(5.4)	295.3	4

Source: Morningstar, Marten & Co. Note: inclusive of sectors with at least two companies
Note: many alternative asset sector funds release NAV performance on a quarterly basis

Figure 9: Best performing funds in NAV terms over Q1

	%
BlackRock Latin American	31.1
Geiger Counter	28.6
abrdn Latin American Income	27.1
BlackRock Energy and Resources	26.4
CQS Natural Resources G&I	23.0
Livermore Investments	15.3
Gulf Investment Fund	14.9
Crystal Amber	14.0
Middlefield Canadian Income	13.4
BH Macro USD	12.3

Figure 10: Best performing funds in price terms over Q1

	%
CQS Natural Resources G&I	32.8
BlackRock Latin American	31.6
BlackRock World Mining	31.4
BlackRock Energy and Resources	27.2
Gulf Investment Fund	25.0
Middlefield Canadian Income	20.2
Livermore Investments	19.8
Doric Nimrod Air Three	19.4
UK Commercial Property REIT	19.4
CATCo Reinsurance Opps	19.2

Source: Morningstar, Marten & Co. Note: excludes trusts with market caps below £15m at 31/03/22

Figure 11: Worst performing funds in NAV terms over Q1

	%
JPMorgan Russian Securities	(94.3)
Baillie Gifford European Growth	(25.9)
JPMorgan China Growth & Income	(22.8)
Scottish Mortgage	(21.6)
BlackRock Throgmorton	(20.6)
Baillie Gifford US Growth	(20.2)
Barings Emerging EMEA Opportunities	(20.1)
Fidelity Japan	(20.0)
Montanaro European Smaller Companies	(19.9)
Montanaro UK Smaller Companies	(19.5)

Figure 12: Worst performing funds in price terms over Q1

	%
JPMorgan Russian Securities	(80.4)
SLF Realisation Fund	(36.5)
Schiehallion	(33.1)
EPE Special Opportunities	(29.3)
Chrysalis	(27.8)
Schroder UK Public Private	(27.2)
Baillie Gifford European Growth	(27.1)
Atlantis Japan Growth	(24.7)
Montanaro UK Smaller Companies	(24.7)
Syncona	(24.5)

Source: Morningstar, Marten & Co. Note: excludes trusts with market caps below £15m at 31/03/22

Figure 13: Money raised over Q1

	£m
Renewables Infrastructure Group	277.3
LXI REIT	250.0
Cordiant Digital Infrastructure	200.0
Ruffer	106.8
SDCL Energy Efficiency Income	100.0
Digital 9 Infrastructure	95.6
Smithson	88.7
Polar Capital Global Financials	84.3
Capital Gearing	82.1
JLEN Environmental Assets	60.7

Figure 14: Money returned over Q1

	£m
F&C	(106.0)
Alliance Trust	(52.2)
Polar Capital Technology	(33.4)
Witan	(29.6)
EP Global Opportunities	(21.8)
Vietnam Enterprise	(21.0)
BMO Commercial Property	(20.5)
Strategic Equity Capital	(19.0)
Herald	(18.5)
Scottish Mortgage	(18.1)

Source: Morningstar, Marten & Co. Note: excludes trusts with market caps below £15m at 31/03/22

SECOND QUARTER 2022

Figure 15: Best performing sectors by total price return over Q2

	Median share price TR (%)	Median NAV TR (%)	Median discount 30/06/22 (%)	Median sector market cap 30/06/22 (£m)	No. of companies in the sector
Insurance and reinsurance strategies	205.4	8.8	169.3	29.6	2
China/Greater China	11.9	10.2	(3.1)	325.5	4
Leasing	8.9	5.1	(40.3)	103.1	8
Renewable energy infrastructure	4.6	1.5	3.1	582.5	21
Hedge funds	3.1	4.0	(12.0)	85.4	8

Figure 16: Worst performing sectors by total price return over Q2

	Median share price TR (%)	Median NAV TR (%)	Median discount 30/06/22 (%)	Median sector market cap 30/06/22 (£m)	No. of companies in the sector
Technology and media	(21.6)	(17.5)	(13.5)	862.7	3
European smaller companies	(17.3)	(14.6)	(13.5)	445.5	4
UK all companies	(16.4)	(12.4)	(13.7)	192.5	9
Growth capital	(16.1)	0.0	(39.2)	192.0	7
Property – rest of world	(15.5)	0.0	(67.1)	28.4	4

Source: Morningstar, Marten & Co. Note: inclusive of sectors with at least two companies
Note: many alternative asset sector funds release NAV performance on a quarterly basis

Figure 17: Best performing funds in NAV terms over Q2

	%
ND Distressed Debt Global	15.6
JZ Capital Partners	15.4
BH Macro USD	14.6
Thomas lloyd Energy Impact	14.4
JPMorgan China Growth & Income	13.5
US Solar	11.6
abrdn China	10.9
Riverstone Credit Opportunities Income	10.6
BioPharma Credit	10.1
Tufton Oceanic Assets	10.0

Figure 18: Best performing funds in price terms over Q2

	%
Literacy Capital PLC	34.7
Syncona	27.5
Doric Nimrod Air Two	18.4
JPMorgan China Growth & Income	17.8
JPMorgan Global Core Real Assets	15.9
BH Macro USD	14.6
Fidelity China Special Situations	14.5
Gresham House Energy Storage	13.9
Africa Opportunity	13.8
Symphony International	13.5

Source: Morningstar, Marten & Co. Note: excludes trusts with market caps below £15m at 30/06/22

Figure 19: Worst performing funds in NAV terms over Q2

	%
UIL	(29.0)
Golden Prospect Precious Metals	(28.6)
Baillie Gifford US Growth	(26.3)
BlackRock World Mining	(23.8)
Keystone Positive Change	(23.2)
Allianz Technology	(22.1)
abrdn UK Small Companies Growth	(21.9)
BlackRock Throgmorton	(21.7)
JPMorgan UK Smaller Companies	(21.6)
BlackRock Latin American	(21.3)

Figure 20: Worst performing funds in price terms over Q2

	%
JPMorgan Russian Securities	(52.2)
Chrysalis	(41.1)
Baillie Gifford US Growth	(39.1)
Geiger Counter	(36.4)
Scottish Mortgage	(30.1)
Montanaro European Smaller	(28.6)
Keystone Positive Change	(28.2)
Smithson	(27.7)
BlackRock Throgmorton	(27.6)
Baillie Gifford European Growth	(26.6)

Source: Morningstar, Marten & Co. Note: excludes trusts with market caps below £15m at 30/06/22

Figure 21: Money raised over Q2

	£m
International Public Partnerships	334.0
Supermarket Income REIT	306.7
Home REIT	260.0
Greencoat Renewables	256.4
Gore Street Energy Storage	165.0
Gresham House Energy Storage	162.4
Bluefield Solar Income	151.2
Capital Gearing	133.3
Ruffer	124.9
BH Macro GP	97.2

Figure 22: Money returned over Q2

	£m
Monks	(60.1)
Alliance Trust	(45.8)
Pershing Square Holdings	(42.8)
Scottish Mortgage	(36.7)
Witan	(36.7)
BlackRock Latin American	(34.8)
F&C	(33.6)
Polar Capital Technology	(33.0)
Finsbury Growth & Income	(22.9)
Balanced Commercial Property	(17.3)

Source: Morningstar, Marten & Co. Note: excludes trusts with market caps below £15m at 30/06/22

THIRD QUARTER 2022

Figure 23: Best performing sectors by total price return over Q3

	Median share price TR (%)	Median NAV TR (%)	Median discount 30/09/22 (%)	Median sector market cap 30/09/22 (£m)	No. of companies in the sector
Insurance and reinsurance strategies	50.8	8.5	(21.3)	33.3	2
India	16.0	17.5	(16.8)	282.2	4
Leasing	15.7	6.6	(26.5)	110.1	8
Financials	10.5	6.0	(10.5)	415.5	2
Biotechnology and healthcare	10.1	10.3	(6.7)	695.0	6

Figure 24: Worst performing sectors by total price return over Q3

	Median share price TR (%)	Median NAV TR (%)	Median discount 30/09/22 (%)	Median sector market cap 30/09/22 (£m)	No. of companies in the sector
Property – UK logistics	(24.5)	0.0	(37.8)	611.2	3
China/Greater China	(22.5)	(16.2)	(11.8)	246.9	4
Property – UK commercial	(13.2)	1.1	(34.3)	248.4	14
Growth capital	(12.7)	0.0	(46.8)	145.6	7
Property – UK healthcare	(12.6)	1.5	(15.1)	491.4	2

Source: Morningstar, Marten & Co. Note: inclusive of sectors with at least two companies
Note: many alternative asset sector funds release NAV performance on a quarterly basis

Figure 25: Best performing funds in NAV terms over Q3

	%
RTW Ventures	27.1
India Capital Growth	24.0
Ashoka India Equity	20.2
Biotech Growth	20.0
Geiger Counter	19.5
Marble Point Loan Financing	18.7
Pershing Square Holdings	17.7
Fair Oaks Income	17.1
Bellvue Healthcare	15.5
BH Macro (USD)	15.0

Figure 26: Best performing funds in price terms over Q3

	%
Doric Nimrod Air One	86.1
Macau Property Opportunities	53.8
RTW Venture	28.4
India Capital Growth	27.6
Fundsmith Emerging Equities	24.1
Biotech Growth	23.6
Ashoka India Equity	21.1
SLF Realisation	19.6
BH Macro (USD)	17.8
Doric Nimrod Air Two	17.8

Source: Morningstar, Marten & Co. Note: excludes trusts with market caps below £15m at 30/09/22

Figure 27: Worst performing funds in NAV terms over Q3

	%
JPMorgan China Growth and Income	(21.6)
River and Mercantile UK Micro Cap	(20.2)
EPE Special Opportunities	(18.1)
Baillie Gifford China Growth	(17.3)
abrdn Smaller Companies Income	(15.4)
Chelverton UK Dividend	(15.2)
Fidelity China Special Situations	(15.1)
abrdn China	(14.9)
Miton UK Microcap	(13.9)
abrdn UK Smaller Companies Growth	(11.7)

Figure 28: Worst performing funds in price terms over Q3

	%
Chrysalis Investments	(40.8)
JPMorgan China Growth and Income	(29.1)
Balanced Commercial Property	(27.2)
Warehouse REIT	(26.0)
Tritax EuroBox	(25.8)
EPE Special Opportunities	(24.7)
Tritax Big Box REIT	(24.5)
Aseana Properties	(24.5)
Schroder UK Public Private	(24.1)
Life Science REIT	(23.7)

Source: Morningstar, Marten & Co. Note: excludes trusts with market caps below £15m at 30/09/22

Figure 29: Money raised over Q3

	£m
HICL Infrastructure	160.0
SDCL Energy Efficiency	135.0
VH Global Sustainable Energy Opportunities	122.0
Capital Gearing	100.3
Pantheon Infrastructure	80.8
Ruffer	61.8
Digital9 Infrastructure	60.0
Personal Assets	36.1
City of London	25.7

Figure 30: Money returned over Q3

	£m
Scottish Mortgage	85.9
Pershing Square holdings	79.1
Monks	48.5
Finsbury Growth and Income	36.9
Witan	35.2
Alliance	32.8
Smithson	30.7
Worldwide Healthcare	28.8
Polar Capital Technology	23.2

Source: Morningstar, Marten & Co. Note: excludes trusts with market caps below £15m at 30/09/22

NOT MUCH TO CHEER

Trust expert MAX KING *reviews the performance of equity investment trusts in this year's difficult market conditions.*

I**T HAS BEEN** a frustrating year for investors and market watchers, both for the bulls and the bears. For the bulls, it has been a year of negative returns, though a setback was clearly flagged in late 2021. For the bears, it has not lived up to their apocalyptic prognosis – though they haven't given up hope that it eventually will.

Equity markets have broadly taken their lead from bonds, falling in the first half of the year as yields rose, then rallying as yields dropped again, then falling as yields climbed once more. Corporate earnings continued to beat optimistic expectations, though analysts started to reduce growth forecasts in the second half. The weakness of sterling partially insulated UK investors from the fall in global markets and the outperformance of the UK provided additional respite.

Holders of investment trusts had the additional handicap of rising discounts to net asset value, with the average for the sector, excluding 3i, increasing from 1.5% at the start of the year to 14.4% as of 5 October. Many funds in the alternatives sector continued to trade at premia, enabling continued new issuance, until late September; but discounts in other sectors, notably property and private equity, increased considerably more than average. Value and defensively orientated funds did better, while many growth-orientated funds were helped by share buybacks and the long-term faith of private investors.

A major blow

The underlying performance of trusts, down 6.4%, was broadly in line with global equities and the All-Share index due to the outperformance of alternatives balancing the growth and small-cap bias of the equity trusts. The widening of discounts, however, extended the loss to a much more serious 18.7% and is clearly a major blow for the development of the sector. Open-ended funds have seen considerable investor outflows (£14.1bn to the end of August, mainly in equity funds) and there has been a corresponding imbalance of sellers and buyers in investment trusts.

Equity funds account for nearly half the sector total (more than half if private equity funds are included). Four trusts are in the FTSE 100 – Scottish Mortgage,

Pershing Square, 3i and F&C – but another three are large enough for inclusion and a further three are within touching distance. Talk of excluding investment trusts from the FTSE UK indices has been kicked into the long grass for now.

Given the poor overall performance, it is not surprising that the list of winners is short and that of losers is long. Much attention has been drawn to the 40% fall in the share price of Scottish Mortgage Trust this year (nearly 50% since its peak in autumn 2021) so that its market value has dropped below £12bn, but it is still the top performer in the global sector over three and five years. The more value-orientated F&C is barely down this year but lags far behind over three and five years. 3i is down 20%, entirely due to its shares being derated while net asset value has risen; and Pershing Square, whose hedge fund mindset causes it to protect against the downside, is down 8%.

Value stocks strongly outperformed growth in the first half of the year, to the detriment of the technology sector, growth-orientated healthcare and, among others, all the Baillie Gifford trusts; but the picture has been more mixed in the second half. The underperformance of small and mid-caps around the world was negative for the specialists in those sectors and also for the generalist trusts overweight in them, while mounting economic problems in China resulted in poor performance for specialists there.

The worst performances came from JPMorgan Russian and Chrysalis. The former – down 90% – was the result of Russia's invasion of Ukraine wiping out the value of all Russian stocks and was unavoidable. The 75% fall in the latter was entirely self-inflicted, as its managers naively charged into blue-sky, early-stage private equity investment.

While discounts for private equity funds widened sharply, underlying performance was often good. The share prices of Oakley Capital, 3i and Pantheon International all fell despite them being in the list of the 20 best performers in the whole investment trust sector. Literacy Capital and JZ Capital were also on the list, but feature in the list of best share price performers. Schiehallion, Seraphim Space and Schroder UK Public Private, formerly known as Woodford Patient Capital, performed poorly in net asset value terms and terribly in share price terms, all three more than halving.

UK small and mid-cap trusts accounted for another 10 of the 20 worst performers in net asset value terms but, since discounts had already widened last year, only three were among the worst 20 in share price terms. Another four of the worst performers were European trusts, one (Montanaro) a small cap specialist. TR Property, which invests across Europe and the UK, was pulled down by the poor performance of real estate equities and its net asset value lost 37%.

There were few winners. BlackRock World Mining was up 33% by the spring but had given it all back by the end of September. Riverstone Energy, now shifting from hydrocarbons to renewables, was up 35% but had been down 88% in the 18 months to March 2020. BlackRock Energy and Resources had a yo-yo year but still advanced 17%.

The "flexible investment" sector has had mixed fortunes and, on average, still lags global equities over three and five years. These funds seek to protect investors in bear markets at the expense of underperformance in bull markets by investing in non-equity asset classes such as inflation-linked bonds, precious metals and infrastructure funds. Ruffer, which has been on a roll in the last three years, has generated a positive investment and share price return in the year to date and trades on a premium. Caledonia (up 6%) and RIT (down 6%) suffered from their exposure to private equity, so their share prices fell 14% and 24% respectively. Capital Gearing and Personal Assets continue to trade on premia but saw modest declines in their net asset values.

In emerging markets, the dreadful performance of China was counterbalanced by some better performances from the Middle East, India and frontier markets. Gulf Investment gained 24%, Ashoka India 4%, JPMorgan India 2% and BlackRock Frontiers 2%. The liquidation of three emerging market trusts – managed by Jupiter, Scotgems and Fundsmith – may be a signal to contrarian investors that it is time to start paying the remaining funds more attention.

A fallow year for issuance

In such a difficult year for trusts with discounts rising sharply, it is not surprising that issuance of new equity was largely confined to the alternative income sector. There were no new issues in the first half, but three sought listings in September – Sustainable Farmland Trust, Independent Living REIT and Welkin China Private Equity. The first two of these would clearly belong in the alternative income sector. Welkin, which claims a compound annual return of 28% and targets one of 15%, will need to overcome an even more sceptical audience than the other two.

More than three-quarters of the £7bn of secondary capital raised in the first nine months was for the alternative income sector, notably for those investing in renewables, but £780m was also raised for Ruffer, Capital Gearing and Personal Assets. Some growth trusts, such as Smithson, were still able to issue equity in the first quarter but their shares then moved to a discount. Among value-investing trusts, City of London, Merchants and Polar Capital Global Financials also raised money – the latter £86m before its shares moved to a discount.

Capital returned was just £1.7bn in the first half but £3.1bn in the third quarter as buybacks were stepped up in response to widening discounts. However, the outflow figure includes £1.5bn and the inflow £1.1bn from the merger of Secure Income with LXI REIT plus £625m and £614m respectively from the merger of Scottish Investment Trust with JP Morgan Global Growth and Income.

Buybacks were £2bn, led by Monks (£187m), Scottish Mortgage (£145m), Alliance (£128m), Witan (£105m) and Polar Technology (£91m). The rest was evenly divided between liquidations (such as Scotgems), special dividends (including £95m from Caledonia) and tenders/redemptions by continuing funds. There is little chance that fundraising will come anywhere near the £16.2bn raised in 2021 but, should market conditions change, a rush of issuance can be expected.

The key to a turnaround in the equity market's fortunes is for bond yields to reach levels where long-term inflation expectations are fully discounted. That point may have been reached at the end of the September, but yields, having been too low for so long, may now overcompensate and rise too high. Growth in corporate earnings has ground to a halt in 2022 and may reverse as economies weaken, but investors should be prepared to look through that to the rebound that will accompany recovery.

Looking ahead

This would make 2023 a good year for equity investors, especially for those in investment trusts. A return to net investor inflows would see discounts narrow again, augmenting returns which should be further increased by the gearing provided by borrowings and the long-term record of underlying outperformance.

That should accelerate the growth of the sector. Total assets have shrunk this year by £7bn to £270bn, and the sector's weighting in the All-Share index has dipped to 6.6%. As the long-term popularity of the investment trust structure continues to increase, that will surely rise significantly further, even if the UK's weighting in global indices stops shrinking. The last quarter will dictate whether the sector bounces back or continues to struggle.

MAX KING was an investment manager and strategist at Finsbury Asset Management, J O Hambro and Investec Asset Management. He is now an independent writer, with a regular column in MoneyWeek, and an adviser with a special interest in investment companies. He is a non-executive director of two trusts.

VCTS: BEST EVER YEAR

ALEX DAVIES, *founder of Wealth Club, gives his annual review of developments in the venture capital trust (VCT) sector.*

INVESTOR APPETITE FOR VCTs appeared insatiable last year. Amati AIM VCT launched its offer on the last Friday of July 2021 – and closed it the following Wednesday, having raised £40m. In October, Octopus Titan, the largest VCT, raised a mammoth £200m in 28 days. Capping them both were the Mobeus VCTs, which filled their £35m raise in just 24 hours. These are exceptional cases, but demand was buoyant across the board.

Indeed, 2021/22 has been the biggest ever year for VCTs. For the first time, total funds raised broke through the £1bn barrier, hitting a remarkable £1.133bn. Not only did this dwarf the preceding year's very respectable £681m, but it was also nearly 40% more than the previous record of £779m achieved in 2005/06, when VCT income tax relief briefly peaked at 40%.

As the pandemic supercharged the pace of digital transformation, investors were keen to pour money into the young and ambitious companies creating technology solutions for the new 'digital-first' world. But just as the tax year was coming to an end, the outlook started to darken – and continued to do so in the new tax year. Russia invaded Ukraine. Energy prices soared. Inflation reached levels not seen in 40 years. Interest rates started to creep up. The pound faltered.

At the time of writing, September 2022, the new VCT season is just getting started. Can VCTs hold their ground against this much-changed backdrop? Can they still be attractive to investors?

We believe that, while the economic outlook has dramatically changed compared to last year, the fundamental reasons for VCTs' appeal to investors are as compelling and current as they ever were – if not more so.

Historic VCT fundraising

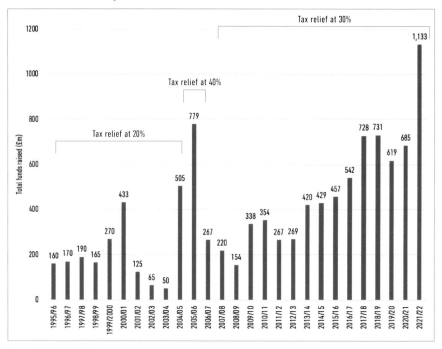

Source: AIC, Wealth Club

Strong long-term performance

Over time, VCTs have well-rewarded investors.

In the 10 years to June 2022, the 10 largest generalist VCT managers have on average more than doubled investor money in terms of NAV total return (current NAV and cumulative dividends paid in the period) – outperforming the FTSE All-Share index. The same is also true of AIM VCTs, which have performed 2.5x better than the FTSE AIM All-Share index.

Ten-year performance: ten largest generalist VCT managers

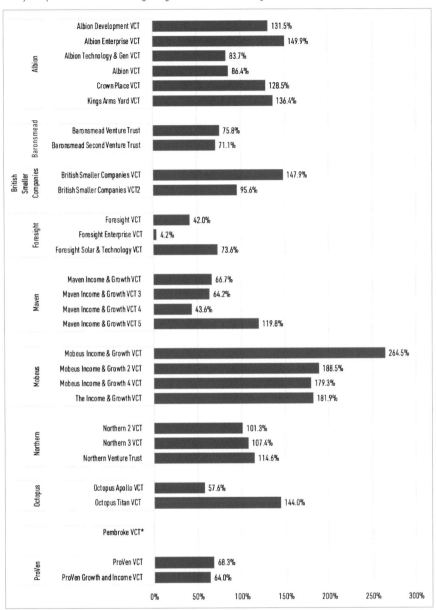

Source: Morningstar, Wealth Club. Data from 30 June 2012 to 30 June 2022

* Pembroke VCT launched in 2013 and therefore doesn't yet have a 10-year track record

Ten-year performance: AIM VCT managers

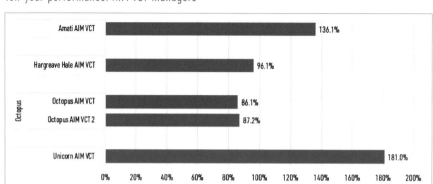

Source: Morningstar, Wealth Club. Data from 30 June 2012 to 30 June 2022

Exposure to growth potential in a hard-to-reach sector

One of the reasons for VCTs' outperformance – and a large contributor to their appeal – is the nature of the companies in which VCTs invest: fast-growing, early-stage, tech-enabled businesses.

Cloud-based banking platform Thought Machine is one example. Its technology can replace a bank's clunky, outdated and often unstable legacy IT infrastructure with a modern, robust and flexible alternative. Thought Machine's core banking system, Vault, is used by more than 35 banks globally; it allows them to easily manage, change and create financial products. Backed by Molten Ventures, manager of the Molten Ventures VCT (formerly Draper Esprit VCT), Thought Machine has received funding from a host of high-profile investors, including US banks Morgan Stanley and JPMorgan Chase, and Lloyds Banking Group. The latest funding round, in May 2022, doubled the company's valuation to $2.7bn.

Another example, from a completely different market, is Popsa. The 'world's fastest photobook app' promises to help people turn the myriad of photos on their phones into photo books – easily and in a matter of minutes. The company, backed by Pembroke VCT and the Octopus AIM VCTs, is growing very fast. It was included in the Deloitte UK Fast 50 in both 2020 and 2021, being recognised as one of the UK's 50 fastest-growing technology companies. In March 2022, the *Financial Times* ranked the company as the fifth fastest-growing technology company in Europe.

These are outstanding examples, but the overall picture is equally promising.

Wealth Club analysts recently looked at 11 VCT managers, covering approximately three quarters of the whole active VCT market, and compared the growth of their portfolio companies with FTSE 350 constituents. We found:

- Nearly half (43.1%) of VCTs' investments are in companies that have grown revenues by more than 25% year-on-year. By comparison just 5.9% of the largest 350 constituents of the UK main market have achieved this.

- 31.0% of VCTs' investments are in companies that have grown revenues by over 50%, compared with just 3.2% for the UK main market.

Growth exposure - VCTs vs. FTSE 350

	REVENUE DECLINE	MODEST GROWTH (<25%)	HIGH GROWTH (>25%)
Octopus Titan VCT	1.18%	14.97%	72.41%
Octopus Apollo VCT	7.98%	11.00%	61.87%
British Smaller Companies VCTs	21.25%	22.50%	53.75%
Proven VCTs	10.00%	37.00%	53.00%
Pembroke VCT	37.94%	5.64%	52.82%
Albion VCTs	3.58%	13.88%	43.86%
Mobeus VCTs	23.96%	40.32%	35.63%
Maven VCTs	21.43%	16.71%	33.42%
Northern VCTs	15.28%	39.67%	30.07%
Baronsmead VCTs	16.99%	34.41%	23.66%
Amati AIM VCT	29.91%	52.46%	11.62%
FTSE 350	62.32%	31.77%	5.91%

All these figures are based on investee companies' financial results in their last full financial year to December 2021.

This striking difference is largely due to the fact the FTSE 350 is dominated by the financial, consumer staples and industrials sectors – these accounted for over 50% of the index as at December 2021. By contrast, the vast majority of VCT-backed businesses are technology companies.

If you're an investor after growth and want exposure to tech, you need to look towards private companies – and VCTs are one of the easiest ways to access the sector.

What about the widely reported 'tech sell-off' of 2022?

It is possible – and some might say inevitable – that the sentiment seen in public markets will percolate through to private markets. The pandemic put a premium on anything digital. There are concerns this led to frothy valuations and that the boom times may not last much longer. That could well be the case, but it's hard to see the long-term trend in favour of technology and digitisation going into reverse, and a large proportion of VCT companies operate in those areas.

What we're more likely to see is lower – perhaps significantly lower – valuations in the short-to-medium term. And this could well present an opportunity for VCT investors.

If company valuations drop, we would typically expect VCTs to revalue their net assets accordingly prior to allotting shares (this is what they did in March 2020, at the onset of the pandemic, for instance). That ensures new investors don't buy today at yesterday's prices and could mean there are bargains to be had – although, of course, there are risks too.

Generous tax breaks add to the appeal of VCTs

There are significant tax breaks associated with VCTs. When you invest, you can receive up to 30% income tax relief. Moreover, any dividends a VCT pays are tax free. The government offers these perks in recognition of, and to compensate for, the risks inherent with investing in young, small companies – and to encourage private investment into them.

VCT tax relief has always been attractive to investors – but especially so in recent years, as taxes have gone up and traditional tax-efficient investments such as pensions have become less attractive, or even completely closed, to wealthier investors.

Currently, UK taxpayers are saddled with the heaviest tax burden since the 1940s. Higher earners have borne the brunt of this: the 10% of income taxpayers with the largest incomes contribute over 60% of income tax receipts.

At the same time, pensions – historically the port of call for high earners looking to invest tax efficiently – have been severely restricted. Over a decade ago, a high earner could invest up to £255,000 per tax year in a pension and get a significant percentage of that back in tax relief. Those days are gone. The tax benefits offered by pensions have been gradually eroded by successive governments. Now the annual pension allowance is £40,000 – reduced to a mere £4,000 for those with income of £312,000 or more in a year.

Meanwhile, the pension lifetime allowance – the total amount most people can put aside tax efficiently in a pension over a lifetime – stands at £1,073,100. The March 2021 Budget announced it will stay at this level until 2026. Any excess in your pension pot could be subject to a 55% tax penalty.

VCTs, with their simple and comparatively generous allowance of £200,000, are a natural alternative for wealthier investors.

The increase in dividend tax also makes VCTs – and their tax-free dividends – increasingly attractive. For instance, if a VCT pays a 5% dividend, you get 5p in your hand for every £1 invested. To match that outside of a tax wrapper, you would need to get a dividend of 7.55% if you are a higher-rate taxpayer or 8.24% if you are a top-rate taxpayer, in the 2022/23 tax year.

Who invests in VCTs – and why?

Contrary to what many may think, there is no such thing as a typical VCT investor. The average age of our clients who invest in VCTs is 61. The youngest is 19, the eldest 102. The fastest-growing group of investors is those in the 30–40 age bracket. 80% are male, 20% female.

In the 2021/22 tax year, they invested £41,335 on average across a number of VCTs per tax year. The average amount invested in each VCT was £12,770. We don't record occupation, but many we speak to who invest are professionals, such as doctors, lawyers, higher earners in the City, business owners – but also, head teachers and civil servants. They tend to have investments elsewhere (e.g., ISAs, pensions, property) to which VCTs add diversification, and they tend to have been affected by tax rises and pension restrictions.

What prompted them to start investing in VCTs?

We asked investors in a recent survey: 71.7% of respondents cited tax as a reason that prompted them to start investing in VCTs. The exposure to high-growth-potential investments (with commensurate high risks somewhat mitigated by the tax reliefs), the diversification VCTs can add to one's portfolio and the opportunity to support UK entrepreneurship were also mentioned. Over 94% believe investing in VCTs helps back the next generation of UK entrepreneurs.

All those reasons are independent of what the economy does or where the next crisis is going to come from.

If you have sufficient assets elsewhere and a certain level of financial sophistication, VCTs may well be a worthwhile option for you to consider, after using your pension and ISA allowances. As a rule of thumb, VCTs should account for no more than 10% of your total portfolio.

When you invest in a VCT, your money would typically be spread over 30 to 100 companies, which provides an important degree of underlying diversification. In addition, it may be prudent to spread your annual investment over several VCTs, preferably with different investment strategies, to further diversify your risk. Don't forget you also have a 30% cushion in the form of tax relief, should things go wrong.

Clearly, for someone who doesn't have sufficient assets or earnings, and doesn't fully understand the risks, VCTs are unlikely to be a suitable investment. Young, small companies are more likely to fail than older and larger ones. If something goes badly wrong for a small company, it is much harder for it to recover than it is for a large and well-established company. Small companies are also a lot more illiquid, as are VCTs themselves – meaning it may be difficult to buy and sell the shares.

One final thought

The VCT season has only just started this year.

The world looks very different from what it did 12 months ago, and investor sentiment has certainly taken a hit. But taxes are still at a record high this tax year. Pensions are still no longer an option for many. Technology and digitalisation are increasingly embedded in all aspects of business, the economy and daily life. And the VCT investment case is just as compelling as it ever was.

The total funds raised may or may not surpass last year's record-breaking £1.133bn. However, if we've learnt anything from the past, it's that the most popular offers always sell out – a reminder to investors that if they spot a VCT they like, they should act quickly whilst there is still capacity.

ALEX DAVIES is the founder and CEO of Wealth Club, the largest broker of VCTs and tax-efficient investments for experienced investors.

A NEW MARKET REGIME

Investment trust expert JOHN BARON *suggests a new era in portfolio construction has dawned and provides an example of a real portfolio from the website www.johnbaronportfolios.co.uk.*

THE TRANSITION TO a new regime of higher inflation and volatility, coupled with lower growth, is necessitating a change in portfolio construction when it comes to both equities and other assets. In particular, those seeking diversification will need to be more creative, and will be assisted by a number of good opportunities across the asset spectrum. As this investment landscape evolves, investment trusts are superbly placed to capitalise given their structure better caters for the long-term investment needed when bucking short-term sentiment.

A new portfolio construct

Poor economic and financial policy, both in the UK and abroad, has not only resulted in inflation, economic malaise and falling living standards for most people, it has also distorted financial markets to the point most asset prices (and the correlation between them) have increased. There will need to be some sort of reckoning, if it has not already happened by the time this book is published. Most likely, either the valuations of financial assets and debt will be eroded by inflation or these values will have to decline and the debt be unwound.

For a variety of reasons, both domestic and geopolitical, inflation will remain stubbornly high. The markets recognise that central banks are restricted in their policy responses given the extreme debt levels and scenario they've created. And while accepting we live in unusual times, it would be truly unusual to tame the current level of inflation with interest rates that remained substantially below that level. The current policy suggests a more severe economic slowdown than perhaps markets are expecting.

It is across this new scenario that markets now tread. Over previous decades, the markets have grown used to a period of falling or relatively stable inflation and low economic growth. This has tended to favour fixed-interest bonds over index-linked bonds and growth (particularly technology) over value when it comes to equities. However, times have changed. These assets – so beloved of the conventional 60/40 equity/bond portfolio – performed well in the last market regime but are unlikely to do so now.

Investors would be wise to embrace a new investment approach to better accommodate this new market landscape. Just as mainstream portfolio construction has evolved to meet changing conditions in the past, it needs to do so again. Certainly the 10 real investment trust portfolios managed on the website www.johnbaronportfolios.co.uk have transitioned within their equity exposure (to achieve a better balance between 'growth' and 'value', having been overweight the former) and also embraced new asset classes when diversifying.

For example, exposure to conventional bonds in particular was significantly reduced some time ago given the inflationary outlook. The only pockets of value are corporate bonds given current valuations – the portfolios' main holding having been CQS New City High Yield (NCYF). And while protecting against inflation and against volatility are two different things, index-linked bonds both home and abroad are also evident in some portfolios as markets (and central banks) may still be underestimating just how stubborn inflation will be.

As for equity holdings, broad market exposure by way of geography will continue to feature but the portfolios have long embraced the concept of thematic investing. Indeed, this concept now represents the larger component outside the UK in most portfolios. This is because sectors such as technology (especially smaller companies), healthcare, private equity and the environment will be continue to be among the secular long-term growth themes of the future regardless of any short-term volatility.

Examples held within the portfolios include Herald Investment Trust (HRI), Augmentum Fintech (AUGM), Bellevue Healthcare Trust (BBH), Worldwide Healthcare Trust (WWH), abrdn Private Equity Opportunities (APEO), Apax Global Alpha Ltd (APAX), HarbourVest Global Private Equity (HVPE), Impax Environmental Markets (IEM) and Jupiter Green (JGC). All should perform well relative to wider markets and volatility should be used to add to positions if underweight.

But something more is required. In addition to reducing exposure to growth investments, a growing component of investors' equity exposure will need to embrace a higher-conviction approach to stock-picking to thrive. Too many funds and institutional portfolios tend to hug the benchmark believing there is safety in numbers. This is becoming an increasingly dangerous fallacy. As Sir John Templeton reminded us, investors have to do something different if they are to beat the benchmark. Fund managers should increasingly do likewise.

For example, the portfolios have been adding to their positions in JPMorgan Global Growth & Income (JGGI). The company holds a high-conviction portfolio of typically 50–90 stocks, while paying a dividend equating to 4% of its NAV. Portfolio construction is steered by bottom-up stock selection rather than geographical allocation. This added flexibility has helped it outperform its benchmark. Other examples of this required conviction approach include Finsbury Growth & Income Trust (FGT) and Edinburgh Investment Trust (EDIN).

In addition to this different portfolio construction entering mainstream thinking, and in contrast to the more conventional 60/40 equity/bond exposure, investors will need to be more creative in embracing other 'uncorrelated' assets when compensating for the reduction in conventional bond exposure. This is especially so given present policies have increased the correlation between asset classes in general – most prices having benefitted from the flood of printed money.

The changing face of diversification

For despite the new market regime, it will remain a truism that it is usually wise to increasingly diversify a portfolio away from equities as the investment journey unfolds, in order to help cushion the effect of any market falls. This investment discipline is particularly important to those near to achieving financial objectives. And while there are no fixed rules as to the pace and extent of diversification, the website's open Diversification page lists and quantifies the portfolios' approach in some detail.

The breakdown of the website's 'Winter' portfolio provides further detail as to how it achieves its task. The portfolio is the website's most defensive, with currently just c. 6.5% of exposure committed to mostly higher-yielding quality equities and the balance to a wide array of alternative assets. It is the culmination of a five-portfolio risk-adjusted investment journey which sees the portfolios increasingly diversify away from equities into other asset classes, to help protect past gains while generating a higher income.

Winter portfolio breakdown (to 30 September 2022)

Bonds	CQS New City High Yield (NCYF)	5.5%
	iShares Index Linked Gilts ETF (INXG)	4.0%
	Invesco Bond Income Plus (BIPS)	2.5%
UK shares	Edinburgh Investment Trust (EDIN)	4.5%
	Montanaro UK Smaller Cos (MTU)	2.0%
Themes	Ruffer Investment Company (RICA)	5.0%
	Personal Assets Trust (PNL)	4.0%

	Aberdeen Diversified Inc & Growth (ADIG)	3.0%
	Capital Gearing Trust (CGT)	3.0%
Other assets	BioPharma Credit Investments (BPCR)	6.0%
	WisdomTree Physical Gold £ ETF (PHGP)	6.0%
	abrdn Property Income Trust (API)	5.5%
	HICL Infrastructure Company (HICL)	5.0%
	International Public Partnerships (INPP)	5.0%
	JLEN Environmental Assets Group (JLEN)	5.0%
	GCP Asset Backed Income Fund (GABI)	4.5%
	BlackRock World Mining (BRWM)	4.0%
	Bluefield Solar Income Fund (BSIF)	3.5%
	CQS Natural Resources Growth & Inc (CYN)	3.5%
	Sequoia Economic Infrastructure Inc (SEQI)	3.5%
	The Renewables Infrastructure Group (TRIG)	3.0%
	Hipgnosis Songs Fund (SONG)	2.5%
	Regional REIT (RGL)	2.0%
Cash		7.5%
Total		**100%**

Previous paragraphs have touched on the make-up of the portfolio's bond and equity exposure. In addition to the themes also mentioned previously, capital preservation companies, such as Ruffer Investment Company (RICA), Personal Assets Trust (PNL) and Capital Gearing Trust (CGT), are listed within the portfolio's 'Themes' section given they hold assets spanning the entire asset spectrum including equities, index-linked bonds and gold. However, these companies are instrumental to the cause of diversification.

Further to this cause, the other 'less-correlated' assets presently include infrastructure companies such as HICL Infrastructure Company (HICL) and International Public Partnerships (INPP), whose revenues have positive correlations of 0.7–0.8% to inflation. Environmental companies such as JLEN Environmental Assets Group (JLEN), The Renewable Infrastructure Group (TRIG) and Bluefield Solar Income Fund (BSIF) are not only assisting with the net-zero agenda but also benefitting from increased power price forecasts.

Commodity companies also feature, such as BlackRock World Mining (BRWM) and CQS Natural Resources Growth & Income (CYN), which are benefitting from higher mineral prices courtesy of the inflationary environment and geopolitics.

Companies within the specialist lending and commercial property sectors are also held – examples include BioPharma Credit Investments (BPCR) and abrdn Property Income Trust (API). Many of these companies also help the portfolios achieve respectable yields relative to remit.

But the portfolio has been seeking further assets which possess an even lower correlation to the economy and markets. Hipgnosis Songs Fund (SONG) invests in a catalogue of songs and associated musical intellectual property rights, and receives revenue whenever they are played. This revenue has grown unabated, including during the pandemic. A recent report from Goldman Sachs saw it upgrade its double-digit annual growth forecast to 2030. While the company's debt is subject to rising interest rates, patient investors will be rewarded.

Other often unfashionable yet underestimated asset classes when markets are volatile include cash and gold. Cash in particular has its critics, particularly during times of high inflation, but it is a known quantity when markets are volatile. Together with gold, history suggests it has been one of the best 'diversifiers' of all given its nature. Both are also a reserve for long-term opportunities given volatility will continue, as evidenced by the appearance of pockets of value after the investment trust sector's recent de-rating.

Performance

When it comes to embracing diversification in the normal sense – that of helping to protect past gains – there is a common concern that diversification away from equities can only lead to underperformance relative to equity markets over time. This is understandable. No one knows what the future holds and humility is important. However, while never complacent, the performance of the website's Winter portfolio gently suggests diversification need not be the hindrance commonly thought – indeed, quite the opposite.

In one respect, performance has been pedestrian. The portfolio has tended to be resilient when markets have dipped and trailed when markets have soared. However, since its introduction in January 2014, it has outperformed the FTSE All-Share index – producing a total return of 54.4% to 30 September, which compares with 43.1% for the index. Good things often come in small parcels. The website's open Performance page has more detail including a year-by-year breakdown.

JOHN BARON *is one of the UK's leading experts on investment trusts, a regular columnist and speaker at investment seminars, and author of* The Financial Times Guide to Investment Trusts. *Since 2009, he has reported on two real portfolios in his popular monthly column in the* Investors Chronicle *– fees are donated to charity. His website www.johnbaronportfolios.co.uk reports on the progress of 10 real investment trust portfolios which achieve a range of strategies and income objectives, and possess an enviable track record relative to benchmarks.*

John is also Chairman of the Baron & Grant Investment Committee which oversees the portfolios of those clients seeking discretionary fund management. The company's website can be found at www.baronandgrant.com. John has used investment trusts in a private and professional capacity for over 35 years. After university and the Army, he ran a broad range of investment portfolios as a director of both Henderson Private Clients and then Rothschild Asset Management. Since leaving the City, he has also helped charities monitor their fund managers.

———————————

INFLATION IS BACK

The return of inflation and the big jumps in energy prices that are fuelling it have been the dominant influence on markets of 2022. Central bankers have been raising interest rates in response. Higher interest rates are designed to choke off demand for goods and services, while encouraging saving over spending. In the face of lower demand, prices should fall – that is the theory anyway. JAMES CARTHEW *explores what this means for investment trusts.*

THE PROSPECT OF higher interest rates first drove a sharp rotation from growth to value and then growing fears of recession. Those fears look justified: in most countries, real interest rates (rates adjusted for inflation) are still very negative, so the central bankers have an awful lot more work to do. The problem is pretty much a global one, but some countries are likely to prove better able at bringing inflation under control than others, and that is likely to have a big influence on stock and bond market returns over 2023.

Within the investment companies market, there were some managers that saw this coming and positioned their portfolios accordingly. Chief amongst them are three absolute return funds (focusing as much on wealth preservation as growing capital): Personal Assets, Capital Gearing and Ruffer. Each of these has assets in excess of £1bn and their shares trade at small premiums to their asset value.

Over 2022 year-to-date (27 September), Ruffer is the only one of these that has actually made money for its investors in NAV terms (slightly down in share price terms as is shown in the chart), but the other two have held up relatively well. This is actually quite remarkable given that for the first two quarters of the year, Ruffer reckons that no major asset class (bar cash) offered investors a positive return.

Figure 1: US and UK inflation (CPI) – stalling?

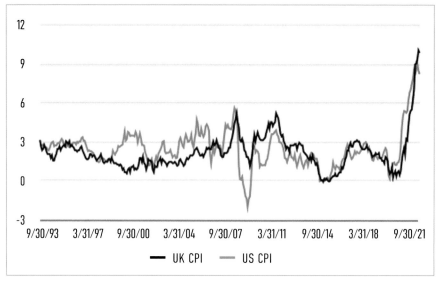

Source: Bloomberg

Figure 2: UK official interest rates

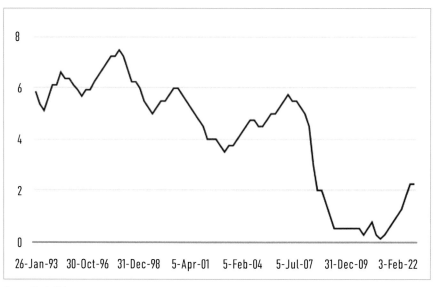

Source: QuotedData

Figure 3: Three absolute return funds' share prices compared with the MSCI All Countries World Index in sterling

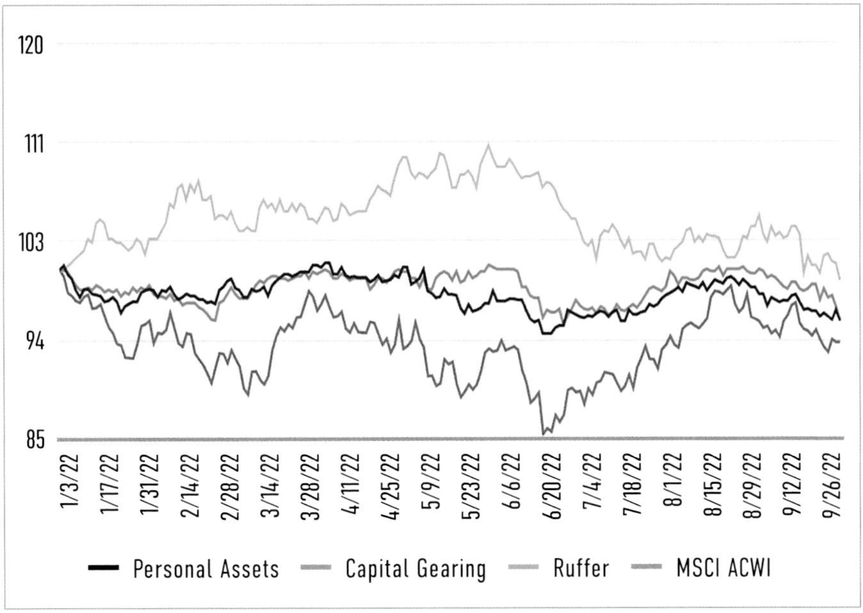

Source: Morningstar, QuotedData

Beware of bonds

Sebastian Lyon, manager of Personal Assets, cautions that – unlike in other bear markets for equities of the 21st century – conventional bonds are not a good hiding place. For some time, any slowdown was met with low interest rates and quantitative easing – the 'Fed put'. These two are off the table while inflation is running out of control.

Funds investing in fixed-interest securities have suffered as government bond yields have climbed, bond prices have fallen and credit spreads (the gap between the yield on a bond issued by a company, for example, and a similar government bond) have widened as investors nervous about debt defaults demand a higher yield to compensate them for the additional risk.

Funds investing in floating rate debt – where the interest rate is expressed as a margin over the official interest rate – should be better off, but again credit spreads are an issue. Henderson Diversified Income Trust, which is largely exposed to fixed-rate debt but does have exposure to floating-rate loans, has responded to market conditions by increasing its exposure to investment grade bonds (increasing the quality of its portfolio).

Its managers have long been selective about which companies they back, and this should mean that the trust's portfolio is less exposed to debt defaults than the market as a whole. That is important as one of its managers, John Pattullo, believes that we are in for quite a pervasive, persistent, and severe downturn. Fortunately, perhaps, he thinks that US inflation has peaked.

Conventional bonds have not featured highly in the portfolios of the absolute return funds for some years, and where they did, they tended to be short-duration bonds. However, since 2017, Personal Assets had been increasing its exposure to US Treasury Inflation-Protected Securities (US TIPS), the American equivalent of index-linked gilts. By the end of July 2022, these were about 37% of its portfolio. Capital Gearing has been holding about a third of investors' assets in inflation-linked bonds for an even longer period. It spread this part of its portfolio across a range of countries, but with a bias to the US. By contrast, Ruffer has a strong bias to index-linked gilts issued by the UK. In the event, inflation showed up just about everywhere.

At first, these index-linked bond investments performed well. However, since March/ April, they have not performed as well as some might have expected, especially the longer-dated bonds. This is because index-linked bond prices are affected by higher interest rates as well as expected inflation. The managers that favoured US TIPS have benefitted as the dollar has strengthened relative to the pound.

In July, Sebastian Lyon said that he remained convinced that Personal Assets' investors would make good, if not great, returns from its US TIPS, which then were offering a real return of about 1% per annum. His dispiriting view was that any return ahead of inflation from any asset class would be gratefully received.

At the end of August 2022, Ruffer's biggest exposure was to cash and short-dated bonds. This accounted for about 34% of its portfolio. Returns on cash are rising, but are likely to be a long way behind inflation rates for some time to come. The main attraction of cash though is not the return that it offers in the short term, but the flexibility that it gives to take advantage of distressed pricing in other asset classes, as and when the manager feels the time is right.

Personal Assets has a fairly sizeable exposure (11% at the end of July 2022) to gold, mostly in the form of gold bullion. However, the other two funds have only a percent or two of their portfolio in this area. Gold is often cited as a good asset to hold in an inflationary environment, and again, initially it seemed to work, but since March the gold price is about 20% off its peak in dollar terms (but steadier or higher in many local currencies, given the strength of the dollar).

One problem is that holding gold costs you money whereas, with higher rates, cash looks like a better option in the short term. In addition, India, which accounts for a lot of the demand, raised import duty on gold from 7.5% to 12.5% in July. Over the long term (100 years), real returns on gold are positive, but there can be extended periods when this is not the case.

Equities and alternative assets

Over the long term, the best real returns come from equities. However, most equity markets have struggled over 2022 as the threat of recession has grown and growth stocks have sold off. Higher interest rates favour near-term cash flows over long-term cash flows. For businesses valued by discounting future cash flows (as yet unprofitable growth stocks, for example), a higher discount rate produces a lower value.

By contrast, stocks that can pay high dividends are prized, provided that those dividends are sustainable. It may be that equity income funds return to favour. It is interesting that Murray International, which has a bias to quality and value, is not only the best-performing trust in its global equity income peer group over 2022 year to date but has also produced returns well ahead of any trust in the global sector.

Talk of discount rates brings us to alternative asset funds. This has been the fastest-growing part of the investment companies industry in recent years. Almost all of these funds have NAVs that are calculated on a discounted cash flow basis. They have tended to trade on premiums to asset value, which has often been ascribed to the desirable yields that they offer. Now, many share prices are dropping as investors fret that discount rates will rise. However, some alternative asset funds come with a degree of inflation protection.

Share prices in the infrastructure sector have fallen sharply and many are now trading on discounts. The sector began life with a focus on UK PPP/PFI-type investments and these tend to come with inflation-linked revenues. HICL Infrastructure, the largest of these funds, said in a quarterly update published in August that inflation was expected to contribute an increase in NAV per share of between 3.0p and 3.6p pence to the 30 September 2022 valuation (adding about 2%). In its annual accounts, covering the 12 months ended 31 March 2022, it said that if inflation was 3% higher than forecast for the next five years, the NAV would be 16p higher.

The weighted average discount rate used to value HICL's portfolio then was 6.6%, down from 6.8% a year earlier. A 0.5% upward move in the weighted average discount rate was estimated to subtract about 8.1p from HICL's NAV. The market appears to be putting more weight on an increase in the discount rate than on the benefit of the inflation-linkage in HICL's returns.

Similarly, many renewable energy funds have also been hit. For those investing in the UK market, the proportion of their income that comes from inflation-linked subsidies is quite high. Subject to whatever happens with power price caps/windfall taxes, they are also beneficiaries of the higher power prices. That ought to mean that these funds' NAVs will continue to march upwards. However, again a higher discount rate could put a spanner in the works.

Take Greencoat UK Wind, for example. The weighted average discount rate used to value its portfolio at 30 June 2022 was 7.7%. That was up from 7.2% at the end of December 2021, reflecting, in part, higher interest rates. The NAV's sensitivity to a 0.5% change in the discount rate is about the same as its sensitivity to a 0.5% move in inflation.

Then there are alternative asset funds which have no direct inflation linkage in their revenues, such as Hipgnosis Songs Fund (held by Ruffer at 30 June). Its discount rate is 8.5%. It had a problem in that its $600m of debt was floating-rate, and was therefore becoming more expensive. It has managed to fix its interest rate expense but at quite a high rate. It also has a cap on the amount of debt it can have relative to the size of its NAV. An increase in its discount rate could trigger a fall in the NAV sufficient to trigger this covenant.

Debt, fixed or floating, sizeable or manageable, is a key consideration when assessing property investments too. Property is often reckoned to be a good investment in inflationary times, but it looks as though it may be different this time. Yields on good quality property had fallen to extremely low levels, but will likely adjust to reflect the new cost of borrowing.

There are some parts of the property market where rents are linked to inflation. Notable amongst these in the investment companies market are the social housing funds – Civitas Social Housing, Triple Point Social Housing and Home REIT. There are stock-specific reasons why these funds' share prices have been weak in recent months, but once again we are faced with a trade-off between higher revenue as a result of higher inflation and the potential for a lower NAV if discount rates (in this instance net initial yields) rise.

The social housing funds are renting to local authorities, whose budget for social housing is funded by the government. The rent should be collectable at least. Other property companies have more to worry about. Tenant quality and the ability to re-let empty space are likely to be increasingly important factors in determining which property companies succeed and which fail.

At its last financial year end, Personal Assets had no exposure to property investment companies or REITs. Ruffer had only minimal exposure at 30 June. However, Capital Gearing has had significant exposure to property and alternative assets trusts. It will have been affected by the widening discounts on these stocks.

Looking ahead

That covers most of the major asset classes, but you might reasonably be wondering how Ruffer managed to generate a positive return over the first half of the year. In part, it comes down to stock selection within its equities portfolio. However, the real driver of returns was its illiquid strategies and options investments.

Hedging against market falls is rare in the investment companies industry, but there are funds that do it. Gervais Williams and Martin Turner have bought a FTSE 100 put for the Diverse Income Trust, for example, and Pershing Square famously made an enormous profit in the market collapse of March 2020 by buying credit default swaps. At the end of August 2022, Ruffer had about 18% of its portfolio in illiquid strategies and options. It is making similar bets and they are paying off.

Another fund that incorporates a similar strategy in its portfolio is RIT Capital Partners. It has done a reasonable job of protecting its shareholders from the worst of market falls, but has been less risk averse than the absolute return funds, producing long-term (10-year) NAV returns that are 4–5% per annum ahead of those funds. Its latest report, published at the beginning of August, reminds us that as the market adjusts, the resulting disruptions will continue to present opportunities.

Markets may gyrate in the months to come as central bankers throw everything at slaying the inflation demon, but there will be some bargains to be had for those that are nimble enough to take advantage. If you do not feel comfortable trying to time markets, it might be best to hunker down in a portfolio of solid, not overly geared, investments. The investment companies market has plenty of these to choose from. It also has the benefit of its closed-end structure, which gives it the ability to take advantage of bargains when open-ended funds are forced to sell assets to meet redemptions.

JAMES CARTHEW *is a director of Marten & Co, which provides research and corporate advice for the investment trust sector and manages the QuotedData website www.quoteddata.com.*

DIVERGING FORTUNES IN LISTED PRIVATE EQUITY

Growth capital and buyout trusts now trade at similar wide discounts. In the view of WILLIAM HEATHCOAT AMORY, *partner at Kepler Partners, this belies very different prospects for underlying earnings and for valuations.*

T HE PAST YEAR has seen a significant shift in risk appetites from investors. Examples abound, but within investment trusts this has been reflected by a general widening of discounts. At the start of the year, according to Morningstar statistics, the weighted average discount for the sector (excluding 3i and VCTs) was 1.2%, which has widened dramatically past 10%. In some cases this may be entirely justified, but in others it perhaps looks overdone. One of the biggest swings has been listed private equity, where discounts for both growth capital trusts and more established private equity trusts have widened significantly, as we illustrate in the following graph.

Sector discounts

Source: Morningstar

Traditional private equity trusts (largely exposed to buyouts, either directly or through funds) have seen average discounts widen by over 20%. However, within the newer growth capital subcategory, discounts have widened by even more. In some cases, shareholder pain has been exacerbated by trusts (such as Chrysalis (CHRY) and Schiehallion (MNTN)) having previously traded on hefty premiums of close to 20% only 12 months ago. Now both groups of trusts find themselves trading on similar discounts of around 40%. The shift in sentiment and discounts widening should serve as a reminder that, however exciting or unique an investment proposition is, anything more than a modest premium to NAV can often lead to tears before bedtime.

Average discounts

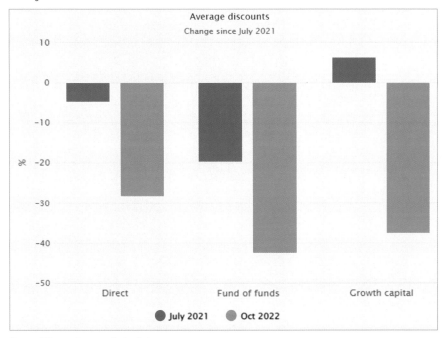

Source: JPMorgan Cazenove, Kepler Partners

In our view, these big moves in sentiment have been driven by concerns on two distinct, but related, aspects: underlying company earnings and valuations. Earnings worries are a result of potential declining growth rates, either a result of inflation or from a looming recession. Valuations, thanks to the decline in public markets, is symptomatic of the former but also directly impacts multiples used to value portfolio companies. We examine each influence in turn, to evaluate whether the significant de-rating in private equity looks justified.

Valuations

When it comes to valuations, we believe the growth capital and buyout portfolios are subject to very different forces. Growth capital companies are typically not yet profitable, but have hitherto been growing earnings fast. With the investment environment giving doubts about future financing rounds, investors like Chrysalis are rightly telling management to conserve cash until the funding environment is more conducive, even if it means a hit to short-term growth prospects. These sorts of companies may find valuations suffer a double whammy, reflecting a higher discount rate (rising interest rates) and lower growth prospects.

Additionally, the valuation methodology arguably works against these companies in the current environment, as witnessed by Klarna, which had a $48bn valuation last September, with the latest funding round done at a $5.9bn pre-money valuation (an 87% valuation slide). Growth capital valuations are in many cases based on most recent funding rounds rather than earnings multiples, which worked well when global investors were falling over themselves searching for the next private decacorn or hectocorn. However, with liquidity now impinged and risk appetites reversed, there is more reluctance to invest in new funding rounds at previous high valuations, leading to mechanistic (and sometimes very dramatic) falls in values within growth capital funds.

On the other hand, buyouts are generally wholly owned and controlled by a private equity manager (aka a 'sponsor' in a buyout deal). Buyouts are usually profitable, and periodic valuations are determined on a mark-to-model basis. This has attracted criticism from some quarters in the past but, for good or for bad, tends to result in a relatively smooth trajectory derived from a highly consistent valuation methodology. Earnings growth is usually the main driver of increases in valuations, outside of that derived from any uplift from selling an asset. Listed company valuations are one input in determining valuation multiples, but also comparable private equity deal valuations.

As we discuss below, private equity managers have record amounts of capital to deploy and so, for buyouts that continue to deliver earnings growth, we understand that deal valuations have so far not fallen by anything like as much as public market indices. Reinforcing this, private equity managers can afford to play the long game and, if a bid for a company doesn't match expectations, they can afford to hold on for a better or more realistic price.

These factors suggest that, absent a change in expected earnings, valuation changes for private equity companies in the current investment environment will not be as dramatic as those seen by growth capital companies or public market equity indices. In many cases, we believe buyout valuations are usually conservative, with the manager not incentivised to write up the value of investments (management fees are generally based on committed capital, and performance fees are based on realised gains).

That said, it is true that valuations across portfolios have been rising: the following chart from Numis illustrates this point. One might argue that, despite buyout valuations potentially being higher than listed equity indices currently (to the extent that earnings growth continues to come through), current valuations may be justifiable. Indeed, as we discuss below, buyout valuations could still be regarded as conservative.

Selected listed PE – multiples over time

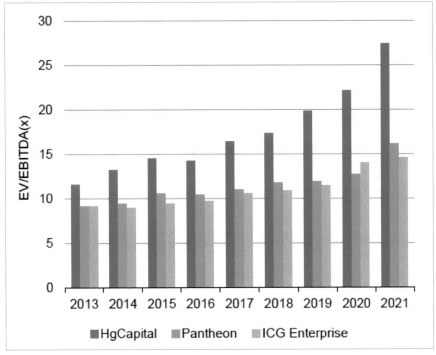

Source: Numis

Evidence for conservatism in buyout valuations (over the long run) is reflected by the fact that it is very rare that buyout managers announce a sale of an asset without reflecting an uplift to the previous carrying value. Examples of this abound in nearly all of the listed private equity RNS announcements over time. Announcements made during 2022 show that realisations are still being achieved, and still at valuations in excess of those used to calculate NAVs.

ICG Enterprise (ICGT), for example, a hybrid fund-of-fund and direct private equity investor, announced Q1 results which showed 17 full exits from the portfolio having occurred in the three months to 30 April 2022, at an average uplift of 23%. This is lower than previous financial years, which have ranged from 31% to 40% on average, potentially suggesting a degree of pressure on pricing to get deals across the line. That said, this is only one quarter, and the average for the full year may trend upwards towards the long-term average.

NB Private Equity Partners (NBPE) is a direct investor in private equity deals (as a co-investor) alongside other private equity managers. It has a more concentrated portfolio than the fund-of-funds (around 95 holdings), and during 2022 has so far reported six full or partial realisations of companies at an average 26% uplift to value three quarters prior to an exit announcement (to 31/08/2022). We understand that the vast majority of investments within the portfolio remain profitable, and so far the managers have seen no alarming negative impact on earnings.

Further support for valuations over the short term is in our view likely to come from the significant firepower that private equity managers have accumulated. We understand that current fundraising has been running strongly, and so pressure to deploy capital remains. For the directly investing trusts, including NBPE, this offers the opportunity to add value through stock-selection. NBPE looks to invest in high quality companies (hard to replicate, barriers to entry, recurring revenues), alongside premier PE managers investing in their core area of expertise, with strong potential earnings growth and prudent capital structures. These sorts of company are exactly those that other private equity managers like to buy.

Oakley Capital (manager of Oakley Capital Investments (OCI)) aims to be the first private equity investor in companies it backs, which means that other private equity managers may make a natural purchaser once the Oakley team have delivered on the first stage of their business plan. Recent evidence would suggest that this is happening, with recent exits such as Facile sold to Silver Lake, Contabo to KKR, and TechInsights to CVC. In many cases, Oakley is choosing to reinvest a proportion of capital alongside these private equity investors, meaning shareholders maintain an exposure to these strongly performing companies.

CT Private Equity Trust (CTPE) (or BMO Private Equity (BPET) before the recent name change) aims to invest with managers at an earlier stage in their development who target 'lower mid-market' deals. In a highly competitive background for private equity, the Columbia Threadneedle private equity team believe this puts them in a good position to continue to deploy capital at attractive rates of return, but also to benefit from realisation activity by feeding larger private equity managers' deals from the CTPE portfolio as investments mature. As well as having net gearing, this has led to a strong NAV performance over 2021, with BPET only marginally the second best performing listed private equity trust over the period.

Over the long term then, buyout valuations look both more conservative and less prone to wild swings than those of growth capital companies. As we discussed earlier, buyout valuation multiples are derived from a combination of inputs, of which public market comparables are the most visible. Public market comparable valuations have undeniably fallen over 2022, but the NAV drawdowns graph provides evidence that, contrary to the assertion that is sometimes put forward that private equity is 'highly geared beta', LPE NAVs have historically proven significantly more resilient than listed equities.

Of course, it is worth highlighting at this point that share prices have not been as defensive as NAVs, with discounts widening out during periods of market stress, resulting in LPE share price returns often lagging public market returns. However, we would argue that NAVs are ultimately the key determinant of total returns, effectively the sun around which the share price should orbit. With buybacks and returns of capital the ultimate recourse for trusts that trade on persistently wide discounts, over the long term NAV and share price total returns should be relatively tightly correlated. As such, we think the following graph should reassure investors that buyout NAVs have historically been less impacted than broader equity markets by significant falls, and suggests that NAVs – assuming earnings haven't fallen faster than listed comparables – should fall less than public equities.

NAV drawdowns

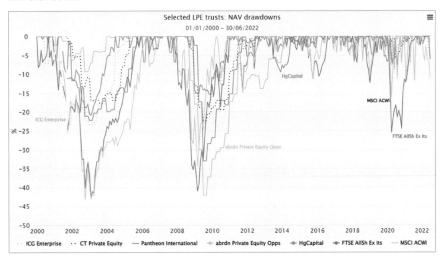

Source: Morningstar

Earnings are key

Having discussed the prospect of valuations falling significantly, we now turn to earnings. With a recession in the US, Europe and the UK more a likelihood than a chance, we think it worth revisiting what impact a recession may have on earnings.

Again, there is a big disparity between growth capital and buyouts. Buyouts are largely profitable companies with demonstrable earnings growth. On the other hand, buyouts are also typically more highly geared than growth capital and publicly listed companies (which might suggest earnings are more volatile). However, many buyout portfolios typically comprise defensive growth businesses that have demonstrated strong earnings growth over the past few years, but which have a relatively low impact from macroeconomic factors (or Covid for that matter). Many of these are niche businesses, and private equity managers exist to drive value through focussing on earnings growth and operational change. This leaves them well placed to navigate changes to the economic environment, such as the one we are entering now.

Anecdotally, mindful of the economic cycle, many private equity managers have been selecting 'defensive growth' companies which may prove more resilient and able to continue to grow earnings irrespective of the wider economy. That said, many companies' management (and private equity managers) haven't necessarily been proven through a recession of any kind, and certainly not a stagflationary recession. The next few quarters will provide useful evidence on how well buyout earnings are holding up. So far, the evidence from buyout managers who have reported seems to suggest that any valuation falls they are seeing are being mitigated by continued earnings growth.

As we have argued before, listed private equity portfolios are very different to those of listed indices, often represented by niche businesses in sectors experiencing secular growth. However, there is a clear distinction between trusts exposed to buyouts and those at the growth capital end of the spectrum. As has been illustrated by Chrysalis's results announcement, companies held by the growth capital trusts are typically unprofitable, and therefore require equity funding channels to remain open in order to continue to grow at a rapid clip. Chrysalis's managers reported that, given the market backdrop and how vicious 'down-rounds' can be, they had advised investee companies to prioritise profitability over growth, so as to extend the 'cash runway'. By implication, with investment and growth prospects moderating (to reduce cash-burn), it is not hard to imagine that the immediate prospects for NAVs in the growth capital sector are not particularly rosy.

Are discounts justified?

A note of caution is clearly appropriate, but in our view it seems a strange situation when many buyout-focussed trusts trade on the same level of discount as those that are growth-focussed. The latter's company valuations rely less on earnings, and to a much greater extent on the vagaries of funding rounds and risk appetites of investors. In our view the current environment points to the fact that, while growth capital discounts might anticipate some fairly steep falls in NAVs, the same cannot be said for trusts exposed to buyouts. As such, the current discounts seen in trusts exposed to buyouts might present an opportunity.

In the following table we show current discounts in the context of the long-term history, with trusts arranged in order of magnitude of the current divergence from the long-term average. In calculating averages, we have taken discount estimates from Morningstar since June 2008, which in our view represents a fair reflection of the modern, post-GFC era. Prior to this, many LPE trusts traded at significant premiums, with investors perhaps too carried away with the concept of Gordon Brown's "goldilocks era" of economic growth. If we were to assume a worst-case NAV fall for 10%, bearing in mind that trusts in the sector are pretty much ungeared, the figures suggest discounts for most trusts would still be wide in the context of their own history.

LPE trusts: current discounts vs long-term average

	AVE. % DISCOUNT SINCE JUNE 2008	04/10/2022 EST. DISCOUNT %	DIFFERENCE %
HarbourVest Global PE	−26.2	−46.9	−20.7
Pantheon International	−28.2	−47.9	−19.7
Apax Global Alpha	−13.9	−30.1	−16.2
Oakley Capital Investments	−24.2	−40.1	−15.9
abrdn Private Equity Opps	−27.1	−42.7	−15.6
ICG Enterprise	−25.7	−40.7	−15.0
HgCapital	−7.9	−21.1	−13.2
CT Private Equity	−23.6	−34.5	−10.9
NB Private Equity Partners	−27.0	−33.0	−6.0
Princess Private Equity Holding	−23.8	−24.4	−0.6

Source: Morningstar, JPMorgan Cazenove

The next graph shows the historic discount of these trusts, compared to a 40% level – which reflects the current average of the fund-of-fund subsector. It suggests that discounts have rarely stayed wider than this for any length of time, aside from the period immediately post-GFC. One might argue that the GFC was a financial recession, and not necessarily an earnings recession. Concerns over the LPE sector at the time were mainly centred on balance sheets, which in many cases were overstretched, and so it might be argued that discounts remaining wide at that time were justified by investor concerns on leverage risks.

By comparison, in the current era balance sheets are in a significantly better position. According to sector data from Numis, 12 out of 16 trusts at the time had leverage and overcommitment levels of over 150% of NAV. By contrast, most now have no leverage and few have overcommitments that exceed 150%. In our view, this means that discounts are not a result of the market anticipating a repeat of 2008/2009.

Average discounts over time

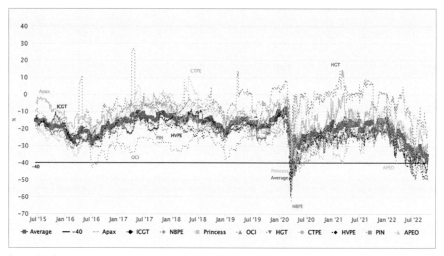

Source: Morningstar

Conclusion

Private equity trusts of all types share one feature that may mean optically wider discounts may be justifiable as markets fall. Valuations take time to calculate and filter through to published NAVs. As a result, there is a risk that investors may find that a 40% discount to a historic NAV may in fact only be a 20% discount, once a fall in NAV is taken account of. Private equity trusts typically revalue portfolios quarterly at best.

We believe that, with respect to private equity trusts invested in buyouts, NAVs will likely not fall as far as comparable equity markets. If this is proved to be the case, this may provide an element of support to share prices and discounts. However, in our view, the greater impact will be from reports on these trusts' underlying portfolio company earnings, and it is this that investors should be focussing on. If, as we suspect, earnings outperform those of listed markets in a recessionary environment, we think this should give a shot in the arm to discounts for trusts exposed to buyouts. For growth capital trusts, unfortunately discount levels are likely to be less to do with 'self-help' and more with market appetites for risk, which are significantly less predictable.

Therefore, for investors looking to take advantage of the current market, the more established listed private equity trusts that are exposed to buyouts look mispriced. Whilst past performance clearly provides no guarantees, looking back at history there are relatively few times when they have traded at discounts as wide as this, and in the past investors have gone on to make significant returns as discounts have narrowed and NAVs have continued to grow.

WILLIAM HEATHCOAT AMORY *is a co-founder of Kepler Partners, which provides research and analysis into investment trusts, including corporate clients.*

IS THE FUTURE FEMALE?

ANNABEL BRODIE-SMITH *is communications director of the Association of Investment Companies. She is also an ambassador for Women on Boards and The Diversity Project.*

D URING MY CAREER I have seen first-hand the considerable benefits that diversity brings. When I joined the Association of Investment Companies 25 years ago, fewer than 5% of investment company directors were female. There was little diversity, and investment company directors were described as "male, pale and stale" in an article at the time. This was harsh, but there was definitely some truth in it. Directors were usually male and former fund managers, lawyers and accountants. When I started to attend AIC board meetings 25 years ago there were no women on the AIC board, which at that time was made up of heads of investment companies from management groups.

I am pleased to say that the industry has made considerable progress. Today 37% of investment company directors are women. As well as fund managers, accountants and lawyers there are directors with varied experience and skills including business, marketing and communications, and ESG. Now five out of the 12 AIC board members are women, and the AIC board has a majority of independent directors. Elisabeth Scott is currently the fourth female AIC chair.

However, there is still much more work to do. This is particularly the case when you look at female fund managers and also applies to heads of investment companies, analysts and brokers in the investment company industry. I want to look beyond the numbers to find out why there's been progress but also why there are still not enough women working in the investment company industry, and what is being done to encourage more.

Investment company directors

For women on boards, the last decade has seen a sea change. In 2012 just 15% of directorships at FTSE 100 companies and 10% at FTSE 250 companies were held by women. By February 2022 this had risen dramatically, with 39% of directorships at FTSE 100 companies and 37% at FTSE 250 companies being held by women, according to the FTSE Women Leaders Review published in February 2022.

Against these benchmarks, investment companies perform well. Across the whole industry, 37% of directorships are held by women – the same percentage as in the FTSE 250 as a whole. The FTSE Women Leaders Review, which highlights progress across the FTSE 350, states: "Investment trusts not only dominate the Top Ten Best Performers list [among the FTSE 250], they also make up around half of the 92 FTSE 250 boards already at 40% or more women." The new target from this report was 40% female representation.

It's also encouraging to see that boards at larger investment companies in the FTSE 350 have more female directors (43%) than comparable trading companies in the FTSE 350 (39%). However, smaller investment companies outside the FTSE 350 generally have fewer female directors and need to catch up with their larger counterparts. The typical venture capital trust (VCT), for example, is £75m in size with only 29% of board seats held by women.

What has driven progress so far?

So in the boardroom, it's encouraging that investment companies have moved forward on diversity. There are several reasons why this is the case. There is a great deal of compelling research which demonstrates the value of gender diversity on boards. A 2021 report from the Financial Reporting Council, 'Board Diversity and Effectiveness in FTSE 350 Companies', demonstrates that higher levels of diversity on FTSE 350 boards positively correlate with better financial performance, with the effect being strongest after three to five years. In addition, the campaigning work of groups such as the 30% Club and Women on Boards has been critical in shifting attitudes.

At the AIC we support greater diversity on boards, and this topic has regularly been covered at our conferences and roundtables. In 2020 we launched Pathway, a website for prospective investment company directors, which aims to encourage a wide and diverse group of candidates to find out more about the role and includes some really useful advice on how to go about getting a directorship. We also run seminars to encourage those who might not have considered becoming an investment company director to give it some thought.

The AIC's 2019 corporate governance code covers diversity of gender, socioeconomic status and ethnicity when it discusses new appointments, the annual evaluation of the board and investment companies' policies on diversity.

Despite the compelling evidence supporting gender diversity, it's clear that government pressure and targets have also been critical in driving progress for listed companies, including investment companies. The Davies Review from 2011 to 2015 encouraged FTSE 350 boards to address the gender imbalance and set a target of 25% female representation on FTSE 100 boards by 2015. Following this, the Hampton Alexander Review was launched in 2016 which aimed to achieve 33% female representation among FTSE 350 companies by 2020.

The Hampton Alexander Review was a gamechanger for the investment company industry. Just 20% of investment company directors were female in 2018 and, shockingly, 30% of investment company boards were all male. By the end of 2020 31% of investment company directors were female and the percentage of all-male boards had halved. It's also important to recognise that institutional investors, voting agencies and more recently the rise of the ESG agenda for institutional investors have all played an important role in achieving change.

Not everything is perfect...

However, it's clear from speaking to senior women that not everything at board level is perfect. There are still instances of unconscious bias towards women and some sexism too.

Sarah Bates, an experienced chair and director, reflects: "I do wonder about the investment trust world on occasion. I remember an AIC dinner some years ago, when someone was getting very agitated about the need to appoint 'the best people'. I looked around the room and made the point that the distribution of the audience was a bit unlikely to represent 'the best people'. Statistically, if we are all white, middle-class, straight women from Manchester (like me) we won't have the best people either. In any case, the concept's a bit unreliable. The best person for a board is the person who makes the board as a whole perform better."

A female director who has held a number of directorships says: "In some ways, yes, it's getting better. There are more women on boards. I have served on three boards where there was a majority of women. I keep being told that it's difficult to find women with the right experience, and in some parts of our industry, that may at first glance appear to have some merit to it. But we need to reach out and be really careful about what experience is actually necessary and what is just a bit conventional. In many ways, though, it hasn't moved as fast as it should have done. I was told last year that the board of something I was applying to had already found a woman in Guernsey, so they didn't need another…"

Mary Ann Sieghart is director of a number of investment companies and author of *The Authority Gap*, a must-read book on gender bias in everyday life. She believes there is still a lot of unconscious bias among some men in asset management. "They assume other men are more competent than women and are genuinely surprised when they see a woman performing as well as, or better than, her male colleagues.

"On an investment trust board, I once mentioned that if we ended up recruiting another female director (obviously on merit), we'd be one of the few majority-female boards, which would make a good story. 'It might make a story, but it wouldn't be a good one,' said one of my fellow male directors. 'I mean, what would the investors think?' This man had been serving on a board with a highly respected and competent female asset manager, who ended up chairing a huge investment trust. Yet he still clearly thought women were less financially competent than men."

Another example of unconscious bias was described by a senior director who had been on a board for a couple of years. She was the only woman on the board, and all the other board members were coming to the end of their tenures. When discussing the specification for a new director at a nominations committee meeting, the chair of the nominations committee stated that they would need to be capable of stepping up to be chair, as the current chair was going to leave within a couple of years. Clearly, he hadn't considered that the female director already in place might be a potential candidate for chair of the board and might be interested. When she mentioned that she was interested in being chair outside the meeting his reaction seemed to be that of pleasant surprise. He was then very supportive and the female director became chair of the company two years later.

But overtly sexist behaviour still occasionally occurs. A senior director witnessed a male chair putting his hand across the mouth of a female director in a board meeting because he perceived she was talking too much. The fact that women are wrongly perceived as talking more in meetings is addressed in Mary Ann Sieghart's book, where she explains that in reality women speak much less than men in meetings but are unfairly perceived as domineering.

Another director says it comes down to a firm's culture. "I think one of the reasons I have never spoken publicly about being a woman in this industry is that sexism is ever-present and I didn't want to put off the next generation of women. Even in the last week I have found myself assumed to be excluded from conversations on cars, car racing and rugby. Ultimately it comes down to culture and the tone set from the top. At some of the firms I am involved with this never crops up, and with others it is a constant frustration – yet I remain the same person at each firm!"

Female fund managers

While there has been encouraging progress on female directors, the same can't be said for female fund managers. In September 2022 Citywire published its annual 'Alpha Female Report'. The research draws from Citywire's database of more than 17,500 portfolio managers worldwide. It revealed that progress had stalled in 2022, with the number of female fund managers growing just 1.7% since 2016 – from

10.3% to 12%. Their analysis very depressingly suggests it would take 200 years to reach gender parity if progress continued at this pace.

Interestingly Citywire found that mixed teams of men and women produced the best investment returns over the past five years. The research by Citywire found that mixed teams beat both men-only and women-only teams as well as solo men and solo women. Morningstar's analysis was slightly more cheering, as although women filled only 11.8% of fund manager positions, they managed 21% of all assets in the dataset.

The AIC's data reveals that 12% of investment company fund managers are female, in line with the wider fund industry. On boards there tends to be a structured plan in place to refresh the team, but this is not the case for fund management roles. It's enlightening to hear female fund managers views on why there are fewer women and what needs to change.

Abby Glennie manages abrdn UK Smaller Companies Growth Trust. "We think progression, especially at the more senior levels, will take time, and a lot of the education work on promoting these careers to females needs to come at graduate level," she observes. "Female turnover does become challenging though, as all fund management houses are trying to hire more women to improve their female ratios. abrdn has put a target in place for 34% of key investment decision-making roles to be held by women by 2025, versus the current level of 25%."

Quotas and targets have worked successfully at board and executive level, so it's encouraging that The Diversity Project has launched the Future Female Fund Managers Programme. This is the first industry-wide initiative to address the under-representation of women in fund management and is aiming for 20% female fund managers by 2026.

Schroders is a founding supporter of this programme. Sue Noffke, head of equities and manager of Schroder Income Growth Fund, says: "My hope for the future is that the pipeline of female talent starting out in investment has an easier path into managing funds and investment companies. Why am I confident? The playing field is more level today with recruitment policies aimed at recruiting widely, rather than from traditional narrow pools. Additionally, more options for parental career breaks that apply to both genders help remove a perceived barrier to appointing women to managing funds."

In private equity only around 10% of senior roles are held by women, which is an improvement from a few years ago but is still not good enough. Helen Steers, manager of the Pantheon International investment company, is working to change this. In 2015 she co-founded a non-profit organisation, Level 20. She explains: "Level 20's mission is to attract more women into private equity, and to support, promote and retain them so that they can progress to senior roles. Over the past five years, there has been an improvement in the number of junior women joining the private equity industry, but it takes time for them to climb the ranks and be promoted to senior positions."

Of course, not everything is perfect for women working in the fund management industry, but it's improving. One female fund manager calls it a "hungry" job, in the sense that it consumes so much time and attention. But in that sense it is no different from plenty of other careers, such as law and medicine, where women are better represented. She adds: "For sure there are elements of sexism and unconscious bias, but it's better in my view to focus on showing that gender is irrelevant to success in this industry."

Brokers and heads of investment trusts

We have analysed the data for female fund managers and directors, but there are lots of other important roles in the investment company industry. There has been encouraging progress here, with recent female appointments to head of investment trust roles at management groups including Melissa Gallagher at BlackRock, Stephanie Carbonneil at Allianz Global Investors and Claire Long at Premier Miton Investors.

There has been change in the broking world too. Emma Bird was recently appointed head of investment trusts research at Winterflood Securities. At Berenberg Gillian Martin and Myrto Charamis are heading up a new female-led investment company team.

There are long-established female participants – for example, Lucy Lewis is managing director, investment companies at Investec Bank, where half of the corporate finance team are female. On the research side, Colette Ord is director of investment company research, heading up research on infrastructure, renewables and real estate, and has been at Numis since 2001; and Monica Tepes has been head of investment companies at finnCap since 2017.

Despite all this good news, it remains true that the lion's share of roles at management groups and brokers are taken by men. In the past, fewer women have applied for these roles – the perception of investment being a male-dominated industry with few female role models with families is off-putting. The hours are also long, especially if there's an IPO or acquisition in the works.

More women are now applying for junior roles, but retaining them can be an issue. Clearly, maternity policies and – more importantly – how companies help women come back to work after having children are critical. One senior woman said post-pandemic she felt staff retention was a problem for both men and women and 'the big resignation' was not just a talking point but a reality in the City. "Men and women are not prepared to put in the punishing hours for an all-consuming job when they have realised they can have a life, and that's much more appealing."

What does the future hold?

Boards have made progress on gender diversity, but there's more to do on this and other forms of diversity – in particular ethnic diversity. The FCA has decided that it needs to do more to increase transparency of diversity on both boards and executive teams of listed companies. The regulator has set out positive diversity targets for listed companies, including investment companies. In their reports and accounts companies will have to make a statement as to whether they have met the following targets: at least 40% of individuals on the board should be women, at least one of the senior board positions should be held by a woman, and at least one individual on the board should be from a minority ethnic background. These targets follow the 'comply or explain' convention, so if companies cannot meet them they need to explain why.

It's likely this FCA initiative will encourage greater diversity. Rachel Beagles, director and former chair of the AIC, says: "The presence of women on investment trust boards has improved hugely in recent years – helped by pressure from the Hampton Alexander review, coupled with pressure from proxy voting agencies, the rise of the ESG agenda for professional shareholders and, more recently, changes to the listing rules. The AIC has done, I believe, a good job in highlighting the issue, despite the unpopularity of this message in earlier years."

But there's more to do. Francesca Ecsery is a director of the AIC and other companies across a number of sectors, including investment companies. "The ice cap is going to melt before we will have parity in the investment trust industry," she says. "So no, I don't think progress is fast enough. I do think that people in finance think that their job is more complicated than other industries, but if you have experience of a number of different sectors you know that's not true."

When it comes to appointing female fund managers, Sue Noffke has useful advice for boards and managers: "Investment company boards and fund managers should consider diverse teams over a known 'star manager' appointment. A partner or team approach can blend individual skill sets together with their personal traits, so that the whole is greater than the sum of the parts."

So is the future female?

Well, the leap forward in the number of female directors of investment companies demonstrates that it should be. The reasons are varied and complex, but the Hampton Alexander Review target had a big impact. Some female directors say they do not like quotas, but targets clearly sharpen the mind and deliver results. Let's hope The Diversity Project's target to increase the underrepresentation of women in fund management delivers similar strong results over time.

Looking back to when I started my career 25 years ago and comparing it to now, it's clear a transformation of women's representation in this industry has taken place. The investment company industry is renowned for its ability to adapt and change to meet investors' demands, and I'm confident this will work in its favour when it comes to diversity. Yes, there's so much more to do, but the momentum is unstoppable and the FCA is now behind it too. This makes me confident that in another 25 years' time the investment company industry will again be transformed. This time it will not just be about female diversity, but ethnic, social and all other forms of diversity will be embraced. So yes, the future of investment companies is female – and it's diverse.

What should women starting their career do?

There is an abundance of advice for women who are keen to develop their career in investment companies. "This is a brilliant job for women who like to be challenged, it's never (or at least very rarely) boring!" says one female manager. Whereas the advice from an analyst is: "Don't be afraid, don't doubt yourself, don't be modest when it comes to letting relevant people know your abilities and achievements. Do ask for what you think you deserve, or ask what you need to do in order to obtain what you want."

When it comes to advice for prospective directors, Gay Collins, investment company director and director of the AIC says, "Learn as much as you can about investment trusts. The AIC is a fantastic resource. Try to build a network in the investment company sector. Many female non-executive directors are very welcoming and inclusive – be brave and approach them on LinkedIn for a virtual coffee. Join Women on Boards. Share relevant investment company conversations and comment on LinkedIn, including the AIC's excellent feed. And if you can, find yourself a mentor or, even better, a sponsor."

The last word goes to Pantheon's Helen Steers, who explains passionately why she thinks being a fund manager is an excellent career for women. "It is intellectually stimulating, interesting, very varied and rewarding. It requires teamwork and collaboration to produce the best results, and the ability to use both quantitative and qualitative analysis to make sound investment and fund management decisions. I encourage young women wholeheartedly to think about a career in asset management, and especially in private equity, for these reasons. It is an apprenticeship business, which requires patience, tenacity and hard work, but women can definitely rise to the challenge."

ANNABEL BRODIE-SMITH *is Communications Director at the Association of Investment Companies (AIC). Her role focuses on communicating the uses and features of investment companies to the media, opinion formers, advisers and private investors. She also communicates the AIC's work and current initiatives to key audiences. Annabel is passionate about financial education and diversity in financial services and is currently an ambassador for Women on Boards and The Diversity Project.*

PROFESSIONAL
PERSPECTIVES

WHERE AND WHAT NEXT?

EWAN LOVETT-TURNER, *head of investment trust research at Numis Securities, looks back on 2022 and ahead to 2023.*

How has the investment trust sector responded to the inflation/ Ukraine crisis over the last 12 months?

I T HAS BEEN a difficult period for equity markets and all investors in risk assets. Persistent inflation has led to a shift in central bank policy to rising interest rates, which has led investors to reappraise valuations, particularly for growth stocks. The MSCI All-Country World Index is down 7.6% in sterling terms (−24.8% in US dollars), while the tech-heavy Nasdaq is down 16.8% (−33.2% in dollar terms).* UK investors have been insulated from some of the worst of the losses by sterling's weakness, and the UK market was relatively resilient given its high-energy and low-tech exposure, until the new chancellor's 'mini' budget led to an equity and debt market sell-off. The FTSE All-Share is now down 7.2% year-to-date.

The volatile markets and uncertain macroeconomic backdrop are evident in the weak performance of many investment companies. It is unsurprising to see JPMorgan Russian as the weakest performer, given the invasion of Ukraine and subsequent sanctions, exchange controls and write-downs to investments. The list of weakest performers is dominated by companies with a growth bias, particularly numerous Baillie Gifford managed funds (BG US Growth, Scottish Mortgage, BG European, Keystone Positive Change and Edinburgh Worldwide) as well as Smithson, Montanaro European Smaller Companies and Manchester & London.

In addition, technology-focused funds (Allianz Tech, Herald and Polar Capital Tech) have struggled. Funds with exposure to private assets have seen asset value write-downs and a souring of sentiment, impacting the share prices of Chrysalis Investments, Schroder UK Public Private and Schiehallion. Several of these trusts have moved from premiums to discounts in the period. A number of UK small caps trusts are amongst the most prominent laggards, most of which have a growth bias, including BlackRock Throgmorton, BlackRock Smaller Companies, Montanaro Smaller Companies, Henderson Smaller Companies and JPMorgan UK Smaller Companies.

The list of leaders includes numerous funds with exposure to energy and commodities (City Natural Resources, BlackRock Energy and Resources and BlackRock World

---

* All data in this section as at mid-October 2022.

Mining) and Latin American funds (managed by abrdn and BlackRock). In addition, funds with a value style have done particularly well, including North American Income, Merchants and Temple Bar). Defensively oriented, multi-asset funds have also held up well, including JPMorgan Global Core Real Assets, helped by currency, and Ruffer, as well as BH Macro. A number of trusts have recovered from a very low base, including aircraft leasing funds. Renewable energy trusts were delivering reasonably strong returns year-to-date, fuelled by the high power price environment, but are experiencing significant weakness at the time of writing due to concerns over possible energy price caps.

What has happened to discounts and where might they go from here?

In a volatile period, the discounts of equity trusts have widened from previously tight levels. Those with growth-biased portfolios have seen their NAVs hit hard and discounts widen, dramatically in some cases. This is notable in the technology sector, as well as sub-sectors with a growth bias such as global smaller companies. Overall, the equity investment company sector discount has widened to around 12%, above the 10-year average of around 7%, and in line with discounts during the Brexit vote in 2016 and the short but sharp sell-off in March 2020 during the depths of the Covid-19 crisis. These weighted averages are significantly influenced by the discounts of some of the industry heavyweights, particularly Scottish Mortgage (which has significantly derated to a double-digit discount), Smithson and Monks.

Long-term discount history: Equity investment companies

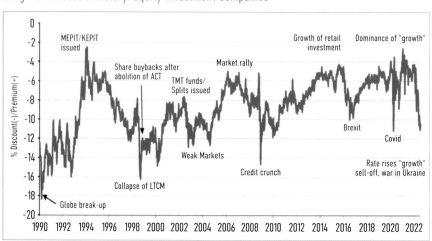

Source: Numis

Alternative asset investment companies started the year at an average premium of 4%, but they are now trading at a discount of more than 15%. However, we caution that such all-inclusive averages can be misleading. For example, many listed private equity funds are trading at wider than 40% discounts, whilst until recent weeks infrastructure investment companies traded on premiums. Infrastructure trusts are now trading on discounts of around 10%, with those of renewable ICs wider still.

The sharp rises in UK gilt yields has led investors to question whether discount rates used to value the long-term cash flows of infrastructure trusts need to rise, reducing valuations. However, we believe that the market's initial response has underappreciated the quality of cash flows, the conservative valuation assumptions and inflation linkage of many of the assets, as well as the benefits of high power prices for renewable energy trusts.

Mainstream UK commercial property trusts are trading on average discounts of around 40% as investors factor in significant asset value declines in the face of rising interest rates. The shine has also come off specialist industrial and long-lease property trusts, which have moved from premiums to wide discounts.

IPOs have disappeared – what has been the driving force behind that and what is the outlook?

Investors are focused on the implications of changing macroeconomic conditions on their existing holdings rather than considering new opportunities. As a result, there have been no significant IPOs in 2022 so far, and we are close to surpassing the 10-month drought during the global financial crisis and the eight-month hiatus during Covid, which are the longest spells without an IPO since 2000 (when Numis started keeping records).

Typically there are more than 14 IPOs a year. It would be unprecedented to see none in the year, but it is becoming an increasing possibility, particular given that a number of potential IPOs that were being marketed were 'pulled' in September, including Chinese private equity, US farmland and UK social housing. Continued volatility and few IPOs in the pipeline mean a fallow year for IPOs is a distinct possibility.

Will some of the new trusts that came to market in 2021 run into trouble now? How have they performed?

There is always attrition amongst IPOs. Ultimately not all deliver on expectations, but we believe it is positive that the investment company structure enables these to be wound down if they disappoint. The 2021 vintage has largely deployed capital, with some taking longer than hoped. Many were focused on infrastructure assets, meaning it is likely to be some time before we can fully assess the performance of the underlying assets. Most are still trading above their IPO price with notable exceptions being Seraphim Space, Schiehallion's C-share issue, which reflects growth investing falling out of favour, and Aquila Energy Efficiency, which has been slow to deploy what it raised.

What has been the impact on secondary fundraising and what is the outlook there?

Investors have been seeking sanctuary in volatile times. Secondary fundraising by investment trusts was £5.2bn in the first nine months of 2022, down 45% from £9.5bn in the same period last year. The first half saw strong demand for fundraising from renewable energy trusts, which benefited from strong power prices. Inflation-linked revenues saw infrastructure and specialist property trusts raise capital. With investors increasingly risk-adverse, secondary fundraising has dried up even in these areas. Capital raising in recent months has been focused on defensive trusts, including Capital Gearing, Ruffer, Personal Assets and BH Macro. Some well-established UK equity trusts, such as City of London and Merchants, have remained in issuance territory. In the near-term that is unlikely to change. We expect issuance to be focused on trusts with defensive return profiles and those that can demonstrate high quality cash flows and benefits from rising inflation and interest rates, such as floating-rate assets.

Manager changes have continued – why? Will they work? Do you expect consolidation to continue?

There has been a changing of the guard for numerous funds, with managers stepping down after long periods in charge. Notable changes included James Anderson, the manager of Scottish Mortgage for 22 years leaving Baillie Gifford, Harry Nimmo is retiring after having managed abrdn UK Smaller Companies since 2003, and Walter Price is retiring after around 15 years in charge of Allianz Technology. In addition, Hamish Baillie left Ruffer.

The succession has typically been well-managed, with successors being clearly identified and a key part of the investment process unchanged, making an in-house solution appropriate. To protect against key manager risk, large management groups have continued the trend of appointing deputy and co-managers well in advance.

Other trusts have sought more radical change. Fundsmith Emerging Equities is planning to wind-up and return cash after disappointing returns. Unusually, this did not come with a rollover option, which can protect investors against crystallising capital gains. We also expect JPMorgan Indian's new lead manager to make changes to the portfolio to improve performance. Rights & Issues Investment Trust is moving to be managed by Jupiter, after Simon Knott, the manager for 39 years, announced his retirement.

"A GLOBAL RECESSION WOULD BE DIFFICULT, BUT ANY TRUST THAT INVESTS OVERSEAS WILL SEE A BOOST TO THEIR DIVIDENDS FROM THE WEAKNESS OF STERLING."

We expect consolidation to remain a key theme in the sector, particularly given the increased focused on alternative asset classes, where valuations are more subjective and portfolios less liquid. This year we have seen the merger of LXI REIT and Secure Income REIT, whilst UK Mortgages merged into TwentyFour Income and JPMorgan Global Growth & Income completed its takeover of Scottish Investment Trust. With more boards focusing on investor demand, having the size and liquidity to appear on the radar of a wide range of investors should continue to fuel consolidation. We are keeping a close eye on the infrastructure and renewable sector: if large discounts persist, we would expect them to become attractive buys for pension funds and other institutional buyers.

What is the outlook for dividends now? Were some trusts in hindsight over-distributing by calling on reserves for a second year running last year? Who is most vulnerable now?

One of the key advantages of investment trusts is the ability to use revenue and capital reserves to smooth dividend payments. This enabled many trusts to maintain or increase dividends throughout the pandemic. Since then, dividend payments from portfolio companies have resumed as business activity has normalised, with many companies also announcing special dividends and increasing pay-outs following an increase in corporate earnings.

As a result several UK equity income trusts have returned to full earnings cover. While others are still drawing on reserves, dividend cover is generally increasing. In the event of a further downturn in dividends from the market, we would expect most UK equity income trusts to be comfortable using reserves to maintain and grow dividends.

The current environment has been good for income generation for many alternative asset classes. In particular, debt funds with investments in floating-rate assets, which see an increase in yield on portfolios as base rates increase. In addition, infrastructure funds have inflation linkage in their cash flows, while renewable energy trusts have gained from high power prices. A global recession would be difficult, but any trust that invests overseas will see a boost to their dividends from the weakness of sterling.

How have enhanced dividend paying trusts performed? Will we see more or less of that in the future?

The important thing that investors need to understand is how the yield is generated, which will impact the risk/return profile of the fund. Income-biased portfolios have typically been focused on mature and relatively defensive underlying businesses, often having low sensitivities to broad market movements. In contrast, paying a yield from a capital growth-orientated strategy can lead to a more volatile return profile.

Several investment trusts have adopted enhanced dividend policies in recent years using capital reserves. They include several funds managed by JPMorgan; healthcare funds, such as International Biotechnology and BB Healthcare; some trusts in the listed private equity sector; and Henderson High Income, European Asset and BlackRock Latin American.

The recent, more volatile backdrop has shown that an enhanced dividend does not solve all problems for a trust. The fortunes of the asset class still impact premiums and discounts. For example, despite enhanced income policies, JPMorgan China Growth & Income and European Assets have derated in line with peers.

Have there been any significant developments on fees over the past 12 months?

There remains pressure on investment company fees, with a continued general movement down. Some funds have adopted tiered fee structures, including Troy Income & Growth and abrdn New Dawn, while several have reduced the tiered rates, benefitting investors as the fund's assets grow. Numerous performance fees have been removed in the last few years, including recently at Henderson High Income, whilst Schroder Oriental Income increased the threshold at which its fee is triggered.

Many wealth managers and multi-asset funds are heavily focused on KID cost ratios, since they now have to report these figures to clients. A change in guidance from the Investment Association has added to the pressure on multi-asset funds to disclose the underlying costs of their portfolios. As a result we believe that many are now limiting their exposure to investment trusts on grounds of cost. We believe this can create opportunities to invest in quality managers with high – but still competitive – fees.

We are in favour of low costs, but note that there is always a competitive tension between what managers can earn from raising capital in listed and private markets. This was demonstrated in 2021 by the ultimatum by Brevan Howard to increase its fees on BH Macro. In addition, a singular focus on fees can reduce the opportunity set of potential IPOs. We know that many interesting managers have decided against listed funds given the expected fee income, both in terms of fee level and expected capital raising, versus what can be achieve in private markets.

Which sectors look well-placed to deliver good returns over the next three to five years?

Given the continued uncertain outlook, defensive investment companies, such as Ruffer, Capital Gearing and RIT Capital, will continue to command a sensible allocation for a portion of investors' capital. We expect, however, that the best returns may be available from being contrarian and investing in areas that currently feel less comfortable. In particular, we believe that discounts of up to 50% on private equity trusts offer exceptional value. Portfolios typically contain more resilient businesses than the market appreciates, in our view, and fund balance sheets are much stronger than before the global financial crisis.

We also believe there may be scope for further recovery in the biotech sector, while out-of-favour geographies such as the UK and China could provide better returns going forward than they have recently. As the macroeconomic environment becomes tougher and liquidity is withdrawn from the system, we also see potential for a greater dispersion of returns for equity strategies, favouring those with more of a stock-picking, rather than a style-driven, approach. This may be a period when active fund managers can build their track records. The potential opportunities in infrastructure and renewable energy have already been mentioned.

What have been the most positive and the most disappointing features of the past 12 months?

The most disappointing thing has been the widespread widening of discounts, particularly in asset classes that are seeking to deliver a consistent return profile to investors. However, the macro backdrop has been impossible to fight for many funds. That said, it has been positive to see the pace of buybacks pick up as boards seek to limit discount volatility. In addition, there has been further consolidation with a number of smaller players leaving the sector. We welcome transparency in costs, but believe that the flaws in KIDs costs ratios have dampened demand unnecessarily in a number of cases.

How positive are you about the outlook for the sector going into 2023?

I continue to be positive on the outlook for the investment company sector. The growth in alternative assets over the last decade demonstrates that the sector continues to innovate and provide attractive investment opportunities. Investment trusts have provided much needed capital for areas such as solar and wind farms, as well as other types of infrastructure.

At a time when regulators are seeking ways to democratise private assets, they need look no further than the investment trust sector which already offers exposure to private assets to a diversified investor base. There is also a wealth of opportunities in well-managed and distinctive equity trusts which have delivered superior long-term performance compared to their open-ended peers. A higher interest rate environment will be a test for everyone, and alternative assets in particular. Nevertheless we believe that, as so often in the past, current volatility and widening discounts will in due course provide attractive entry points for many trusts.

UK REBOUND?

JONATHAN DAVIS *talks to* SIMON GERGEL *of Allianz Global Investors, managers of The Merchants Trust, and* ALEX WRIGHT, *manager of Fidelity Special Values, about the UK market's prospects.*

T HE UK EQUITY market has been such a poor performer in relative terms for so many years that it sometimes seems that it has become a fact of life. Over the past 10 years the total return, including dividends, of the FTSE All-Share index has lagged the FTSE World index by around 6% per annum. In capital terms, the FTSE 100 index is, remarkably, still trading at around the same level it was in early 2000, meaning that virtually the entire return investors have had from the 100 largest stocks in the UK market over more than two decades has come from reinvested dividends, with virtually no increase in capital values.

Going into 2022 the disparity between valuations of similar UK and non-UK companies was about as wide as it has ever been. Those who have been declaring (some, it has to be said, for several years) that the UK market looked remarkably cheap have had a long wait to be vindicated. Nevertheless, the first half of 2022 was a period in which you could say – or at least hope – that the tide looked like it was finally about to turn.

Over the nine months to the end of October, while inflation surged and the war in Ukraine triggered an intensive decline in most stock markets, the UK for once stood out as the best performer of all the biggest developed country stock markets, with the FTSE All-Share offering long suffering supporters a total return of minus 7.9%, while the S&P 500 fell by 23% in local currency and the FTSE World index by not much less.

In absolute terms the avoidance of loss is hardly the most ringing endorsement an investor could wish for, but at a time when both stocks and bonds were falling sharply together, it offered some hope that it could mark the end of the UK's pariah status in the eyes of international investors. It is true that the UK's stronger showing was largely confined to its largest constituents. The total return of the midcap index, the FTSE 250, was down more than 25% over the first nine months of the year while small cap stocks and even more so, those listed on AIM, suffered even more.

There are many reasons why the UK market in aggregate has been out of favour for so long. A lot of it has to do with the composition of the indices, dominated as they are at the top of the market capitalisation scale by banks and insurance companies, oil majors, utilities and tobacco stocks, none of which – apart from periodically the oil companies – can realistically be described as inherently high return companies. In a period characterised by low interest rates and easy money, so-called value stocks, of which the UK has plenty, have been thumped in performance terms by anything with higher growth potential.

In addition, the political turmoil of Brexit, whatever your personal views about its merits, has been mostly seen by global investors as a negative, limiting their desire to invest in companies listed here. The same is less true of foreign businesses, which have been happy to make a number of bids for undervalued UK-listed companies. In reality the impact on UK companies is of only limited importance to index performance, given that some two-thirds of revenues of UK listed stocks come from abroad. In that context the changing value of the pound against the dollar has more impact on the reported profits and valuations of UK companies than any direct consequence of Brexit per se.

In preparation for this year's *Handbook*, I caught up with two of the more talented and experienced managers of UK equity trusts to share their thoughts about the UK market's prospects and how they were dealing with the exceptional challenges posed by rising inflation, higher interest rates, the war in Ukraine and turbulent political developments in the UK, including the appointment and rapid resignation of a new prime minister.

Although the two trusts are broadly similar in size, the two managers, Simon Gergel of Allianz Global Investors, managers of The Merchants Trust, and Alex Wright, manager of Fidelity Special Values, have different mandates and different investment styles, so provide an interesting contrast in thinking. They certainly give good reasons to think that the medium-term outlook for UK equities is much improved, even if the challenges facing the recent prime minister, Liz Truss, have already proved insurmountable.

Income Merchant

SIMON GERGEL HAS been managing The Merchants Trust (ticker: MRCH) since 2006. The trust sits in the UK Equity Income sector and has been in the Allianz Global Investors stable since 1997. The trust itself has a long history that dates all the way back, in common with a slowly dwindling number of peers, to the nineteenth century (1889 in this case). It has a market cap of around £700m.

The trust has recently been in demand. After a strong performance in 2021, making it the best performing equity income trust over five years, Gergel and his team picked up a number of industry awards. This combined with a near 5% dividend yield and recognition that the UK market might have been oversold produced strong inflows for the sister open-ended fund they run in the same style. It also pushed the shares in Merchants to a premium for a sustained period, enabling the board to issue 11.4m more shares over 12 months – not that common an experience for most UK equity income trusts in recent years.

Sustaining a reasonable dividend is at the heart of the case for considering UK equity income trusts and recent market conditions have been challenging for that endeavour. The pandemic in 2020 led to UK listed companies cutting dividend payments by some 40%, forcing many investment trust boards to use their discretion to draw on reserves to avoid having to do likewise to their own dividends. Dividends from UK companies, while mostly restored, have still to recover fully their pre-pandemic levels.

In the case of Merchants, it has had to draw on its revenue reserves for two years running in order to maintain its record as one of the AIC's dividend heroes, meaning it has increased its dividend every year for more than 40 years. The dividend should be fully covered by earnings in 2022, but, says Gergel, "It is going to take time to rebuild the earnings cover to a point where dividend growth can accelerate again, but I think our shareholders understand that and prefer a steady and growing dividend to one that may grow more quickly but have to cut the pay out during a market downturn."

How does the recent surge in inflation affect the thinking of an equity income manager? With UK inflation forecast by the Bank of England to reach a peak well above 10% in the second half of 2022, even the 4.5–5.0% dividend yield Merchants offers, while very attractive in a period when interest rates were converging on zero, is less so when the cost of living is into double digits.

"It is a challenge of course" Gergel replies, "but it also emphasises the opportunity in equities. Equities are real assets, businesses that can grow over time. Many of our companies have either direct pricing power, like regulated utilities, or indirect pricing power because the goods and services they provide go up in price over time. They certainly look a better bet than bonds in an environment of higher inflation, to state the obvious."

In terms of portfolio management, he says that the focus is not on making sure that dividend growth keeps ahead of inflation in every year, although that is something Merchants has comfortably managed over longer periods. "It is going to be difficult to do that again in the short term" he acknowledges, "in part because during the pandemic so many companies cut or rebased their dividends."

"We try not to get too obsessed by day to day dividend movements. We look for value and we look to buy good companies at sensible prices to make money in the long term. Yes, we want them to pay dividends along the way, but we don't buy and sell a stock because the dividend is at a certain level, or because we are trying to achieve a certain income target. That would be quite dangerous."

Gearing, or borrowing to enhance returns, has an important part to play in sustaining the track record of the trust. Merchants has a policy of looking to use gearing in almost all market conditions, within a range of 10% to 25% of total assets. The range is higher than many of its peer group. In mid 2022 it was standing at around 13%, towards the lower end of the range, but a level with which the trust is "more than comfortable," says Gergel, given current valuations and the liquid nature of the stocks it owns.

Provided that the portfolio can generate an income return which is higher than the cost of its debt, currently 3.6%, there is an obvious and immediate benefit to shareholders in using gearing to help underpin the dividend, with any capital return as an added bonus. Because the trust allocates a proportion of the cost of the debt to its capital account, it enables the trust to pay a higher dividend from its revenue account than would otherwise be the case. In this context the fact that the trust has finally been able to repay or refinance all the more expensive fixed rate, long term debt with which it, like a number of other trusts, was burdened has helped returns. The overall cost of its debt has halved over the last five years, from 8% to under 4% today.

The board of Merchants reduced the level of gearing from over 20% a short while before the pandemic struck in 2020 and has since reduced it a little more. What would it take to get back to the maximum 25%? "It is not on the table in the short term, because the macro environment is challenging and complex at the moment" says Gergel, "but valuations are also very interesting at these levels, so you have to trade these things off against each other."

What about valuations then? Is the UK market as cheap as many people make it out to be? Gergel is not in much doubt about that. "Yes. The UK market is cheap. It is quite a bit cheaper than its long term average, though not however at bargain basement levels. There have been times when it has been cheaper. Company profitability is still pretty good, but the market will obviously look less cheap if profitability turns down, as is quite possible as we move through the second half of the year."

More important than the absolute level of the UK market, he says, is the polarisation that has characterised its behaviour this year, between value and growth stocks, on the one hand, and defensives and cyclical stocks on the other. Despite selling off sharply in the first half of the year, growth stocks were still trading at a premium mid-year, while many cyclical shares had been hit very hard and were sitting on exceptionally low earnings multiples.

Gergel's team were adding to their holdings of cyclical stocks in the first half of the year for that reason, the upshot being that "while the UK market overall looks cheap, our portfolio is even cheaper." A quarter of the Merchants portfolio in August was valued on a price earnings ratio of less than 8, and another 20% on a p/e ratio of less than 10. If those earnings can be sustained – admittedly a key question given the backcloth of rising interest rates and fears of an economic slowdown or recession – historical experience would suggest that the portfolio should produce good returns over time.

"Of course it could take time for this to work through and I think we are going to have a rocky patch in terms of company news flow for the next six to 12 months. We have seen some big profit warnings already and there will be more. But if we get to a point where inflation starts to fall and the economy starts to recover, then these beaten-up cyclical stocks will become very interesting indeed."

It is always prudent to expect the unexpected in investment, and recent experience has fully borne out the necessity of doing so. given the series of shocks that has confronted every fund manager in recent years, culminating in the inflation/ Ukraine developments that have dominated 2022. "I think we just have to get to used to dealing with uncertainty and not becoming too obsessed with one particular economic view, but rather concentrate on scenarios and positioning the portfolio more broadly."

The positive side of the market turmoil this year is that "if you take a long term view, and can look through some of the noise, you can find great opportunities. We have certainly found a lot of new ideas in the last 12 months. The portfolio we have today is very different to how it was a a couple of years ago, both before and during the pandemic. Dealing with periods of volatility and uncertainty is never easy and we will get things wrong, but we do consciously aim to maintain a focus on the long term and that gives us the confidence to back our views."

Delving deeper into the portfolio, the analytics show that Merchants has indeed seen a high degree of turnover in its portfolio. One cyclical sector that looks particularly promising when we spoke was housebuilding, with at least two stocks in the sector trading at discounts of 20–25% of their asset values, an unusual event. Other companies whose shares had sold off sharply and Merchants was buying included Unilever, with its strong array of global branded goods, and CRH, the buildings materials company.

"At some point the cyclical stocks that have sold off will do a lot better" Gergel concludes. "It is almost impossible to know when that will be and it could get worse if we have a deep recession, which I am not sure we will. I think there is certainly better value in the cyclicals area than in the defensives and we have been gradually moving some of the portfolio in that direction."

Although it is a UK equity income trust, Merchants recently changed its mandate to allow Gergel and his colleagues to invest up to 10% of the portfolio in overseas listed stocks, with the idea of enabling greater diversification, given the lopsided sectoral makeup of the UK equity indices. A notable addition to the portfolio from the change in portfolio rules is the German carmaker BMW, which despite hefty cash holdings was on a p/e ratio of around five at the time of purchase.

Despite the relatively limp performance of the UK market over the past two decades, and sterling's recent weakness, as you might expect Gergel is happy to make a case for its continued resurgence. One positive factor is the often cited fact that more than 60% of UK listed company revenues (and nearer two thirds in the Merchants portfolio) originate overseas. Another is that corporate governance standards are higher here than in many overseas markets. As a global investment management house, Allianz Global Investors votes on resolutions at AGMs in most markets. In the UK only 5% of resolutions are ones it votes against, compared to 20% in the rest of the world, where governance is more problematic.

Both those factors help to dilute the importance of political issues, which many investors use as a reason to avoid investment in UK stocks, Gergel argues. Not only is Brexit done, for better or worse, but the risk of a hard Left government has also receded, as the Labour and Conservative parties converge on more common ground. The resignation of Boris Johnson as prime minister may also prove to be a positive, given a perception abroad that he was not particularly pro-business.

Whether or not Gergel is right about that, what does seem clear, he says, is that behind the massive and challenging uncertainties created by the Ukraine war and higher inflation, the broader investment environment is changing. "The period of low and falling interest rates that we have had for the past 40 years is over, and that is a big change. I am not saying that inflation is going to keep going up. It is almost certainly going to come down from where it is now and may eventually hover around the 3–4% level. It is very hard to predict."

"But will people continue to go on being willing to pay ever increasing prices for high growth companies in this environment? I am not sure. The mood is changing. Undoubtedly the economic environment is very hard to read. There was an article in the *Financial Times* the other day which said that anyone who finds the current environment easy probably doesn't understand what they are doing!"

"So yes – investing in these uncertain times is more difficult than it was three years ago. But there are always challenges in investing. I started my career just before the 1987 crash (when the UK stock market fell by 20% in a day). That was pretty interesting. We had a big recession in the early 1990s, which was much worse than anything we have seen, apart from the 2007–8 financial crisis. You tend to forget how difficult it has been in the past. It always looks much easier with hindsight."

Contrarian Stock-Picker

ALEX WRIGHT HAS been the manager of the Fidelity Special Values investment trust (ticker: FSV) since September 2012, meaning he has just had his tenth anniversary as manager of the trust. The trust was originally set up as a closed ended vehicle for the much-lauded stock-picker Anthony Bolton, a hard act to follow. Alex originally joined Fidelity as a graduate in 2001, working as an analyst in a number of sectors, including building materials, beverages/leisure companies and emerging market banks, before opting to specialise in UK equities.

He was given the Special Values mandate after proving his credentials as manager of the open-ended Fidelity UK Smaller Companies fund and running a pilot UK equity fund investing across the market capitalisation scale. By then he had come to the conclusion that he was most at home in UK equities, which is not only a broad and mature market, but one in which stock selection is more important than in emerging markets, for example, where macroeconomic factors have more impact on share prices.

Does he regret opting to make his career investing in a market that has performed disappointingly in relative terms? "Absolutely not. Clearly if you had 2020 hindsight you would always choose somewhere that is going to perform the best. But the UK market is still one of the world's best markets in which to seek to add value, because company access is so much better in the UK and corporate governance is so much better. It is a good place to be an active manager."

Like Simon Gergel, Wright has the FTSE All-Share index as his benchmark and a mandate that allows him to invest in companies across the whole market capitalisation range, including AIM. Unlike Merchants, which is an equity income trust, Fidelity Special Values sits in the UK All Companies sector, which places a greater emphasis on growth over dividend yield, and as a result the trust's fees are charged to income rather than capital. The market cap of the trust is around £850m, compared with £700m for Merchants. The dividend yield is around 2.6%, compared to the 4.5–5.0% yield on Merchants.

In terms of performance, time horizon is a critical factor. Over the 10 years Wright has been in charge, Fidelity Special Values has produced an impressive annualised share price total return of 10.6%. For Merchants this figure is 8.5%. Over the last five years however, the honours are the other way around, with Merchants delivering 6.0% per annum and Fidelity Special Values a more modest 2.1%.*

---

* Source: Trustnet. As of 17 October 2022.

While Merchants has traded at or around par since 2018, FSV has ranged between a premium and a discount, in part reflecting its more volatile performance and contrarian investment approach. Merchants has the better risk-adjusted performance over the past three years, though ironically perhaps Fidelity Special Values, despite its lower yield, has experienced the fastest dividend growth of 12% per annum over five years, against just 2% for Merchants.

Such comparisons are fairly meaningless, however, given the different mandates and the different audiences to which the trusts are appealing. While both trusts have strong followings, and have comfortably outperformed the FTSE All-Share index, the single digit annualised rates of return which they have produced in the last five years do bear witness to the difficulty of producing consistently exceptional returns from an out of favour market, as the UK has been. The difference in performance is largely driven by their different styles and discount movements.

Like Gergel, Wright shares the view that market conditions have been challenging for some time, and this year more challenging than usual, with so many external factors affecting the way that markets have moved. After suffering a strong downdraft when the Covid-19 pandemic broke, he was able to capitalise on the vaccine-powered share price recovery in November 2020, with shares in the trust appreciating by 80% in 12 months from the lows of the initial Covid-induced sell-off.

By contrast, the increased uncertainty in 2022 saw the trust's shares experience a double-digit decline as the discount widened towards 10%. (In NAV terms, the trust was only slightly behind its benchmark, the FTSE All-Share index.) When Wright took over the management of the trust in 2012, the discount had moved out to about 15%, but gradually rerated from there towards a small premium over the next five years as its performance improved and the manager's reputation spread. Shareholders who backed Wright at the time of his appointment have benefited from the "double whammy" of rising NAV and discount narrowing.

Wright sums up his contrarian stockpicking approach as being focused on seeking unloved companies which are in the process of undergoing change for the better, but which the market has not yet come to appreciate. "Investors tend to hate companies where something has gone wrong, but things are never quite as black or white as they appear. Even small changes can have a very big effect on stock prices. You can have quite spectacular success where other investors are scared about an unpopular stock."

He gives me a couple of examples. One is the specialist lender Paragon, which issued and then securitised packages of buy-to-let mortgages in the run up to the global financial crisis. "After the severe liquidity issues the banks had in the financial crisis, everybody thought that the business model was dead, but in fact the default rate on their loans was surprisingly small. It was an incredibly unpopular business in an incredibly unpopular sector, yet their product turned out to be surprisingly low risk. The shares traded on an incredibly low valuation, given that it actually had a very high quality underwriting business. When the funding was sorted out, the stock shot up by 750% in the time we owned it."

The reason that Fidelity felt able to defy the conventional wisdom and buy into Paragon when it was trading so cheaply was, ironically, because the firm had earlier been heavily shorting the shares, on the basis that the banks would surely remove Paragon's funding and there would have to be a massive rights issue at a discounted price, which is what duly happened. "With the balance sheet sorted out, because we understood the business really well as a result of shorting the shares, we were able to spot it as a valuable turnaround proposition when the general market view was still very negative."

Another more recent example was Indivior, a specialist drug division (previously known as RB Pharmaceuticals) that was spun out of Reckitt Benckiser in 2014. The thing about spin outs, says Wright, is that unlike IPOs, where investment banks and brokers are heavily incentivised to tell a company's story, spin outs are typically a small part of the parent company's business and as a result often not well followed or understood. In the case of Indivior, which specialised in treatments for opioid disorders, it was seen as a one-drug business with poor prospects. When the company lost a court case over the exclusivity of their patent on their product Suboxone film, the share price tanked from £5 to £1 in short order.

Fidelity started buying the shares at that point because they were very positive on the prospect for Indivior's follow-on product, Sublocade, which had at the time a very slow launch. The stock then fell further because of a Department of Justice case, to a low of 30p, at which point Fidelity bought more. Although the Department of Justice was claiming $3bn in its suit, a sum that was more than Indivior's entire market capitalisation, Fidelity researched similar cases and thought the outcome was likely to result in a much less onerous penalty. This again turned out to be accurate, paving the way for the shares to rise from a low point of 30p to £3 today.

Such extreme cases are the reward for intensive research, for which Fidelity is well resourced. Nevertheless, Wright says, it is not just external factors which make current market conditions so difficult to navigate. Another is that the average calibre of competitor active fund managers is much higher than it was 30 years ago, when the trust was first launched. "There are a lot of clever people in hedge funds and algorithms out there looking for anomalies, and information travels so quickly that there is no longer an information edge that allows you to eke out small gains from relative value trades. Those value opportunities have all been arbitraged away."

On the other hand the inexorable rise of index funds and ETFs, so-called passive investing funds, has helped to make momentum a more dominant factor in the way markets trade today. The share prices of some of the biggest post-Covid winners, such as Peloton and Netflix, went up much further than they should have done, Wright says, because of this "dumb money" momentum factor. That creates opportunities for contrarian bottom-up stock-pickers like him.

In these conditions, even before you factor in the recent global inflation and Ukraine shocks, he says that active fund managers have to be much bolder and learn to live with more volatility than used to be the case. The sharp sell-off we saw in the first half of 2022 has to be seen in that light, although Wright makes the point that the most speculative stocks in the post-vaccine sugar rush market move actually peaked back in March 2021, and inflation was becoming a problem even before Putin's invasion of Ukraine raised the stakes much higher.

What we have seen this year therefore is the market pricing in the inevitability of an economic slowdown. "We are obviously now going into an economic downturn, but the question is how long lived and how deep is it going to be?" He thinks it was much more likely to be a "common or garden variety" recession driven by parts of the market being overheated and interest rates rising than another big sell-off like 2000–03 and 2007–09. While inflation may well peak in 2022, the question is how rapidly it will then fall and how quickly the central banks feel able to draw back on their anti-inflation policy moves.

What has also made investing more challenging has been the fact that, unlike in the big bear markets of 2000–03 and 2007–09, the big moves around Covid and now inflation have all happened so quickly, giving managers less time to plan their moves into and out of different types of stocks and sectors.

Taking heart

Nevertheless, Wright has taken heart from the strong relative performance of the UK equity market in 2022 and expects it to continue. Between 2016 and 2021, the UK underperformed the rest of the world for six years in a row. In 2022 so far, the UK has outperformed European, Japanese and Emerging Market equities and is marginally ahead of the US market. Does he think the phase of underperformance is over? "I don't see any reason for the current inflection in trend to change. In fact I think we have got a long way to go. The US market has fallen sharply, but is still expensive when measured against its history, while the UK remains very cheap on almost every measure."

The gearing that Fidelity Special Values can draw on is created differently from Merchants and many other investment trusts. Fidelity uses derivatives known as contracts for differences to enhance its returns. Gearing averages around 5–6% per annum, but the range has been as wide as −5% (i.e., 5% net cash) to +20%.

The advantage, Wright points out, is that "you only pay for the CFDs when you use them – and you only pay about 40 basis points above overnight interest rates, which recently have been incredibly low. So the overall gearing costs have been unbelievably low, around 1.5%."

The CFDs also have a role to play in hedging out the currency exposure embedded in the trust's holdings of non-UK listed shares, which ranges from 15–18% (a slightly higher range than Merchants). The non-UK holdings give the trust more diversification and have helped performance during the recent weakness of sterling. The trust held four companies in the portfolio that were subject to bids when we spoke, where there was a high conviction those bids would go through but the shares had yet to fully reflect the bid price. The use of gearing enabled the trust to hold onto those shares and wait for the discount to close.

As for the future, Alex Wright says he thinks there is a "really interesting opportunity" to make positive absolute returns from the UK market over the next three to five years. The p/e ratio is at 9–10 times earnings. "Even with a 20–30% downgrade in earnings, which would mean a big recession, that is still an attractive level and you also get a 5% yield from the Footsie index. That is a better prospective return than from many other asset classes, including global equities."

The current situation, he says, although challenging, is nothing like as bad as the 1970s, but it would still be a surprise if the double-digit annualised returns of the past decade were to be repeated in the next one. The Fidelity Special Values portfolio has been trading at a discount of between 20% and 30% to the market overall and, as a value investor, Wright naturally believes that the disconnect will be rectified in due course, whatever short-term shocks may still be in store.

MULTI-MANAGER FIX

JONATHAN DAVIS *takes a look at how one of the oldest investment trusts is faring in its effort to refit itself for life in the 21st century.*

THE NEED TO adapt to changing circumstances is one of the constants of life in the investment trust sector, and nowhere has the need to adapt been more evident than in the challenges facing some of the venerable 'big beasts' with long and glorious histories in the global sector. Thirty years ago two of the oldest trusts of them all, Foreign & Colonial (founded in 1868) and Alliance Trust (founded in 1888) were dominant forces in the investment trust world, followed not far behind in the vintage rankings by the likes of the Scottish Investment Trust (1887), Witan and Scottish Mortgage (both 1909).

In the days before the onset of low-cost index funds and ETFs, these venerable names offered steady but practical one-stop-shop solutions for the private investor looking primarily for diversified global equity exposure. With the arrival of much cheaper and readily accessible passive alternatives, a phenomenon that has accelerated notably this century, they now face the challenge of remaining both relevant and competitive in the retail funds market. The name of the game has become differentiation, with each trust adopting a distinctive new direction, albeit with mixed results. The Scottish Investment Trust sadly failed the challenge altogether, being absorbed this year into the JPMorgan Global Growth and Income Trust after a long period of poor relative performance.

While Scottish Mortgage has prospered hugely (until this year) by investing in large stakes in private unlisted companies, Foreign & Colonial is attempting to differentiate itself from its peers and competitors by branching out into assets other than global equities, such as private equity and bonds. Meanwhile Witan and Alliance Trust have opted for "a pure multi-manager" approach, giving a piece of the overall portfolio to a number of different stock-pickers, rather than having a single manager or team to run their portfolios. This is a popular approach in the institutional investment market, but has been less common in the global investment trust sector until now.

The experience of Alliance Trust makes for an interesting test case of what re-invention can do. It is now just over five years since its new strategy was first implemented. It followed a period of several years where the trust lost focus and drifted sideways, with its future much debated in the media and the markets. In due course it attracted the attentions of Elliott Management, an activist investment firm which took a significant shareholding and agitated successfully, along with others, for change.

Long based in Dundee and self-managed, the trust's board was beefed up and re-energised and in due course adopted a new business strategy. This involved disposing of the trust's hodgepodge of non-core investments including private equity and mining, selling its fund management business to Liontrust and getting rid of its shareholder saving scheme, leaving just the investment trust and its then £2.7bn of net assets to be invested as a pure global equity offering.[*]

After reviewing a number of different options for how best to do this, the board opted to go down the multi-manager route, hiring WTW, a well-known investment firm, to do the job. Part of the rationale for this was the belief that running a pure global equity portfolio in a manner that was popular in the institutional market, but not readily available in the wealth manager and private investor market, would give Alliance Trust and its shareholders a much clearer and more distinctive identity in the global investment trust sector, as well as holding out the prospect of better returns than a simple index fund. A multi-manager approach that can be used as a one-stop-shop in equities should be even more appealing to an individual investor than a well-resourced institutional investor.

What is different about Alliance Trust's new approach is that instead of simply allocating chunks of the trust's investment portfolio to other already diversified funds, the WTW approach is instead to ask a number of fund managers known for their stock-picking skills to choose only their best stock ideas. These are then combined and allocated to a single global equity portfolio whose risk and style parameters are managed centrally by the consultancy firm specifically for Alliance Trust. It is a formula that has proved successful in the professional market, where WTW is a big player, providing discretionary investment management over some $181bn of institutional assets.[†]

The firm is probably still better known for its actuarial and pension fund consultancy and services business. Its investment division is well-resourced however, with around 1,000 employees, of whom around 10% are engaged in the business of investment manager selection. The decision to hire WTW raised a few eyebrows at the time, because as Craig Baker, its Global Chief Investment Officer, says "we hadn't managed assets directly for UK retail investors before. While we had advised a number of investment trusts on manager selection, we had never done discretionary management for an investment trust before." It saw the Alliance contract as a great opportunity to expand its reach into the UK wealth manager and private investor

---

[*] As at 31 December 2017.
[†] As at March 2022.

market by applying its time-tested methods to a well-known and established name in the trust world.

While a novelty in the trust sector, employing a panel of fund managers to submit only their best 10–20 stock-picking ideas in their chosen specialist areas and using them to construct an equity portfolio has some obvious attractions. One, says Baker, is that it avoids the problems that the traditional individual or small team fund manager appointment can create if performance turns out to be disappointing. Replacing a manager is normally a lengthy and time-consuming process – notice has to be given, shareholders have to be consulted, legal documents have to be produced and so on – that tends to see the trust's share price fall and stay at a discount while the process is underway.

With the multi-manager approach, however, changing a manager is much simpler. Alliance Trust has nine managers in its current line up, so typically only around 10% of the portfolio is affected if a manager is dropped, and in the Alliance Trust model it can be done immediately. There is no notice period. The panel of "best in class" managers can also be refreshed over time. More importantly, perhaps, by concentrating on their "best ideas" rather than on their whole portfolios, the process isolates the factor, WTW says, that academic research suggests is the most consistently discernible value that active fund managers can add. By this it means stock selection rather than other factors such as momentum, growth or value.

"What we say to them [the fund managers]" says Baker, "is we don't want you to fill the portfolio with stocks that you are holding primarily for risk control purposes. That is pointless. We can deal with that by how we blend the various stock-pickers. We just want your very best ideas, and think about the risk in terms of long-term, permanent loss of capital rather than in terms of your short-term performance relative to a benchmark or your peers. Our view is that you get a much better bang for your buck in return per unit of risk from pure stock selection than you do from everything else."

High active share

The upshot of this approach, critically, is that while the resulting portfolio looks very much like the benchmark index, the MSCI All-Country World Index, in its geographical and industry make up, it still has a very high "active share", meaning that its holdings of specific stocks are very different to those that make up the benchmark. In other words, if the stock-pickers really can find the best stocks, and the active share measure suggests that they are indeed trying to do just that, that should show up in superior performance.

But what about the costs? One of the main criticisms of the multi-manager approach is that shareholders face paying a double set of fees for the privilege of having a third party choose external fund managers. Baker's counter to that is that WTW's existing extensive relationships with potential investment managers means that it can extract much better terms from the skilful stock-pickers it identifies than most other investors could do themselves. And there is some truth in that: Alliance Trust's ongoing cost ratio ranks fifth for cost effectiveness in the global sector, behind only Scottish Mortgage, Monks, Bankers and Brunner.[*]

So why then does it appear that the shareholders in Alliance Trust have yet to see these theoretical benefits of WTW's superior strategy show up in the relative performance of the trust versus the MSCI All-Country World Index? Making a realistic assessment of the trust's performance since the new approach was adopted in 2017 is complicated by the fact that it was not until the summer of 2019 that the last legacy asset of the trust, its saving scheme, was finally relinquished. Nevertheless the trust has so far failed to beat its chosen benchmark convincingly, or meet its long-term target of delivering 2% per annum of outperformance, described as being targeted over rolling three-year periods (noting that some will be easier than others to achieve).

Over the five years to the end of September 2022, for example, the share price total return of Alliance was 41.3%, somewhat lagging the MSCI ACWI Index's 49.4%. The NAV total return, on preliminary estimates, was 39.5%, including the legacy assets, or 41.5% if excluded.[†] WTW's answer, crudely summarised, is that the shortfall in performance is almost entirely due to the remarkable and unusual extent to which just a handful of very large capitalisation stocks (so-called mega caps), such as Apple, Microsoft, Alphabet, Amazon and Tesla, have contributed such a large proportion of the world index's return in the last five years.

Alliance Trust's index-like performance stands in contrast to the success which WTW has had over the long term following the same approach. "Obviously we think that over the long term we can beat the benchmark, as we have done in our institutional portfolios that have a longer track record. Over the 10 years to 31 December 2021 we have outperformed by about 2.7% per annum and over 15 years by 4–5% per annum for the client where we have been doing this for the longest time. Normally you would say that five years is long enough to have as a full market cycle. So why haven't we managed to do it over the most recent five years?"

---

* PRIIPs KID costs as disclosed on individual company websites, as at 17 January 2022.
† Source: Numis calculations.

"THE MULTI-MANAGER APPROACH IS POPULAR IN THE INSTITUTIONAL INVESTMENT MARKET, BUT HAS BEEN LESS COMMON IN THE GLOBAL INVESTMENT TRUST SECTOR UNTIL NOW."

An unusual market

"The strange thing" Baker says, "is that we haven't really had a full market cycle," in the sense that returns have been so dominated by those mega cap growth stocks. "There has been such an extraordinary situation over these five years of large and mega cap stocks driving everything. That's been a real headwind to our performance." According to his analysis, the stock-pickers have earned their corn over the period, with stock selection within size buckets being very positive, but this has been more than offset by the impact of the trust being underweight in the mega cap and large stocks and overweight mid and small cap stocks. Alliance Trust has not been alone in this – indeed performance relative to the peer group has been strong. Alliance Trust has significantly outperformed the equal-weighted version of the MSCI All-Country World Index, and its performance has been among the best 5% of randomly selected equal-weighted portfolios with the same number of stocks. The only trouble is that the index has done even better, in the top 0.5% of all of these, indicating quite how extraordinary the performance of the index has been.[*]

Shareholders are entitled to ask how well this argument stands up. The whole point of indexing is that it takes such anomalous periods in its stride and the onus is on the active management industry to justify why it should be given the benefit of the doubt, just because the market has chosen to behave in what may appear to be an irrational way. Nevertheless in this case it is possible to have some sympathy for Baker and his colleagues, as the timing of their introduction to the job of managing the Alliance Trust portfolio was outside their control and in hindsight looks unfortunate if solely comparing the returns to the index rather than in absolute terms or relative to the peer group. As it is, the trust's performance in both NAV and share price total return over five years has turned out to be broadly in line with its index and ahead of most, but not all, of its peers in the global sector. Roughly half of its nine managers have beaten the index while the other half have underperformed, more or less cancelling each other out.

Given that the objective of the trust under its new mandate is to outperform the world index by an average of 2% over the very long term, something it has yet to achieve, the board appears to have accepted the argument that the period has been sufficiently unusual to justify sticking with the new approach, particularly given the fact that the performance looks strong on most other measures.

Chairman of the Alliance Trust, Gregor Stewart says that the board has examined the trust's performance at length, regularly challenging the manager, and is satisfied that the strategy is fit for purpose over the long term. He says: "The board

---

[*] WTW and MSCI Inc., data to 31 March 2022.

is disappointed that we haven't outperformed the index since adopting the new investment strategy in April 2017. But absolute returns have been strong and we've done better than many of our peers. We understand that, through most of the last five-plus years, it's been an exceptionally difficult market for core, active global equity managers to deliver outperformance when judged against an index whose returns have been driven by a small number of US mega cap growth stocks. Now that market returns are becoming less concentrated, both by countries and industries, we are optimistic that there are better times ahead. Indeed, we are already seeing early signs of that. While global trusts with a strong growth-style bias have had a torrid time since inflation and interest rates started rising, we've achieved steadier returns and are confident that, over the full market cycle, we expect to deliver meaningful outperformance of the index and consistently rising dividends."

"We have done better than the majority of other active approaches, but clearly we would have hoped to do better relative to the index," is Baker's conclusion when I raise the question of performance. "We are however very excited about the future prospects, in part because of the portfolio we have in place, in part because of the skill of our stock-pickers and in part because we have delivered outperformance in stock selection since inception. If that edge in stock-picking continues, and we see the market's recent bias towards the mega caps neutralise, or even reverse, then we should see considerable outperformance of the index as well as the peer group."

The composition of the 200-share Alliance Trust portfolio is different from many actively managed funds in that there are no big single bets. Apart from the small emerging market exposure, which is made up of many very small positions, it is rare, says senior portfolio manager Stuart Gray, for any single stock position to be more than 1% above its index weight. The largest holding as at 31 July 2022, Alphabet A+C, was 3.6% and the average holding size 0.6%. "It is not a big bet on two or three companies, whereas the passive approach, the MSCI All-Country World Index, has effectively consisted of a very large bet on just five companies." From a risk control perspective, this diversification should ensure that the absolute performance of the trust – as opposed to its relative performance against the index – is reasonably reliable and steady.

In terms of market strategy, Baker says that macro considerations will never play a dominant part in shaping the portfolio, but can influence the degree of gearing that the trust employs. The average gross gearing the trust employs is 10%, and can be varied by WTW without recourse to the board in a range between 7.5% and 12.5%. When we spoke it was between 7% and 8% and Baker's view was that "we are cautious but not totally negative about the equity market. Equally we are not about to increase the gearing and plough into equities because we are near the bottom." The trust, he says, will always have a well-balanced portfolio. "We are unlikely to be a top decile fund in any year, and we are unlikely to be a bottom decile fund in any year. We think we will continue to produce good outcomes in most environments."

One encouraging sign for the board and managers is that its performance in 2022 has shown signs of greater resilience, with first half returns being roughly in line with the index, but well ahead of its peer group. The discount at which the shares trade has remained narrower than that of F&C, Scottish Mortgage, Monks and Witan, helped by the company's willingness to buy back shares. Although it has no formal discount control target, in the 12 months to September 2022 the board has sanctioned the buyback of shares equivalent to 6% of the issued share capital. It has also made a conscious decision to increase the dividend payout.

In common with a number of its peers, Alliance has invested in improving its communication to shareholders and attempting to get across the message that its new strategy offers investors a reliable core global equity holding around which they can, should they so wish, add other investments with different risk profiles. There is no doubt that the trust is clearly differentiated today from the listless, drifting vehicle it appeared to have become five years ago.

Without an improvement in its index-relative performance, and until that vaunted faith in stock-picking is reflected in results, there still remains work to do to meet the challenge of remaining relevant and competitive against passive alternatives. Nobody likes to see the grand old names of the past go out of business, but the board at Alliance Trust is clearly making a determined effort to remain a valid 21st century competitor and avoid the fate of those, like the Scottish Investment Trust, which have sadly lost their independence. Look out for more progress to come.

PRIVATE INCOME

By JONATHAN DAVIS

L IKE ALLIANCE TRUST, another trust that has taken steps to adapt and renew its offering to investors in recent years (and more than once) is Aberdeen Diversified Income and Growth. It makes for an interesting case study in the positives and negatives of making repeated changes in a trust's management arrangements, with the final verdict on its latest incarnation still to be determined.

The trust (ticker: ADIG) dates back as far as 1897 when it was originally launched with the somewhat bulldog-like name of British Assets. It was founded by James Ivory, also the founder of the Edinburgh investment firm Ivory & Sime, with the original objective of investing in undervalued Australian banks and insurance companies. Today, after a number of iterations over the years, it has retained its global focus with a market capitalisation that currently ranges between £350m and £400m.

Ivory & Sime continued to manage the trust for many years before it moved to F&C Investments and then briefly on to BlackRock, where it traded as BlackRock Income Strategies Trust. That did not work out well, and in 2017 the board decided, somewhat unusually, to go back soon after to the drawing board. After running another selection contest the job of managing the trust was given to abrdn, the listed asset management company, with a mandate to run a diversified, multi-asset portfolio with an income bias. Two years ago the board reviewed the strategy and made further changes to the way that the trust is run, including replacing the previous management team with another from abrdn.

Since passing the mandate to abrdn the trust has traded under the name of Aberdeen Diversified Income and Growth and sits in the flexible investment sector of the AIC's classification. As such, it is up against some stiff competition in the shape of the Ruffer Investment Company, Capital Gearing Trust, and Personal Assets, all companies that have large and growing followings and promise to protect the capital of their shareholders through most market conditions. Their absolute return approaches have held up particularly well through the twin tests of the Covid shutdown in 2020 and the inflation/Ukraine war shock of 2022, so the challenge for the new look abrdn-managed trust to cement its future in this sector after so many changes has not been an easy one.

The revised approach that abrdn offered the board two years ago centres on expanding the range of asset classes in which the trust can invest, drawing on the many specialist teams that abrdn employs to create a genuinely broadly diversified global investment vehicle. In particular there is a new focus on adding private assets of all kinds to the portfolio mix. These include not only private equity, but also privately owned credit instruments and a range of alternatives, including infrastructure, renewable energy, venture capital and royalty companies.

Although Baillie Gifford has led the way in the last few years in broadening the scope of its family of equity investment trusts to include mature unlisted companies that have yet to join the public listed markets, arguing that they have the potential to offer superior returns to public companies in many cases, the canvas that ADIG has opted to work on is wider still. By broadening its policy to include more private asset classes, while it remains in direct competition to some of its popular bigger peers in the sector, it can still be seen as a distinctive multi-asset offering, with the highest yield in the sector and a distinctive risk profile.

When announcing the latest change in management arrangements, the board said it would also be adopting a new investment objective as Libor was being abolished, a 6% per annum net asset value total return over any rolling five year periods. Although not committed to a specific dividend target, it also made clear that the primary focus would be on delivering a dependable and sustainable income, with capital growth as an important but secondary objective. In this way it also hopes to differentiate itself from the Ruffers and Capital Gearings of this world, for whom capital preservation has always been the priority.

According to the new lead manager of the trust and head of private market solutions at abrdn, Nalaka De Silva, the essence of the new arrangements lies in the simplicity of the 6% total return objective, designed to make the trust more readily comprehensible to private investors in particular. The recent changes follow a lengthy period of consultation with the shareholders. Although the portfolio is exceptionally well diversified, with more than 640 underlying individual holdings held through a wide range of funds, the way the different asset classes are combined is designed to give confidence that the attractive dividend will be resilient in difficult market conditions and capable of growing in better ones.

This was in response to complaints that the portfolio had proved to be too volatile under previous arrangements. "The essence of what the shareholders and the board were telling us" says De Silva, "is that they wanted a portfolio that was less correlated with the equity markets but had a more consistently stable and dependable dividend." The best way to achieve that, his team decided, was to gradually increase the share of private market investments towards an eventual target of 55% of the portfolio while increasing the holdings of real asset classes such as infrastructure to provide protection against higher inflation and diversifying the sources of risk. Among other moves, including cutting the exposure to emerging market debt and asset-backed securities, the weighting in listed equities was reduced to allow these changes.

A work in progress

The transition to this more resilient portfolio remains a work in progress. De Silva is able to draw on the full resources of abrdn, including 465 investment professionals, more than 350 private market specialists and relationships with 400 general partners of specialist private funds. At the end of April 2022, the portfolio was invested in three main broad asset buckets: private markets 48%, fixed income and credit 23% and listed equities 29%. The strategy was further reviewed this autumn and some further refinements added.

Balancing the requirements of sustaining an attractive dividend and the desire to add some potential for growth on top is hard enough in normal market conditions and made doubly so when markets have been as volatile as they have in the last couple of years. The board has committed to paying 5.6p dividend for the current full year, which with the shares trading below 90p in mid-October translated into a yield of around 6.5% at one point, comfortably the highest in the flexible sector, ahead of most pure global equity funds and also ahead of many infrastructure trusts following their autumn sell-off. The trust has two years of revenue reserves to draw on to support the dividend if need be.

Adding capital growth has been a tougher task. "My core challenge over the past 12 months has been how to preserve value in what has been a pretty challenging environment," De Silva says. The NAV performance of the trust has been dull but steady, up 2.5% since the new team took over in August 2020 and creditably flat through the first eight months of 2022, maintaining its dividend while both the bond and equity markets were tumbling.

The trust, in other words, has largely delivered on its commitment to reduce correlation with the equity markets. According to Kepler Intelligence, the correlation with the All Countries World Index was actually negative over the period from the start of the new strategy in October 2020 and the end of the first quarter 2022. The main problem has been that the discount at which the shares trade has come in, but remains wide in the 15–20% range (and moved out to 22% at one point during the September 2022 market sell-off).

This means that the share price has not quite kept pace with the published NAV over the period since the new strategy was agreed. The board has bought back a few shares, but it has yet to lay out a definitive discount management policy, preferring to wait for the markets and the new approach to settle down. In any event, having a higher proportion of the portfolio in private assets limits the scope for buybacks.

There could be a number of reasons for the stubborn persistence of the discount, including the fact that there is typically a lag in the reporting of NAVs for some kind of private investments. De Silva says that he always expected it to take some time to convince potential buyers of the trust that its risk profile had changed. "We have seen a lot of retail investors coming onto the register through the execution-only platforms, but the institutional base seems to be still sitting on the fence, waiting for better value to appear." However, he says that the spread between the buying and selling price of the shares has remained quite tight, and he has noticed that every time the prospective yield approaches 5.75% more buyers have come back.

The chopping and changing in the management of the trust, however necessary, cannot have helped. Experience suggests that it typically takes 2–3 years for a new manager to win the confidence of the market. The key to reversing former negative sentiment lies in delivering on the promises made at the outset, and ADIG has clearly made a start down that path. If it can sustain its record of steady NAV performance and low correlation with equities while continuing to maintain and grow its 5.6p dividend, there is clearly room for the shares to rerate in due course.

Q&A WITH
MIKE SEIDENBERG

2022 has proved to be a tumultuous year for all kinds of growth shares, with the high-flying technology sector among the worst affected. MIKE SEIDENBERG, who succeeded Walter Price this year as lead manager of the £1.1bn Allianz Technology Trust, offered us his comments as the year unfolded. Despite a sharp NAV decline in the first nine months of 2022, the trust is still the second best performer in the investment trust universe over the past 10 years.

When we spoke back in 2020 you said valuations in the tech sector were high, but not insane. They got a bit more insane after we'd spoken, but this year we've seen some sharp sell-offs in tech and the best we can say is that valuations are obviously a bit more sane now than they were. Can we say any more than that?

I think the comment that I made to you last time we spoke was reflecting what was a different interest rate environment. We're in a more aggressive interest rate environment now as we're trying to get inflation under control, which obviously has an impact on growth assets, including technology shares. What we saw this year was a broad sell-off across all sectors and all types of growth assets. It wasn't just tech.

In the second half of 2020, not so long after Covid started, you could have bought almost anything with a tech flavour to it, and it would have done well. Is it now time to be more discriminating?

That is right. A rising tide no longer lifts all boats. In 2022 we have started to see some dispersion in performance between different parts of the tech sector space. Cybersecurity and digital transformation come to mind. That's something we wanted to see. I've just come back from an investment conference where I met with lots of tech companies, as well as people who buy technology. What I heard consistently was that people aren't thinking of this as another 2008–9 potential recession.

Like you, I lived through that, and when you start to worry about the safety of the cash in your bank account or a money market fund breaking the buck, that's a really scary scenario. I don't think we're going back to that, even if we do go into recession. I'm not an economist, but I do need to have a macro view when I'm thinking about the portfolio. I think we're in an environment where companies are looking much more closely at their spending on tech. So I think we are going to see more of this dispersion.

Difficult markets like this really test your conviction and your process. Having said that, they do come round and we are long-term investors. I've been investing for something more than 20 years now. I've been through cycles and what I have observed is that right now is a great time to start a business because, generally speaking, if you have an innovative idea a down cycle is the best time to start.

Would it be too simplistic to say that as a tech company it does help to have a few earnings these days?

I don't think it's simplistic at all. I agree with the statement. I don't believe in profitless prosperity. We want to invest in businesses that have good long-term operating margin structures. You could play the devil's advocate, and say "well what about Amazon, which had no profits for many years?" I understand the business well enough to know that Amazon has method to their madness. It is about building competitive moats around businesses and then monetising them later.

AWS, Amazon's cloud business, is a classic example. When I first started looking at it, Wall Street thought it would be something like a 12% operating margin business. However, when I've spoken with people there, I came away feeling that it could achieve a higher long-term operating margin. At the end of the day, businesses have value based on future cash-flow streams and earnings streams.

I look at a lot of sectors and there are some where I just don't like the margin structure. Maybe they have low barriers to entry. Maybe there are lots of customer acquisition costs. Part of my job as portfolio manager, and for the team, is to really try and figure out the sectors that are genuinely profitable and going to turn into good long-term businesses. By the way, just because a company's gone public doesn't mean it's a good business. In the public markets it is very much a case of buyer beware. Maybe I'm too cynical. But I keep that thought as my North Star when I'm thinking about a company's future.

Is not the problem that a lot of more recent tech stocks that have come to market haven't really succeeded yet in converting their big initial market share into something sustainable. Would that be a fair comment?

Yes, I think that's true as well, although I think you need to distinguish between consumer- and business-facing businesses. For example, we've never invested in Peloton, even though I have one myself and really like riding it. In a post-pandemic world, which I think we're in, people are going back to normal. Those businesses that did well during the pandemic period now have to figure out what is a normal demand environment. You have to have a business model and a cost structure that reflects the longer-term demand environment. If you don't, you can have fairly painful consequences, as Peloton and others have found.

I don't particularly want to pick on Peloton. We don't own it, but I do know the story pretty well. You have this bike which was pretty cool before the pandemic, but then it catches on like wildfire during Covid. What do you do? Do you go out and buy a factory to increase capacity, as opposed to subcontracting out? They thought it was a great idea to go out and build a factory, but what it means is that they now have a cost structure that isn't supportive of the new demand environment. It is a painful period of adjustment.

What did happen in the pandemic was it persuaded people that they wanted to conduct their lives digitally, at least to some extent. Think about ordering food digitally, for example. I never did that before the pandemic. Now it is commonplace. Sometimes when my kids say "great, let's get a pizza, it's only $20," I have to remind them, "not exactly, once you've added in the delivery and other fees." But I think we can all agree that we're going into a period of blending digital and physical – it is something that has happened and it's not going to change. It's occurring on the high street and it's occurring all over the world.

The same thing also applies in business-to-business, although not in quite the same way. Businesses want to decrease the amount of friction they experience when they're doing business with other customers. So if you're Caterpillar for example, and you're selling a tractor or excavating equipment to one of the big users, one of the big contractors, you want to make that process as easy as possible and as frictionless as possible, which you can now do by combining digital research and before you get to the physical delivery.

One of the issues is that not everybody is moving towards at least a semi-digital kind of business structure and they are vulnerable to rising costs.

Software applications really do make people more efficient at the margin. Go back to that example of selling our excavator. I can show you the brochure via Zoom, or look at a digital catalogue, and you can decide on the features or benefits you want without having to go to a dealer or direct to the manufacturer. I try never to lose sight of the fact that even in this inflationary period we're in now, software technology can help you do more with less and more efficiently. That's obviously a way to go.

Sometimes, when I'm in London, I go into these offices and you can see all these old leatherbound ledgers lying around. Photos from the 1920s and 30s had lots of people in rooms inputting sales and so on. Now that's all done digitally. Most companies are now shifting from legacy platforms to digital platforms. They don't want to get stuck with expensive legacy systems to maintain. They want to be in a world where they can be flexible and nimble, and that is really the notion of moving to the cloud and moving to digital.

These things go in cycles, don't they, though? The newspaper business, for example, has gone through at least three distinct phases in my lifetime, from union-dominated working practices to digital technology to competition from the internet and now to pay-for-content? It is not easy for companies to navigate through them.

Yes, I don't think that's easy. It requires an ability to think through to what lies ahead. As it happens I am a content junkie. Whenever I look at my bill for the *Wall Street Journal*, I'm like "you've got to be kidding me. It's such good value." The *Wall Street Journal* is a tool in my toolbox as part of my job. It's no different from a cowboy putting on a pair of boots and a hat when going out to herd cattle! I love to learn new things and newspapers do an amazing job of making us more informed. I think that people will pay more for content going forward, primarily because it's of value to them. All it needs now is to be monetised.

One of the issues for you is that every business is a technology business to some extent. Does it actually make sense to be a specialist technology investor?

That is a great question and something we talk a lot to the board about. Essentially the question is: where does technology start and stop? As investors we try to make sure that if we're investing in a particular company it truly is a tech company, and that isn't always easy to figure out. I'm old enough to know there was a company called BASF, which was a large chemical company. It used to say something like "We don't make things. We make things that go into other things." I think that's a good way to think about technology, especially on the b2b side.

On the consumer side, it's not entirely the same because clearly you've got some companies, like Meta and Google, that while they *are* technology companies, what they *really* are is in the consumer business. But to focus on the reason why you need a technology trust, that's a nice, easy question. Because we're specialists with domain expertise. I've got colleagues such as Rich Gorman, who focuses on cybersecurity for us, who really understand the nuts and bolts and the nitty-gritty. That gives our investors the ability to outperform by properly understanding the companies in that sector and how their products are differentiated from others.

Let's deal with this issue of your benchmark. This is not unique to you, of course, but it's more exaggerated in the tech sector, because you have three large holdings that dominate your benchmark

(Apple, Microsoft and Amazon are some 30% of the Dow Jones technology index). You're underweight in all of them but if you don't own them, you will be a long way away from the benchmark. How do you manage that?

That's a big issue. As a trust we are benchmark aware, but we're not benchmark tracking. We're happy with that. I think credit for that really goes to the board. They're looking out, as they should, for the investors of the trust. What they're really saying is they don't want to take too much single-stock risk, even if that happens to be a large portion of the benchmark. That in turn means that I have to find companies that are going to do better than those mega caps, which from a performance perspective can be quite difficult at times. It is something we need to live with. It doesn't always look great in any given 12-month period, but if you look over a multi-year period, even with these very large mega cap weights in our benchmark, we've done well by investors and been able to outperform.

How important do you think Apple restricting the data that other companies can get from iPhone customers is going to be?

I think it's a big deal. An e-commerce company I was meeting the other day said not only are they having to pay more per ad, but they are less able to identify the customers and don't get such good analytics after the transaction. That's all a result of the iOS changes introduced by Apple. For e-commerce providers, especially in first-world markets, that data had given them a very good insight into their customers. Its restriction is a headwind, there's no doubt about it.

I think Apple has every right to do what they want to do in this matter, though I don't think they're acting altruistically. I don't think anybody's altruistic right now. But they were in a position to put this up as a win around privacy and consumer protection. I think most people would embrace that idea. As for me, when I go to a website I just accept all the cookies. That's because I'm one of those people that want the website to know me better. That's a win for me.

But there are a lot of other people who feel differently. I've got a colleague who's the exact opposite. He wants to be as anonymous as possible on the web. So it's a matter of the individual, but net it is a headwind for the sector. Companies like Meta have become less effective because they just can't get the same signals back from the market.

Is Mark Zuckerberg spending billions of dollars on this new frontier known as the metaverse a concern for you?

I think it's really helped us being underweight, or in this particular case not now owning the shares at all. They are facing a multitude of headwinds. TikTok is grabbing a big chunk of the younger demographic that Meta desperately want and they're having to respond to that. It is potentially an existential threat to Facebook over time. I knew the company very well when it was going public. The transition from desktop to mobile was very important for them, and they handled that well, but they didn't face a huge competitor at that point. But now when you have a competitor like TikTok, which is grabbing the eyeballs of people like my daughter and my son, what they are trying to do is like overhauling the engine of a racing car while driving on the track. That's not such a fun place to be.

It doesn't mean they won't get there. But as I often remind myself, no one is as fickle as a consumer. If you're in that new demographic, which I'm not (but I wish I was!), once they leave you, they rarely come back. Facebook is having a lot of negative feedback about the split between digital pictures and reels on Instagram. Some of the complaints are valid. They've probably been far too aggressive in introducing reels.

They are also losing Sheryl Sandberg, who has definitely been a positive. She's a sales machine! She's beyond motivational. She's the type of person that you say "okay, I'll go to war alongside you." She's got that type of charisma. But look, they've got some good people and the stock is really cheap. So while it's helped us not owning it, there could be a point where the tide turns and things get better.

Software is still your biggest sector, though not quite as big as it was. What's going on in the software world at the fundamental and the stock level?

Well, from a fundamental perspective, as I alluded to, I don't think it's a case of a rising tide lifting all ships anymore. I think companies are going to be far more picky where they spend their money to get to move their business on. Software budgets generally are still fairly robust when you look at it from a high level, but within that we are seeing areas of strengths and weaknesses, with things like cybersecurity, which is now a must-have, growing strongly. Since the pandemic it's made the lives of chief information officers and chief security officers even more difficult.

For example, I'm working in Colorado today. I was 100 miles away at a conference yesterday. I am going home later and then I'll be in the office tomorrow. Who knows where I'll be on Friday? As a company your employees are working from multiple locations and using a network the way it wasn't designed to be used. That requires a lot of security. Digital is also still an interesting space, as transition to the cloud is a multi-year journey which most companies simply have to make. Companies will continue to spend, because once you start down this road you've really got to go right through with it.

I think we're also seeing some interesting things in software companies that work on semiconductor design. You can see large auto manufactures saying to themselves that they need to go to more electric vehicle working practices. Hybrid is just an interim stop. In Detroit, all the big auto manufacturers are spending all their R&D dollars on the transition to electric. They're not going to combustion engines anymore.

If software can help facilitate the design of chips and systems it is going to be really important for electric cars. Nothing is more important than how much power you have, how that power is used and how it's distributed. Tesla has done such an amazing job of vertically controlling that aspect of their business.

We have also seen the impact of large companies having to think more about ESG. Industrial and oil companies, if they care about decarbonisation and carbon capture, are going to need a lot of software to capture those metrics and help facilitate the transition. So the core market in many cases is process-based software. We're spending more time on learning how to figure out what the best options are in this space.

What about your investment in Tesla? It is one of your biggest holdings – why?

It is one of our larger absolute holdings and our largest overweight. I think the company just thinks differently. If you're listening to one of their conference calls, they're really focused on operational excellence. They really think hard about manufacturing and they think about it differently. They're saying, "We need to control all the electronics that go round our car." Sure they work with other companies, but they're really vertically integrated. When you look at their cars you think "wow, these cars are really beautiful." I still think they can improve the fit and finish internally if I compare it to say a Range Rover. But having said that the people who have these cars love them.

We think Tesla is going to be very difficult for the others to catch, which is why it's such a big position in the portfolio. Hopefully Elon Musk will clean up this whole Twitter thing. What I can tell you is I feel much better about the management team at Tesla today than I would have done say 18 months ago. Since then, he's brought in a deep bench of people that have been there, done that. It doesn't mean other car makers won't do well, but Tesla has a brand, it has as a halo around it.

If you think about it, that's amazing given that they've never spent a dime on marketing. Zero. They have such high brand awareness and that will help the cars hold their value. Obviously, there's scarcity at the moment for all kinds of cars. Tesla isn't the only one. But I think the company is really well positioned and they're going to be doing some interesting things around trucks as well in future, the big industrial trucks that carry trailers. I think there could be a really good area for them. I think a lot of cities will be very receptive to having materials moving in and out of the ports with fewer emissions.

What's your opinion of Elon Musk?

He thinks differently and he seems to get more done in a day than I probably got done in a year. I just don't know where he finds the time to do anything else. He is clearly just wired differently. I wouldn't bet against him. I think he deserves the benefit of the doubt. He's earned it. Yes, some of the things he does seem really kind of wacky at the time. But overall, you look back and he's done really well. I'm sure there's some method to his madness on some of these side projects.

Can I ask you about valuations in the tech sector? Obviously, they have been affected by the movements in interest rates. But suppose we projected a 10-year US Treasury yield of 3% for a sustained period? What sort of rating should tech stocks command in that kind of environment? Should it be a premium or discount?

Well, my view is that interest rates are probably going to come down at the margin over time, but I don't operate on that assumption. We're making investments. I want to own something for fundamental reasons. I looked at the valuation of some companies in the S&P 500. Campbell's Soup, which isn't going to go out of business anytime soon, grows maybe at 5% per year and things are going a little bit against them at the moment. Yet look at some of the tech companies and where they're trading, they have multiples which are lower than Campbell's Soup.

If you think about what it is tech gives their customers, it is competitive advantage. I don't think that goes away. Companies become irrelevant and companies become obsolete all the time. Our job is to find those companies that are not going to fail because they can use tech. Tech to me warrants a higher valuation than the overall market primarily because of the competitive advantage it affords people. Most of the companies have got superior margin structures at scale, when compared to lots of other businesses.

I always say you only buy technology companies for three reasons: they are helping to grow sales, they are helping to make you more efficient operationally, or they're providing you with a better customer service. Those are basically the three reasons why people buy tech. In my opinion, given the inherent characteristics of tech, it should outgrow the S&P 500 on average. It's not going to sell at a premium all the time, but over time it deserves a premium.

We're talking about a p/e ratio at the moment of around 20 times.

Yes. I feel good about that. In this job you have to turn over a lot of stones to figure out where the opportunities are. But I'm starting to have a good sense of some interesting ideas at the moment, in companies that have been pulled back too far, along with everything else. Tesla is probably one of the more expensive companies we have. It's an expensive stock relative to its profits today. I don't think that's the case over time because it is in heavy investment mode. Some of the growthier software companies have high valuations relative to their earnings because here again they're building up the moat around their business.

What are the risks that you worry about most?

Well, obviously you have the risk of a broad consumer slowdown, which would certainly translate through to people feeling insecure about their jobs. That tends to have an impact on tech spending. Global conflict also of course. I would never have said this four years ago, but there could be another pandemic which causes us all to go back inside. That wouldn't be good either.

What this means is that we have to make the investing process even more rigorous before we commit our money. I worry about people being able to hire enough people to go out and really generate the sales they need. If we invest in cyber companies, we worry about what would happen if the company we invested in proved to be at fault for a major breach. On the other side I think the decline in VC funding is probably a positive for some of our companies, because their competitive landscape has actually gotten rather better. They don't have so many people throwing money at companies saying "spend, spend, spend!" and that means we have seen more rational pricing behaviour.

We do have some stocks which haven't really worked out well. We've lightened our load in memory as of late, probably just because we're worried about capacity issues. They may be cheap for a reason. Like a lot of investors, we're wrong at times. Everybody is. If an investor tells you they are right all the time, you should probably run for the hills. But we try to make sure we get more things right than wrong. And when we do that we do it with conviction, so when we get things right, we really are able to monetise that. And hopefully, if we do get it wrong it's a small mistake, not a big mistake.

Are there any advantages that the trust has which an open-ended fund doesn't have?

Yes. There are some companies that we're able to invest in that we probably wouldn't be able to invest in with an open-ended fund due to the liquidity issue. A trust structure is a less volatile product at the margin. It allows us to have a longer duration on some of our ideas because we think that the people who invest in it, for the most part, have longer-term horizons.

And I really like the clientele. It's fun for me when I'm in the UK marketing, because generally speaking we're being used as a part of a bigger portfolio and therefore our goal is to make sure when they allocate whatever – 5%, 4% – to tech, that we're on the order form. We have great competition; I really like our competition. I've been on a panel with Ben (Rogoff) at Polar, who I consider our main competition. He has done an amazing job. It is fun to be in a space that's full of interesting companies and really good competitors because I think it's a bit like watching two good teams play soccer or football against each other.

You must get asked often why the tech business is so US-centric?

That's hard. One of the common questions we get asked when I'm in the UK is, "How come you don't have more international exposure?" My answer is usually twofold: a) just because a company is domiciled in the US, it does not mean that much. The reality is that most of these companies are global in nature, just as GlaxoSmithKline is; b) generally speaking, as crazy as this sounds, multiples are usually cheaper in the US relative to European and UK tech. They usually trade at discounts. I don't know why that is, but it tends to be the case.

Finally, would you like to have the ability to invest in unlisted stocks as well?

As much as I might think it's an interesting opportunity, I think it's a different business. I really do. Walter and I get asked about it all the time. The team has really good relationships with the companies we invest in. It's a different game to get allocation into those early stage businesses. My argument would be that you'd need to hire someone who's a full-time employee to do that because the notion that you're going to go down to Sand Hill Road where all the VC companies are and cherry-pick their best ideas to get an allocation is a dreamer's notion. They don't just show you the Facebooks.

Q&A WITH JAMES DOW

JAMES DOW *joined Baillie Gifford after a number of years as a financial journalist and has been involved in running the Scottish American Investment Company, commonly known as SAINTS since 2013 and has been joint manager since 2016.*

T HE TRUST STARTED life in 1873 and has been managed by Baillie Gifford since 2004, when it took over the mandate from First State Investments. It is distinctive amongst the firm's large stable of 13 investment trusts in being managed in a different style to the others. While most have a bias towards high rates of capital growth and in several cases unlisted private companies, SAINTS is a global equity income trust aimed at investors whose priority is a reliable and growing long-term income. In this Q&A James Dow explains his philosophy and the trust's recent history and performance.

You've obviously got a good family name for both investing and journalism (Charles Dow was a journalist who started the Dow Jones index among other innovations). How did you get involved in the stock market and with managing the trust? Was that through journalism or was it something you were interested in before?

I had previously worked for a few years as a business reporter for *The Scotsman* newspaper, and that experience confirmed to me that the stock market is an endlessly fascinating world, with so many companies doing so many different things. Fund managers seemed to know all the answers to why the news was happening – they pretended they did anyway. It all seemed to be far more interesting than journalism.

And then there's the added interest of doing something which is fundamentally quite difficult. Being an active manager and adding alpha or value over time, it's not easy [*Not half! Editor*]. So as well as being infinitely varied and interesting, the actual application of the job, allocating capital and making investment decisions, to me that was clearly a better job than being a journalist.

So I switched careers and have been here ever since. After the first few years I occasionally fed in ideas to the managers of SAINTS. I became involved directly with it around 2013 and started being one of the decision-makers on it, then deputy manager and finally fund manager in 2016. In this profession you are learning about the world and thinking about the future. It is a good place to be.

What did you take away from your experience in the newspaper industry?

It was a crazy period. When I joined in 2001, the business section was a 32-page pull out, published on pink paper, rather like the *FT*. In fact it was the biggest business section outside the *FT*, bigger than any of the broadsheets. But within the space of the three years I was there, it shrunk down to tabloid size and effectively became six pages folded into the rest of the paper, three of which were yesterday's FTSE closing prices.

That, to me, was a startling sign of an industry that was on a rapid descent path and forced to change by the economics of the business. It was a salutary lesson in how businesses and economics can change. The Business Editor when I started out was a man called Ian Watson and there's still a diaspora of *The Scotsman's* staff peppered around in lots of different places. Fraser Nelson, who is still editing *The Spectator*, is one of them.

The newspaper industry has been through a remarkable cycle of change, from rapid expansion after the breaking of the print unions to another decline after the arrival of the internet and back to a point where people are now charging for content once more.

Exactly. There was a time where you would've said if you want a business with a competitive moat, if you want a guaranteed future, it is hard to beat the classified ad section. It is effectively a licence to print money forever. And you'd have been so, so wrong, extrapolating the past and assuming it would always continue into the future. I think that's a good lesson for investment. You're buying the future, not the past. You need to think quite carefully and critically and coolly. I see a large part of the job as looking for those businesses which do have enduring earnings growth, the things that power SAINTS. It's easy to get caught up in a lot of stories.

Another thing I like about investing is that it is a place where experience really should benefit you over time. When you feel that you've seen all the movies, kissed all the frogs, however you want to describe it, that should make you better over time in being able to discern between the businesses that genuinely are enduring and growing and the ones that are actually rather fragile, or are likely to be in the long run.

Of course the fund management business has its own issues, not least the false god of relative performance, benchmark tracking and all the rest of it. Did you know when you joined Baillie Gifford that they weren't really into that style of business?

No I didn't. I just knew that they were in the interesting business of fund management and I think it only dawned on me later that I had been incredibly fortunate to join somewhere that was very stable and had a long-term outlook. That is partly because the firm has not always been terribly good at talking about itself. Back in the day, if you rang up all the different investment houses around Edinburgh for a quote, Standard Life would be back on the phone within 30 minutes, eager to speak. And then Baillie Gifford would send you an email from their PR agency three days later, saying "no comment".

The culture was all about getting on with the job, not tooting your own horn. You're genuinely trying to find good companies on a 10-year view. I was quite surprised when I joined and found that the same is still largely true today. It's not immediately obvious because the firm doesn't like to talk about itself very much, compared with others. It's a fortunate thing, of course, because, as I know from seeing other investment management firms, if your one-year relative performance is bad, then it is a case of "You had better mind your eye." Then after three years it is, "You probably should start looking for another job."

I think there are stats on this, but I don't think any fund manager has consistently outperformed forever over all three-year periods. It just doesn't happen. There are going to be times when whatever you do, whatever you believe in, it's not going to be the in-thing with the market. So you need to be somewhere where you're given the opportunity to have that learning and keep at it for a very long period of time.

In the long term that is very much to the clients' benefit. SAINTS is a good example because there have been periods, like 12–18 months ago, when rapidly growing, zero-dividend paying, cash-flow negative companies were all the rage. The steady compounding style of SAINTS was not really any help – "How boring! God, who cares about that?" But that's fine, because I've got the room to keep going, keep learning and keep planning the fund without fear. It's not "Oh, sorry, we're shutting you down and starting up a new fund that will bring in more assets." That's just not the mentality at all. You can get through those periods because you have got a genuine long-term commitment to the business.

How did you come to develop your own different style of investing when Baillie Gifford is mostly known for its focus on high growth and increasingly private companies?

The great thing is that even before SAINTS came over to us, we'd always had core anchor clients interested in long-term, steady compounding, resilient income and growth. Sometimes BG is characterised as a lot of people who've gone crazy for hyper growth. But the reality inside is that there are lots of different people interested in lots of different styles. It so happens that one of those has been incredibly successful in the last five to 10 years, which is the very high growth style. There were always lots of people who are interested in other ways of doing it.

My own interest in our steady compounding style came about because this was an area which needed more senior resource and there was the chance to build something with my own imprint on it. There was an opportunity for autonomy and to create our own philosophy and process from a blank sheet of paper, and that was what we did. We have really turned it over and built up the team for both SAINTS and the open-ended equivalent fund (Global Income Growth) from three to nine people.

What are the differences between the investment trust and the open-ended fund?

The Global Income Growth Strategy has about £3bn in total, of which SAINTS accounts for approximately £900m [this and all other performance figures quoted are current as of 30 June 2022]. As well as the Global Income Growth open-ended Fund we also have a responsible version which has some additional exclusions in it. At heart however it is the same 60-stock portfolio. It just has different flavours. The difference with the investment trust structure is that for income investors who want that absolute peace of mind that year-in year-out the dividend is almost certain not to drop, whatever could go wrong, you have that because of the revenue reserves, as was evidenced in 2020.

The other quirk, apart from the revenue reserve and the independent board and all that goes with it, is that we can borrow. The trust has £95m in long-term debt and we can put that into property, infrastructure and fixed income to generate a little bit of extra income above the cost of borrowing and pay that out. As a result the trust has a slightly higher yield than the open-ended fund, because of that ability to borrow long term. But by and large the three variants – as we call them – are at heart fundamentally the same thing, and it's fundamentally the same set of stocks. You can pick the one you want depending on the particular flavour that appeals to you.

The gearing impact on the dividend capacity will be improved now that you have succeeded in refinancing the old expensive debenture?

Yes. We had a dinner recently and one of the old board members came back and said: "Do you remember when we borrowed at 8%?" It didn't look as foolish as it does now. If you had said that one day interest rates would be at 0.5%, you would have been laughed out of the room. It turned into a millstone, but now with our debt cost around 3%, things would have to go pretty drastically wrong with the world for that to be an onerous borrowing rate. Somebody might even say "If you can't make 3%, probably it is you who needs to change, not the borrowings!"

Does the cheaper borrowing mean that you might also change the mix of assets in the portfolio somewhat, as you have done recently by including infrastructure and fixed income?

There is a school of thought that says if the trust was purely in equities, it would be easier for some people to market. It would not be so confusing. The board hears that, and at the end of the day they and we are agreed that because we're seeking real growth over time ahead of inflation in both income and capital, the bedrock or close to 100% of the NAV probably should always be equities. We could borrow more and gear up to put even more into equities, but our clients or shareholders are typically not looking for a very racy outcome, which is why we keep the gearing at modest levels, currently around 10% of net assets.

Looking to invest in property and infrastructure and fixed income where we can beat the cost of borrowing not only generates extra income, it has benefits as well in terms of the resilience of the income stream. We can buy into things which should not be correlated with equity income, because they are on different cycles. Now, will the exact mix of property bonds and most recently infrastructure always remain the same? No, probably not. That will evolve over time, depending on what opportunities we see out there.

How far have you had to modify what you're doing given that we appear to be moving into a new environment after years of suppressed interest rates and low inflation? Might that actually favour your investment style more?

Do I think that the future is going to look different from the past in terms of that regime change? Yes, I think so, in terms of the awareness of inflation and what normal real interest rates should be. A lot of people have had a sharp reminder of that. I don't think we're going back to some of the excesses of the recent past, where companies without revenues are apparently worth $200bn. I don't think that's coming back anytime soon.

On the other hand, do I think that we're going to completely the polar opposite of that, where the right thing to do is invest in deeply distressed value companies because interest rates will be 10% or something like that? No, I don't think that either because I think economies have structurally changed since the days of double-digit inflation like the 1970s, which means that inflation is not likely to be quite as persistent as it was in years gone by. That doesn't mean that inflation goes back to 1%. It just means it's not going to become embedded at 10% either.

So with the caveat that macroeconomic forecasts are invariably wrong, I think we're going back to somewhere between the two. What does that mean for SAINTS? For the past 10 years I've been involved in it, we've tried hard to focus on real world companies with good resources, secular growth opportunities that are not dependent on a fad or a fashion, with good people managing them, good balance sheets, things that look desperately dull when interest rates are zero and crypto is the new, new thing.

But in that environment, where inflation is a bit higher and rates are a bit higher, and people have come to their senses, these companies can carry on delivering steady growth ahead of inflation year after year. In a way that doesn't really require us to do very much with the portfolio because it's what we've always done. It has just been out of favour. I think now it's going to be more in favour than it has been in the recent past.

In terms of your shareholders wanting reliable income, won't your current dividend yield of 2.8% look less attractive when the bank is paying you 3.0% rather than when, as up until now, it was paying nothing?

The last time I checked my bank rate, they weren't anywhere close to 3%, so this is a hypothetical world! But if we're talking about a world of rates at 3%, then I assume that we're talking about a world where inflation isn't zero either, and so you know, people are going to be aware that if the bank rate is 3% and inflation is 3% as well, then you're not actually growing your income or capital in real terms.

I think what we would hope is that people would look at the SAINTS yield and say, yes it's slightly below, but on the other hand, if I'm getting good real growth in my income and capital every year, then that is more attractive than something which is going sideways, particularly over long periods of time. You're going to be much better off owning something that's growing in real terms.

When we're looking at the equity portfolio, we're typically hoping to see something like 10% nominal earnings per share growth over long periods of time, i.e., for a decade or more. We won't get all those right. Some of those will disappoint, but that's the sort of benchmark that we're using to get excited about things. If we can get close to that, then that doesn't need to compound for very long at all, before even with a 2.5% yield, it will very soon look more attractive relative to the 3%. It doesn't take very long to catch up.

How will companies react to this new environment in terms of share buybacks and dividend payout ratios?

There is always a wide range of approaches across companies. The important thing for us as stock-pickers is to try and find the companies where the management do have a commitment to continuing to grow the dividend. It doesn't necessarily have to be a progressive dividend. But over longer periods of time, we hope they've got a strong commitment to say if the earnings go up by 50% or 100% over the next 10 years, then the dividend should also do that.

We put a lot of work in bottom-up stock specifics to see if we can genuinely believe the dividend commitment. In some ways the tenet has had the biggest test it's ever had in the past couple of years. Not only have we had Covid, with dividends collapsing in that huge shock; but then later we've had inflation coming through, and in that short space of time it's unlike anything that SAINTS has seen before. The great thing is that having done all that bottom-up analysis – is this company actually resilient? What is its cash flow going to be like when the world economy blows up? Are the management really committed to growing the dividend rather than switching to buybacks – we've really only had it tested in the last few years.

And what we found in 2020 was that the dividend income went down by just 3%. Many of the companies actually raised their dividends in 2020. And then this year, the board just put up the second quarter dividend by a little over 10% and that's reflecting actual underlying growth in the dividends coming through in the portfolio, not because they're drawing on reserves. The beauty of active investing is that you can stock-pick your way around the companies that favour share buybacks and are genuinely committed to growing dividends with earnings, and that's exactly what we're trying to do for SAINTS.

And it helps that most of the revenue in the portfolio is internationally, not locally based?

Yes. I find it fascinating that many equity income investors prefer UK equity income to global equity income. When you go global, you have a global universe of about 5000 dividend-paying stocks of any reasonable size that you can invest in. That sheer number makes it possible to stock-pick your way around the companies that may have great growth, but there is no dividend commitment whatsoever. For sure there are attractive, dividend-paying companies in the UK and we own five or six of them. But once you get to number 10 you are definitely getting to the point where in my opinion you just cannot reliably build a properly diversified portfolio with resilient dividend growth.

About 80–85% of the income in the portfolio is coming from non-sterling sources and historically that has just been a great thing over the longer term. Sterling has continued its depreciation over many, many years and there are good reasons to think that is probably going to continue for many more years too. Sterling weakness is a tailwind for us.

If your stock-picking is good, and your horizon is long term, turnover in the portfolio should presumably be quite low?

Yes. Many of our investments date back more than a decade, and in any given year we will typically only make about half a dozen new ones. During 2021, for example, we disinvested from four companies and made investments into five new companies. The sales included SMTH, a Japanese financial company which had not grown as fast as we had hoped. On the new purchase side, we have for example taken holdings in Starbucks, the coffee chain, which we believe still has many years of growth ahead of it. And also Valmet, which is a world leader in making machinery for the pulp and paper industry, where we see years of good growth as its customers reduce their carbon emissions. We also made a small investment into infrastructure, through a limited number of names, such as Greencoat UK Wind. In 2022 so far we have added just two names, L'Oreal and Intuit, and sold another two, Hiscox and Kimberly Clark de Mexico.

How would you compare yourself to a quality growth investor like Terry Smith – aren't you just fishing in the same pool?

I suppose I should bash him and say, "Oh no, our approach is much better," but I think in a lot of ways we *are* both fishing in the same river if you like, looking for those high quality long duration businesses with good moats. One difference is that we do have the explicit requirement for a dividend payment, and I would argue that that enhances returns over long periods of time if you've got that discipline and that commitment. Dividend discipline, even if you're not an income investor, is telling you a lot about the characteristics of the business, its capital allocation thoughtfulness, and so forth. There is a reason the Dividend Aristocrats index in the US has been such a great performer over long periods of time. And so, I would say that philosophically, that's a difference and I personally feel it's an advantage that we have.

What is the most important thing you have learned from the extraordinarily volatile experience of the last few years?

Just how valuable diversification is, but it doesn't look like what the textbooks say. The textbooks say diversification is about things like geography and sector, but actually I think a much more important element is different types of growth case and business model. It's easy for investors to buy essentially the same idea over and over again, and inadvertently end up with little diversification. And one of the things that's really benefited SAINTS is the fact that if you look at our underlying holdings, you see very, very different growth cases underneath them.

If you look at UOB, which is a bank in Singapore, expanding into the rest of Asia, or if you look at USS, which is a Japanese second-hand car auctions business, or if you look at Intuit, which is small business software in the US, we've got very, very different types of investment case and I would say true diversification in the portfolio. I don't think I appreciated just how valuable that diversification was, or how it came about, until we'd seen the stress across economies and markets in the last five years. That has benefited us in a way and together with the dividends would be my guess as to why SAINTS as has held up pretty well this year.

One notable difference between you and your peer group is that the US allocation is much lower. Is that a deliberate policy?

I would flip the question around and say, "Isn't it remarkable that so many managers have an almost identical weight to the global benchmark in North America?" When you have 5,000 stocks to pick from and you are a proper bottom-up active stock-picker, what an extraordinary coincidence that the percentage of holdings in the United States is exactly the same as the benchmark! Yes, the US is a broad market. It is a deep market. There are some fantastic dividend-paying companies with great growth prospects. But they are also competing against some fantastic European-based and Asian-based companies. We don't underweight the US by design. It just comes from our bottom-up stock-picking approach. The interesting thing is that it has always worked out at around a third in America, a third in Europe and a third in the rest of the world. It has been stable over time.

Shares in SAINTS have traded at a premium for most of your time as manager, with the exception of the Covid sell-off and this year – what is the policy?

For the most part, there's been a modest low single-digit premium and the board has kept that under control with a reasonable amount of issuance, but not going crazy. It's not been something the board's had to manage dramatically. If you go back 25 years, SAINTS did trade at a huge discount for a period of time. It was very out of fashion and the board aggressively bought back shares during that period. The problem with that was that the gearing on the trust then went up much higher and that memory is not lost on us or certain board members.

One of the lessons from that is: if the trust ever found itself at a very large discount, the board will be thinking "what's the cause of the discount?" and "how do we address that?" rather than saying "lets just buy back a lot of shares and cross our fingers that everything will be all right." I'm talking purely hypotheticals now, but it's about trying to be thoughtful about premiums and discounts and not just having a mechanistic response. Sometimes buying back shares isn't the right answer.

The future will be more of the same, I am sure, but is there anything that could prompt you to change course?

The heart of what we do is about long-term compounding. It is not as if we have reinvented the wheel. The average company can do 1–2% ahead of inflation over long periods of time, but there are some companies that can do much better than that, and those are the ones that we're searching for. As long as we don't overpay for them, that should give our clients better returns, both capital growth and income.

Because we've got that focus on genuine long-term compounding, even when we've had something like Covid or high inflation, that hasn't really thrown us off course. As long as we've got our companies right, we've picked the ones that are resilient, are well managed, don't have too much debt, with good capital discipline, all those things, then we should not be thrown off course by macroeconomics.

If anything was going to throw us off course it should have been Covid. We never game planned anything like that. What, everything shuts down and everyone goes home! Yet the companies continued doing what they do and in some cases, they got even stronger because they had competitors who went out of business. It sounds glib to say I'm fully confident that my fund is not going to be thrown off course, but I do think by the nature of what we do and the tests that we've passed, we have conviction that – to the extent that any fund manager can before they come crashing down in a small bubble of pride – we have a portfolio that can continue to deliver that long-term compounding.

Q&A WITH EVY HAMBRO

JONATHAN DAVIS *talks to* EVY HAMBRO, *long-serving manager of the BlackRock World Mining Trust, about the outlook for the mining and precious metals sector and for the trust as it approaches its 30th anniversary.*

Capital at risk. The value of investments and the income from them can fall as well as rise and are not guaranteed. Investors may not get back the amount originally invested.

IF YOU VALUE experience in your investment trust manager (and I certainly do), then Evy Hambro is certainly one worth listening to, as he has one of the longest unbroken connections of any with the trust he manages. His appointment as lead manager may only date back to 2009, but his involvement with the trust goes back a lot further, all the way back in fact to his second year at university and the imminent launch of what was then known as the Mercury Global Mining Trust.

During his summer vacation, he was offered a summer internship at Mercury Asset Management, to work with Julian Baring, probably the best known gold and mining analyst of the day. Baring and a colleague, Dr Graham Birch, were busy planning the launch of the new global mining trust. This was in 1993, a year in which George Soros and Jimmy Goldsmith and other high profile investors were making a mint in the gold market. The price of gold jumped from $300 to $400 in a short space of time and ten of the firm's holdings of mining shares – many of which are effectively geared plays on the gold price – went up 10 times in the course of just a few weeks.

"From that moment on" says Hambro "I was completely addicted." He was asked to come back in the winter vacation for another stint, which started just 10 days ahead of the launch of the trust on 15 December 1993. "I remember being involved in the final bits of the roadshow that raised the money and then watched as Julian and Graham put the money to work." He must have made an impression because he was then asked to stay on straight away, rather than return to student life, an offer he sensibly declined as he wanted to finish his degree, a BSc in agricultural and food marketing. Mercury kept the job offer open for him, provided that he started work as soon as the university term had ended, which he did, over-riding his original plans to find a job in advertising. In that way started an association with the investment trust that has continued to this day.

The Mercury trust was rebranded a few years later, following Merrill Lynch's takeover of Mercury Asset Management, and then rebranded again when BlackRock absorbed Merrill Lynch in 2006. After a number of years doing research and acquiring hands-on knowledge and mining contacts in Australia and Canada, Hambro was named a co-manager of the trust in September 2000 and lead manager in 2009 when Graham Birch retired. Since 2015 he has been supported by Olivia Markham as co-manager.

BlackRock World Mining Trust – performance

GBP	YTD END SEP 2022	2021	2020	2019	2018	2017	2016	2015	2014	2013	2012
Share price (TR)	11.2%	17.5%	46.7%	19.4%	-10.7%	24.2%	100.6%	-37.0%	-30.4%	-17.5%	-4.1%
Undiluted NAV (TR)	2.5%	20.7%	31.0%	17.2%	-11.5%	23.8%	92.9%	-35.3%	-26.4%	-24.6%	-5.0%
MSCI ACWI Metals and Mining 30% Buffer 10/40 Index (reference index)	-1.2%	15.1%	20.6%	15.4%	-12.0%	21.4%	92.1%	-35.6%	-12.2%	-21.0%	-4.2%

Source: Datastream and BlackRock as at 30 September 2022-Performance in sterling terms, net of fees with income reinvested
Note: The figures shown relate to past performance. Past performance is not a reliable indicator of current or future results and should not be the sole factor of consideration when selecting a product or strategy. Please refer to page 281 for BlackRock's disclaimers on trust information.

The result of having started so early on in the trust's life means that Hambro has had plenty of time to understand – and learn to live with – the intensely cyclical nature of the mining sector. He has been involved in the trust much longer than any of the directors sitting around the board table. "It has been an amazing journey. We have had incredible volatility. We have had plenty of highs and lows, luckily more highs than lows. We have seen amazing cycles in the way the industry is perceived, from it being regarded as old economy and left behind in the 1980s, through the Asian crisis in 1998, then the dot.com boom, the global financial crisis and then the collapse of the sector in 2012 and 2015."

And today? It is rare to find an old hand in any sector who has such a strong and enthusiastic opinion about the outlook for his sector as Hambro does for mining this year. "We are probably in one of the most exciting cycles that I've seen. It is what keeps me going really. There is an incredible outlook for the space in so many different ways. It really is very exciting, the value that is available."

So what evidence does he have for being so optimistic, despite the clouds that have hung over the economic outlook in 2022, with soaring inflation and growing fears of recession in the face of rising interest rates and massive energy price hikes? The starting point is the fact that the mining industry, once notorious for its boom and bust behaviour, has never been as strong financially as it is today. Balance sheets are more conservatively financed today than those of any other stock market sector. Average net debt to EBITDA* ratios for the biggest mining companies were down from more than 1.5x in 2015 to just 0.4x at the end of Q1 2022.

At the same time valuations remain very attractive by historical standards. The average Enterprise Value to EBITDA ratio of the World Datastream Global Mining index has fallen from an average of around 10x to under 5x this year, the lowest it has been since 1991 (that is, before Hambro had even started working in the sector). The mining companies are throwing off huge amounts of cash and hiking their dividends, unlike in the past when periods of strong cash generation invariably led to huge spikes in new capital investment on mining projects which subsequently had to be written off in the next downturn.

"I think the biggest differences from today from where I started is that the industry is massively more consolidated. We've seen that in many other industrial sectors, but I would say mining is one of the most concentrated sectors out there. If you just look at the data of the mining universe by market capitalization, it's dominated by just six companies. The top 10 companies account for more than half the index.

"The other thing is that the companies that are biggest today were not the biggest companies back then. The biggest company when I started was an aluminium company called Alcoa. It was the dominant player, had the most successful track record and so on. It is now just a modest player in the space. Not only have we had the consolidation, but the constituents and where they rank have moved around enormously."

Capital discipline key

Even so, he concedes, investor attitudes towards the mining sector have been slow to change. "The mining industry is carrying less debt today than in the past. We have got mining companies today with net cash on their balance sheets. Yet the extraordinary shift in leverage and strategy has gone pretty much unnoticed by investors. You saw that most recently in June when the mining sector experienced a big downdraft in share prices." The sharp sell-off (down 15%) wiped out in one month almost all the impressive gains that BlackRock World Mining had made in the previous five months.

---

* Earnings before interest, taxes, depreciation, and amortization.

"IF A COMPANY IS PAYING OUT $1BN IN DIVIDENDS A YEAR, THEN, IF THE SHARE COUNT HALVES, THAT SAME $1BN NOW PRODUCES A DOUBLING OF THE DIVIDEND."

The shares had however bounced back off that low pretty well when we spoke in early autumn, prompting Hambro to say – to hope might be a more appropriate word – that share prices should not be as volatile today as they were because leverage in the businesses is so much lower. Picture a normal distribution curve of sector returns, he says, and you could say that the extreme left hand side of the curve, where the most leveraged companies sit, has been taken out of commission. "If you can exclude those outcomes the entire curve should shift to the right, creating a more positive outcome. That has been our thesis for five or six years now," says Hambro "and we are frustrated that it has taken investors so long to understand that."

But do leopards ever really change their spots? "Well this is a bit more subjective, but we have also seen a much tougher capital allocation process in the industry." In the early 2000s, companies would plan to buy or build a project, only to find that it fell short of the target hurdle rate because it was funded with too much debt and could not raise any more equity to finish it before the cycle turned. These days in contrast companies are much more careful to avoid putting strain on their balance sheets, financing more of their projects with cash, for example, or sharing the risk with a partner.

The lessons that have been learned from the most recent cycles are still fresh in the minds of executives and board members, Hambro believes, and very much in the mind of their investors as well. "I would say that more sensible allocation of capital is very much alive and well. It takes generational shifts to go back to the old ways and I am sure that at some point people will make mistakes again, but right now, and probably for the foreseeable future, we are in a period of strong returns for the industry. Those returns will be shared between investors and reinvestment back into the business, but they won't be shared with the balance sheet. The claim that shareholders have on the cash flows are far higher than they have been."

Several global factors have influenced the supply and demand of commodities in the time that Hambro has been involved in investing in mining. China's entry into the world economy is probably the biggest. He recalls Bob Wilson, the former head of Rio Tinto, saying in 2001 that the world was going into a period of rising demand while supply was still constrained by the under-investment of the past decade. That in turn, he predicted, would produce a violent reaction in commodity prices and see prices for commodities rise in real terms for the first time for a very long period. "He was absolutely right, and those words fed into our thinking in the investment team, encouraging us to be more aggressive in our portfolios."

That all came juddering to a halt in 2015 as most of the capital projects started in the next expansionary phase between 2000 and 2011 were completed and no more was being invested. The important thing to understand today, he argues, is that we are entering a very similar environment again to that which prevailed at the start of the century. The demand this time round is coming mainly from the huge investment in green infrastructure to which the world has now committed itself, while supply remains constrained once again by under-investment since the 2015 cycle peak and by ESG concerns that slow down or prevent completion of new capital projects.

"It does look as if we have got this gap between supply and demand, which will be positive for prices and therefore profits. It is obviously going to be volatile, there are going to be mini-cycles, whether from rising interest rates, recession fears, conflicts and so on. But I don't think we will see those extremes of outcome that I mentioned on the left hand side of the distribution curve, and that is largely because of the absence of debt. In our view that makes investing in mining companies higher quality on a risk-adjusted basis. They should be trading at better multiples, whereas right now they're trading at the lowest multiples we've seen in 30 years."

Over the long run, though, is it not the case, I say, that the very long-run real return on commodities is around zero – so what makes him so sure the outlook is quite so bright? Hambro says he is not quite brave enough to say "it's different this time" – the four most dangerous words in investment, according to the late Sir John Templeton. He does point out however that since inception the share price of the BlackRock World Mining Trust has produced a total return that is three times the return on the FTSE 100 index. "That doesn't sound much like zero to me, especially as we aren't even remotely close to our share price peak. No, we aren't even anything close to the top of the cycle."

What has underpinned the strong performance of the BlackRock World Mining Trust in recent years, he believes, is its decision in 2010 to refocus its strategy around maximising total return (capital and income combined), rather than simply prioritising capital gains. The strategy review highlighted the fact that more than half the trust's return – and more than 100% of the return when the share price had fallen – had come from dividends.

"We therefore decided we wanted to make sure we don't leave any income behind on the table. We felt that if we weren't maximising the income that was available from the sector then it would be very hard for us to deliver a superior total return. As a result our returns have risen and been less volatile than they would have been. We also have achieved more diversity of income. Even when companies were cutting their dividends to zero in 2015–16, we were still paying them. And that is why I think we have moved from trading at a considerable discount for 25 years to something much closer to par."

Since the change in strategy the trust has managed to diversify its income beyond portfolio company dividends in a number of ways: through the careful use of derivatives ("minimal but very profitable"), from mining royalties and – until recently – from the use of gearing to leverage the spread between corporate bond yields and the cost of borrowing. The board has also reaffirmed its commitment to pay out effectively all its income in any year as a dividend to the trust's shareholders.

The shift in emphasis towards income has "paid off in spades" Hambro says. "It has been exactly the right thing to do. We have done what it says on the tin. The shareholders like it because they don't want us to hold income back when they need it." One alternative would have been to adopt the kind of small but persistent regular dividend increases that have earned a number of equity income trusts the Association of Investment Companies' "dividend hero" status. But while the dividend stream from BlackRock World Mining Trust is inevitably more volatile as a result of its new policy, varying from year to year depending on the dividends it receives itself from mining companies, the rerating the trust has seen strongly suggests that the policy has indeed proved popular.

In terms of the dividend polices of the portfolio companies themselves, Hambro says he is not against share buybacks as an alternative to dividends. "What we are biased towards is generating the best possible return for us as an investor. If the company that we are invested in thinks that the shares are trading at very low multiples, and the best thing they can do with their surplus cash is reduce the share count, rather than building new capacity, then that's exactly the right thing that they should do." Some mining companies these days are generating free cash flow yields of more than 20% and trading at two or three times EBITDA.

EV/EBITDA – World DataStream General Mining Index

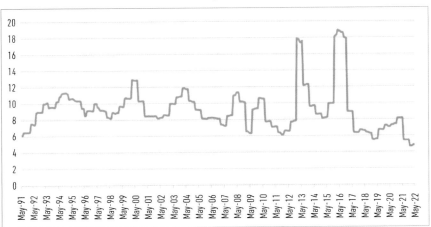

There is "no way" that they could get a better return from investing in a new mine with share prices on such low ratings, quite apart from all the risks (the development risks, the operational risks, the employee risk, the country risk) involved in completing new projects. Three of the bigger holdings in the portfolio have cut their share count dramatically in the last 20 years and "it wouldn't surprise me if by 2025 a number of companies have share counts that were half what they had in 2020." The point is that if a company is paying out $1bn in dividends a year, then, if the share count halves, that same $1bn now produces a doubling of the dividend.

Supply dynamics

On the supply side what about the risk of big new discoveries and new developments changing the supply/demand balance? Hambro says it is unlikely – success rates from exploration have fallen and development is increasingly capital-intensive and time-consuming because of regulation. Widespread recycling of metals such as copper and aluminium could in time increase supply, but that too will take time to come by – according to management consultants McKinsey – as the recycling industry is undercapitalised, fragmented and often family-owned.[10] (He likes the potential of the sector and is looking to invest in it.) On the demand side, rising interest rates and the risk of recession are clearly potential short-term negatives, but he is confident they will be more than offset by the inexorable rise in green infrastructure spending.

The question of how managements deploy their surplus cash flow at a time when their balance sheets are so strong only brings us back to the issue of companies' capital allocation. The biggest risk to the positive outlook for the sector Hambro sees is precisely that managements shift their strategy towards more undisciplined spending, as has often happened in the past.

"If the industry went back to aggressively focusing on building new supply at any cost, that could be very damaging to our story. We see no sign of that right now. I would put that down as a very low probability event, but it is something we spend an enormous amount of time looking at." Mining shares' volatility is evident in this shrewdly managed trust's recent performance: an annualised return of 5.5% over 10 years, but 15.5% over the last five (data as at 30th September 2022), Shareholders in BlackRock World Mining Trust, which was yielding more than 7% at the time of writing, will be hoping that this cycle is indeed different.

---

1 Source: Datastream, September 2022
2 Source: Bloomberg, September 2022
3 Source: MSCI, September 2022
4 Source: Alcoa, July 1994
5 Source: Reuters, 2015
6 Source: Rio Tinto, September 2022
7 Source: BlackRock and FTSE 100 returns, September 2022
8 Source: BlackRock, September 2022
9 Source: Reuters, December 2015
10 Source: McKinsey, 2020

DEMOCRACY RULES, OK?

JONATHAN DAVIS *looks at how one of the UK's biggest fund management firms is exploring new ways to give private investors access to privately owned assets.*

S CHRODERS IS ONE of the biggest players in the investment trust market, managing a total of eight equity and three property trusts, together with an interesting hybrid trust with a social impact objective. While the bulk of the equity trusts specialise in the Far East and UK public markets, it has more recently expanded into the private and mixed private/public equity space, in keeping with the group's strategic ambition of advancing what it calls the "democratisation" of private investments.

By this it means making it easier for individual investors to access privately owned assets that have historically, for a mixture of technical and regulatory reasons, been mainly only open to larger financial institutions. Investment trust shareholders have of course been able to invest in listed private equity funds for more than 30 years, so in this respect are the exception to the more general investment rule. It is, you could say, further evidence of the wider range of opportunities that are opening up buyers of investment trusts compared to conventional open-ended funds.

Schroders has been actively looking to develop its private investment capabilities for several years now. When he was appointed in 2016, current CEO Peter Harrison identified expanding its private asset capabilities as one of his strategic objectives. Through a combination of acquisitions and organic growth, its subsidiary Schroders Capital now has $88bn of funds under management across a range of private assets, including $15bn in private equity.[*]

According to Rainer Ender, head of private equity at Schroders, "retail clients are a growing share of the asset management market, but are significantly under-allocating to private assets. Investing in private equity has historically been out of reach for the vast majority of investors apart from big institutions, but this is changing quickly, and we are well placed to support investors taking advantage of this shift." Schroders expects private market assets globally to reach $21 trillion by 2025, rising from around $14trn in 2020.

---

[*]   As at June 2022

Toward a mixed model

In the investment trust space Schroders has demonstrated a particular interest in developing a mixed public/private model, meaning funds that invest in both listed and unlisted companies. In 2019 it took on the Woodford Patient Capital investment trust after the departure of Neil Woodford. The trust, now renamed Schroder UK Public Private (ticker: SUPP), was an opportunity to take an existing struggling portfolio of early stage private companies, weed out the worst performers and then build on that foundation with new investments.

Despite the best efforts of the Schroders management team, the problems of the former Woodford portfolio have so far proved to be deeper and more persistent than it hoped, and the rescue mission has taken longer to bring to fruition. On a positive note, the balance sheet has been repaired, nine new private equity investments made and the mandate expanded to include non-UK investments. In its latest interim report (to 30 June 2022), Schroders said that despite market weakness it remains optimistic about the long-term potential of the portfolio.

In 2020, as the UK stock market was recovering from the pandemic, Schroders launched a new investment trust, Schroder British Opportunities, designed to develop a new version of its mixed private/public model. In a difficult market, the trust raised £75m with the stated aim of building a portfolio of attractive, fast-growing British companies, split roughly 50–50 between listed and unlisted shares.

The idea was to draw on the experience, contacts and resources of Schroders Capital's private equity arm to source investments while simultaneously investing in a more conventional portfolio of mostly small cap listed equities, thereby offering a differentiated vehicle capable of having the best of both worlds. A specific objective was to target retail investors, whether clients of wealth management firms, or private investors investing directly through platforms.

According to Pav Sriharan, investment director in Schroders Capital's private equity team, "the logic behind the push into private assets for retail investors is coming from the demand side. We are seeing significant and increasing demand from individual investors, both wealth clients and retail." This is a consequence of a number of factors, he says. One is that governments recognise the increasing importance of privately sourced capital for economic growth and job creation and regulators have been looking at ways to make it easier for private investors to access private assets.

At the same time "there has been a lot of product innovation designed to produce funds that are more liquid than the traditional private equity model, including evergreen vehicles that allow you to get in and out if you want to but still give you access to superior private equity returns." These permanent life vehicles differ from the traditional fixed-term private equity model in which large institutions typically agree to tie up their money for 10 years, with potentially a further two years to complete the process of realising the value of the investments.

The move towards mixed private/public funds is another aspect of this general trend. The past decade has seen an increasing number of conventional equity investment trusts adding private investments to their portfolios. Baillie Gifford's Scottish Mortgage has been a prominent trailblazer in this regard, but far from the only one.

In that sense the Schroder British Opportunities trust is treading an increasingly common path. It is important to note however that private equity is a blanket term that covers a wide range of different approaches. The range goes from venture capital (high-risk, early stage companies that have yet to prove they have a viable future), through growth capital (companies that are either profitable or on their way to profit, but need capital to fulfil their full potential), all the way up to large and established mature companies that in some cases may go on to list on the public markets. Pursing a different tack are buyout firms that look to move in the other direction, buying listed companies and taking them back into private ownership.

Refining the model

All these approaches carry different risks and offer potentially different kinds of return. In the case of Schroder British Opportunities, its private equity holdings focus on private companies towards the smaller end of the growth capital spectrum, with a market capitalisation between £500m and £5bn. It aims to avoid venture capital (too risky) and pre-IPO companies (on valuation rounds). Most of its publicly listed equity holdings are similar types of company, typically fast growing businesses across a range of sectors. When the trust was launched in December 2020 the board said it would aim for a 50–50 division between public and private holdings, with an annualised target return of 10% per annum.

In September this year however the board announced that it was proposing to relax the 50–50, allowing it more flexibility in switching between the two types of holding. This in turn goes back to the more fundamental question of the rationale for offering a mixture of public and private equity. According to Sriharan, this has less to do with liquidity issues than with the idea of "investing without boundaries", meaning "having the opportunity to invest in the best companies, irrespective of whether they are public or private."

Allied to this is the belief that there is value in a fund management firm which has resources in both areas being able to compare valuations and insights and "compete for capital – a phrase we use a lot in Schroder British Opportunities." There will be times, Sriharan says, when public holdings look more attractive to privately listed ones, and vice versa. It makes sense, therefore, to be able to switch focus between the two, subject to liquidity, and focus really where there are attractive opportunities at compelling entry valuations. Equally important, adds Rory Bateman, co-manager of the trust, is that having a dual mandate makes it possible for the trust to continue to own good companies when they move from the private to the public markets, or vice versa, rather than having to sell them because of mandate restrictions.

Still early days

It is still relatively early days for Schroder British Opportunities, and it is fair to say that the turbulent market conditions of the past year have not made for an easy start to its ambition of building a larger and more sustainable vehicle. With equity markets sliding, the majority of private equity trusts have seen their discounts widen, smaller companies have been hammered and the recent style shift away from growth towards value has not helped the kind of growing companies that make up the majority of the trust's portfolio. It has been something of a perfect storm.

As a result, while the trust's net asset value has been resilient, growing by 15% towards the end of 2021 and the shares mostly trading at a modest discount, 2022 has proved a much tougher year. It has been a frustrating time for the managers, who point out that the operational performance of many of the companies the trust owns has been in line with their expectations. Presenting the half-year results in July, Sriharan noted that it had taken some time to bring the private equity holdings up to the original 50% target, as in its first year the trust had walked away from a number of investments that it felt were too richly priced. Its nine private holdings had grown their fair market value by an average of 56%, balance sheets were healthy and six of the nine were already profitable. The NAV has fallen back to around the original launch price, while the discount at which its shares trade has widened sharply, reaching 28% at the end of September 2022. Inevitably that has put on hold any plans the trust might have had of issuing new shares to increase the market capitalisation and bring it nearer to the £150m threshold that most wealth managers these days say they need to see before they will commit client money to it.

On the public equity side, Rory Bateman said, five of the trust's 29 holdings had been the subject of bids, underlining the potential value in the unloved UK market. The growth rate of the portfolio was around twice that of the UK Smaller Companies benchmark, balance sheets were generally strong with half the leverage of the benchmark and 80% of the overall portfolio was profitable. The portfolio was

"THE PAST DECADE HAS SEEN AN INCREASING NUMBER OF CONVENTIONAL EQUITY INVESTMENT TRUSTS ADDING PRIVATE INVESTMENTS TO THEIR PORTFOLIOS."

well diversified across sectors. Liquidity was also good and the trust had 10% in cash to help meet further commitments on the private equity side.

Yet, while the managers say that they are excited about the potential of their stocks, it seems that the market has yet to give the trust the benefit of the doubt. As the publicly held shares are marked to market daily, the implication of the current discount at which the shares trade is that the 50% of the portfolio which is in private holdings is being valued by the market at less than half their reported valuations, despite strong operational performance. The fact that private equity trusts which specialise in growth capital, such as Schiehallion and Chrysalis, though not directly comparable, have suffered an even more significant derating is only small consolation.

For the moment, therefore, the innovative mixed private/public model that Schroders is pursuing remains a work in progress. The firm has a reputation for being a patient long-term investor and, given the progress in NAV to date, will be looking forward to the return of more favourable market conditions that allow the trust to rerate and expand, building on Schroders' undoubted experience in this sector.

INVESTOR FORUM

We asked some of the most experienced investment trust investors we know to give their answers to some topical questions.

Who's who?

Alan Brierley is the director of investment company research at Investec and has covered the sector since the early 1990s.

Richard Curling is an investment director at Jupiter Fund Management with wide experience of the investment trust sector, including managing the Jupiter Fund of Investment Trusts.

Nick Greenwood has been the manager of Miton Global Opportunities (MGO), a specialist trust that invests only in other investment trusts, since its launch in 2004.

Peter Hewitt is a director and fund manager in global equities at BMO Global Asset Management and is responsible for managing the BMO Managed Portfolio Trust, listed in 2008.

Alastair Laing is CEO of Capital Gearing Asset Management, where he has co-managed the funds since 2011.

Which trusts have been the most creditable performers over the past year?

Alan Brierley: BH Macro stands out – a strong feature is an inverse correlation with equities, which has tended to be most pronounced during times of peak distress. The manager has demonstrated that higher returns are achievable when risk assets underperform. In a world of low fees, it showed its real value at high fees!

Richard Curling: Within the context of my fund's objective and the sector it operates in, I would highlight a number of creditable performances – Global Opportunities finally delivered after several years, Ruffer preserved capital with a positive return, Murray International delivered in global equities and Odyssean stands out in UK small cap.

Nick Greenwood: Dunedin Enterprise, the gift that just keeps giving. It is a private equity trust which has been going through an orderly wind down for some years. It keeps selling assets at useful premiums to book and handing back the proceeds to shareholders. Despite the numerous tenders, it is still one of our largest holdings. Two other private equity plays, Oakley and NB Private Equity, have done a sterling job with their portfolios only to be rewarded for their efforts by being left on wide discounts.

Peter Hewitt: By a mile BH Macro, a unique trust that does what no other does and shows you don't always have to have the lowest fees to do well. Next, I would mention Murray International. It's great to see a traditional investment trust using a value approach, run by an experienced manager, return to form. It has had some criticism over the years, but dividend has never missed a beat. All this and a Dundee United supporter as well! Lastly, I would pick Oakley Capital. The trust has reinvented itself, improved corporate governance and bought in shares.

Alastair Laing: Secure Income REIT – they recognised that conditions could not get much better so sold themselves at the top of the market. An example of a management team that were highly invested in their company so took decisions in the interests of shareholders rather than to maximise management fees.

And on the other hand, which have been the most disappointing trust performers?

Alan Brierley: Chrysalis: the bubble burst just as they were paying a truly egregious performance fee – not the sector's finest hour! Property discounts have widened sharply in anticipation of forthcoming challenges, while UK small caps have experienced a double whammy of falling NAVs and widening discounts. In the UK small cap sector, given its ability to short, the experience of BlackRock Throgmorton was particularly disappointing.

Richard Curling: The biggest disappointments come when a trust does not deliver during circumstances when it should – for example, Throgmorton is an excellent trust but it should have done better this year given its ability to short stocks. In more general terms it is probably the growth capital sector that has been most disappointing to investors.

Nick Greenwood: The little-known EPE Special Opps has had a dreadful time. Its principal investment Luceco makes and distributes LED lighting and other products typically sold by DIY chains. During the Covid pandemic DIY was popular, but that left the stores overstocked as recession fears grew. A further concern was that their manufacturing plant is based in China, leaving them vulnerable to lockdowns and exorbitant shipping costs. River & Mercantile suffered terribly as growthy small caps underperformed. Schroder Public Private (Woodford that was) moved from one setback to another, culminating in Rutherford Cancer Centres going bust and, finally, a mispricing error with Benevolent AI which cost shareholders a further slug of their capital.

Peter Hewitt: Top of the list for disappointing performers has to be Chrysalis. Among other issues, their board is a series of full-time non-executive directors with precious little private equity experience. Next would have to be Schroder Public Private. Schroder's been managing this for nearly three years and no sign of recovery. Finally, I would have to include Scottish Mortgage. Lots of recent shareholders now underwater. A recovery would be welcome.

Alastair Laing: Phoenix Spree – they did the opposite to Secure Income REIT. They identified a fantastic opportunity to sell significant chunks of their portfolio at the top of the market but completely failed to act on it because they were reluctant to shrink the company. Phoenix Spree shrunk anyway, by the share price collapsing rather than by the managers grabbing the obvious opportunity they had identified.

Have you seen any surprises or over-reactions in the market response?

Alan Brierley: A highly supportive macroeconomic backdrop and unprecedented actions by financial authorities have been catalysts for some exceptional returns since March 2009, but this party was never going to end well. And it hasn't.

Richard Curling: The market seems largely rational. Where there is uncertainty discounts have tended to move out to reflect this. For example, many listed private equity companies appear to trade on big discounts, but that may be because investors do not believe the NAVs (given the lag in valuations may not have reflected the derating seen in quoted markets). More recently, I think the infrastructure and renewable ICs have overreacted to the rise in bond yields following the recent fiscal statement. One genuine surprise this year has been the recovery of the aircraft-leasing companies.

Nick Greenwood: The width of discounts that private equity and property sectors have fallen to. There are challenges, but these seem to already be comfortably discounted in prices. In the case of private equity it is selling from shareholders, following new regulations, who now have to declare the high costs incurred by private equity trusts within their own literature. Investors in property face uncertainty over what trusts' cost of capital will be going forward.

Peter Hewitt: I feel Oakley has been harshly treated with its discount, however time will tell if the NAV is set to fall back.

Alastair Laing: The most amazing market to witness was the gilt market during the September meltdown. The long UK index-linked gilt – Feb 2073 – fell from £393 in November 2021 to £41 on September 28 2022. For a government bond to fall that far was truly extraordinary. It does not bode well for the UK economy or for mortgage holders.

"THE SECTOR NEEDS MORE CONSOLIDATION. THERE ARE TOO MANY ZOMBIE COMPANIES THAT ARE NOT DIFFERENTIATED, LACK CRITICAL MASS AND HAVE POOR LIQUIDITY."

ALAN BRIERLEY

Have discount movements been understandable or overdone? If so in which sectors?

Alan Brierley: Discounts had traded close to historically narrow levels for a number of years, but as we entered a more challenging environment there was no margin of safety. We are now seeing discounts at a similar level to the last crisis, and we would now look for companies to provide more support.

Richard Curling: Largely understandable – see my comment on private equity. Widening discounts may also reflect uncertainty about the future earnings of underlying companies as the world approaches recession. A wide discount presents a great opportunity, because when markets recover a narrowing of the discount can supercharge returns. The discount on some REITs looks quite large, although this may be the market discounting future falls in asset values.

Nick Greenwood: I think it is more of a size issue than a sector one. The traditional buyers of trusts are now lost in the big wealth management chains and are managing pots of money that are just too big to be able to include small- and medium-sized trusts, say sub-£500m. On the positive side, self-directed investors have been much more interested in the attractions of closed-ended funds. Up until the Russian invasion of Ukraine there seemed to be a nice equilibrium between wealth chain selling and individual investor buying. Once the shooting started the appetite for risk amongst individuals evaporated, leaving just wealth chain selling. Turnover in smaller trusts was low but heavily biased to the sell side. Market makers did not want inventory to build, so prices fell faster than NAVs and discounts widened. At one point the average discount in the 12 largest holdings in MIGO exceeded 29%.

Peter Hewitt: Most discounts are understandable, however that does not mean to say they have not been overdone. Many decent private equity trusts are on 40% discounts. If we experience only a mild recession, then there is a real opportunity. Perhaps something similar with property, although with both sectors if we do go into a recession then that is when leverage comes into play and can make a bad situation a lot worse.

Alastair Laing: Understandable. We are facing a very serious recession and bear market!

Is more consolidation on the way? Which trusts are most vulnerable?

Alan Brierley: The sector needs more consolidation. There are too many zombie companies that are not differentiated, lack critical mass and have poor liquidity. The listed private equity sector has seen corporate actions over the past decade, and with private equity dry powder of $2trn, the current discounts (and quality of portfolios) have obvious attractions. Hipgnosis Song has not sought to address its discount with the same vigour that it did when fundraising and, on a 45% discount, it looks vulnerable. Likewise Witan, where poor strategic management and the slow response to the dynamic evolution of global equity markets have been a dragging anchor on returns.

Richard Curling: I hope the process of consolidation continues. Almost any company with a market cap less than £100m is certainly vulnerable, as are companies with upcoming continuation votes.

Nick Greenwood: Long-only equity funds are under greatest threat. Unless they are using the closed-end structure by owning a conviction portfolio, taking out gearing or holding illiquid stocks, they are not offering anything that an open-ended can't. Open-ended funds don't have the problems of discount volatility or the hassle of having to trade in the market to get in or out.

Peter Hewitt: I'm not sure if there is a wave of consolidation on the way simply because it is so difficult to pull off. There will be a continual stream of manager changes, which is a good thing.

Alastair Laing: I suspect many trust boards will retreat to the bunker for a while, licking their wounds as a bear market unfolds. However, these conditions could cause a shake-out a few years from now.

What about liquidity – better, worse or about the same?

Alan Brierley: Worse. For many years there has been healthy two-way flow, but risk aversion and profit taking has resulted in a supply/demand imbalance. Market makers no longer have the capital to address this, while many companies have not shown the same appetite for buybacks as they did for issuance. With discounts now approaching levels last seen during the last crisis, we would now look for companies to provide more liquidity via share buybacks.

Richard Curling: Liquidity always seems to deteriorate in a down market – this year has been no exception.

Nick Greenwood: About the same, but unpredictability is the problem.

Peter Hewitt: Liquidity has definitely deteriorated, although that has to be expected given the level of the equity market and the very adverse sentiment. However, you can still get things transacted if you are patient.

Alastair Laing: Absolutely terrible!

What has been your biggest regret this year? What were you most pleased by?

Alan Brierley: I regret that no one was prepared to put an arm around Boris Johnson and tell him that, if he continued to behave like he did, he would do significant damage to the conservative party, government and country. Or if they did, he was too stubborn to listen.

Richard Curling: I have been really pleased with the way the new breed of alternative income investment companies, such as infrastructure and renewables, have expanded this year and widened the opportunity set for investors, giving access to normally illiquid assets.

Nick Greenwood: Our uranium call has worked at last. We were actively selling into some of the trusts that proved to be losers over the last 12 months, typically shifting half our holdings before prices broke. We should have been more aggressive.

Peter Hewitt: Having taken profits in a series of tech-orientated growth trusts back in January and what seem like great prices now, the big disappointment has been UK equity trust performance. A few who are mainly exposed to FTSE 100 companies have done relatively well. However, most of the rest have underperformed due to the horrible performance of the FTSE 250 Index and FTSE Small Cap Index. Discounts have also widened in these areas.

Alastair Laing: My biggest regret has been that property and core infrastructure trusts proved not to have the defensive properties that we had hoped they would. I was pleased that renewable energy infrastructure trusts enjoyed a huge tail wind from power prices, so performed well despite a general infrastructure rerating.

What has been your trust of the year?

Alan Brierley: Pantheon Infrastructure. It brings institutional-grade infrastructure private equity co-investments to the masses at low fees.

Richard Curling: I think the prize must go jointly to Secure Income REIT and LXI for pulling off a merger, which seems to have benefitted both companies' shareholders. In the equity sector Ashoka India has produced a positive return this year and nearly doubled investors' money on a three-year view. In Alternatives, Gresham House Energy Storage has had a great year – in fact almost any of the renewables companies could make a claim to be trust of the year, given the confluence of positive factors that have impacted that sector. Finally, a special mention for Fundsmith Emerging Equities for winding themselves up and returning cash to shareholders – so rare in the sector but it is always good to see this being done.

Nick Greenwood: Dunedin Enterprise…yet again.

Peter Hewitt: For performance alone BH Macro, the ultimate diversifier. I have owned it since its IPO in 2007 and it genuinely does what it says on the tin. When equity markets fall it makes significant absolute gains.

Alastair Laing: Is it a cop-out to say Secure Income REIT again? They definitely deserve the accolade of trust of the year.

What are your hopes and fears for the future?

Alan Brierley: Hopes: (a) Russia to withdraw from the Ukraine; (b) death to KIDS (useless Key Information Documents)! Fears – how long have I got? The Goldilocks environment is over and we are now transitioning to a new regime of higher inflation, interest rates and volatility, and lower growth. This will be extremely challenging for global financial markets, and to compound matters, we have geo-political headwinds that have not been experienced since the Second World War. Meanwhile in the UK, the recent mini-budget debacle appears to have shattered any confidence that was left in the government.

Richard Curling: My hope is that widening discounts which exaggerate the fall in markets will not put investors off investment trusts, and that boards will continue to focus on doing the right thing for investors – including consolidation of sub-scale trusts and buying back shares when appropriate to enhance NAV. I hope also that directors of trusts in the alternative space are careful not to issue equity at a discount.

Nick Greenwood: I hope that the trust sector fully exploits the attractions offered by closed-ended funds – they are superior vehicles providing managers inflows and outflows in increasingly tricky markets.

Peter Hewitt: Being generally a glass half full man, I hope for not too deep a recession with a peak in inflation and interest rates early in the New Year. That implies bond yields are moving sideways or even down. That would clear the way for an equity revival. It would be great if that were seen in the FTSE 250 and Small Cap Indices performing strongly. If these circumstances were to happen, watch out for a tech revival also. However, there is no guarantee, and we could still be in the mire this time next year.

Alastair Laing: We hope that all investment trusts with liquid underlying portfolios will adopt a zero-discount model, of the sort pioneered by Personal Assets Trust. Not only does this protect shareholder interests, it also allows well performing trusts to grow in scale and to meet the needs of a wider range of potential investors.

FUND PROFILE: BH MACRO

STUART WATSON *explores BH Macro (tickers: BHMG and BHMU), the largest trust in the AIC Hedge Fund sector with net assets of £1.3bn.*

B H MACRO INVESTS solely in the Brevan Howard Master Fund, which in turn invests in a number of other Brevan Howard funds as well as having its own core portfolio. The Master Fund focuses on fixed income and currency investment and seeks to exploit pricing anomalies and increased market volatility. Although the Master Fund uses an unspecified amount of leverage, it says that most trades are structured to minimise downside risk. After a period of impressive returns following its 2007 IPO, BH Macro's NAV was largely flat between 2012 and 2017. It shrunk dramatically in size after two large tender offers and Brevan Howard's fees were reduced from 2.5% to 1.0%. Returns have significantly improved since 2018 onwards leading to Brevan Howard demanding a fee increase to 2.0%. This was approved, but the trust's largest shareholder soon after succeeded in pushing for a merger of BH Macro with its sister fund, BH Global. Many of BH Macro's best months occur when equity markets fall heavily and its recent increased popularity has seen its premium to NAV climb to over 20%.

The history of BH Macro

Hedge funds have generally not been a happy hunting ground for trust investors, or indeed investors of any persuasion. Roll back to 2009 and the AIC Hedge Fund sector consisted of around 30 trusts as various hedge fund managers were attracted to the pool of permanent capital that investment trusts can provide.

Of those 30 trusts, only BH Macro, Third Point Investors, and Boussard & Gavaudan now remain. Once sizeable trusts such as Dexion Absolute, Thames River Hedge, BlueCrest AllBlue (now Highbridge Tactical Credit), Goldman Sachs Dynamic Opportunities, and Bramdean Alternatives have either been wound down, sold off, or are in run-off mode. Hedge fund indices tell an equally sorry tale of lacklustre returns.

BH Macro has had its difficulties but appears to have stood the test of time and has flourished in the extreme volatility of the last few years. The trust was launched in March 2007 as a feeder fund for the Brevan Howard Master Fund, which had begun trading a few years earlier in April 2003. In 2008, a sister trust called BH Global was launched, which invested in a different Brevan Howard fund.

BH Macro dealt with the global financial crisis with relative ease, and five years after its IPO its shares had doubled with minimal drawdowns along the way. But as markets calmed during the 2010s, the volatility that Brevan Howard sought to exploit dried up.

After around six years of flat returns, buybacks and two large tender offers saw the trust shrink in size significantly. The trust's directors negotiated a reduction in the annual management fee from 2.5% (2.0% at the trust level and 0.5% at the Master Fund level) to just 1.0% and Brevan Howard's notice period was slashed from two years to three months.

BH Macro's performance was a lot better in 2018. Although global markets declined after the Fed continued to raise rates, the trust returned a reassuring 12.4%. The Fed eased rates in 2019 and global markets had a bumper year with BH Macro delivering a more modest 8%. Then the pandemic struck. The extreme volatility in early 2020 saw BH Macro return 5.5% in February and 18.3% in March. It added to those gains when stocks bounced back, ending the year up 28%.

In January 2021, Brevan Howard decided to demand a large fee increase for both BH Macro and BH Global and threatened to resign if the changes were not put before shareholders. Brevan Howard wanted fees to increase to 2.0% (including the 0.5% charged within the Master Fund) and its notice period to be lengthened from three months to a year. Just prior to Brevan Howard's deadline for an EGM to be called, BH Macro's Chairman, Colin Maltby, retired with immediate effect and Richard Horlick took his place. The day after, the EGM was called.

At the end of March 2021, 82.5% of BH Macro shareholders approved the fee increase although support was more muted at BH Global where just 65.6% voted in favour. A couple of weeks later, Investec Wealth & Investment Limited, the largest shareholder in BH Macro and a significant holder of BH Global, suggested a merger to create a larger and more liquid vehicle, given that both trusts had fairly similar underlying portfolios. A few months later, the merger was all done and dusted.

BH Macro has mostly traded at a premium since 2020 and, despite plenty of new share issuance over the past 12 months, its premium had widened to around 20% by the end of September 2022. From its IPO up until the end of July 2022, its shares returned an annualised 9.4%.

When BH Macro was first listed it had three classes of shares – euro, sterling, and dollar. Each month, shareholders have the chance to convert between the share classes. The sterling shares were initially in the minority but soon proved to be the most popular. Indeed, the euro shares were retired as a separate class in 2017.

This table shows how the share count of BH Macro declined significantly from 2013 to 2017 and how it has since rebounded, thanks to the merger with BH Global in 2021 and subsequent share issuance:

AS OF 31 DEC	EURO (M SHARES)	STERLING (M SHARES)	DOLLAR (M SHARES)
2007	28.7	14.0	53.9
2008	21.5	19.1	55.0
2009	17.3	26.4	40.7
2010	14.8	34.3	31.8
2011	9.5	39.6	30.4
2012	7.4	41.7	29.6
2013	6.8	43.6	25.0
2014	5.1	37.7	18.3
2015	4.2	33.4	17.2
2016	1.5	22.4	10.0
2017	-	14.0	2.8
2018	-	14.1	2.7
2019	-	14.3	2.4
2020	-	15.0	2.2
2021	-	25.9	2.7
2022 (2 Sep)	-	29.8	2.9

Source: compiled from BH Macro announcements

A quick overview of Brevan Howard

Brevan Howard was set up in 2002 by Alan Howard, Jean-Philippe Blochet, Chris Rokos, James Vernon, and Trifon Natsis, all traders at Credit Suisse. I believe most of its founders have now moved on or stepped back. Howard was CEO up until late 2019 but then passed the reins to Aron Landy, who has been with the firm since 2003.

Brevan Howard has been on a recruitment drive in the last few years and says it has "over 500 team members and over 100 Portfolio Managers, Traders, and Sub-PMs with offices in London, New York, Geneva, Jersey, Hong Kong, Edinburgh, Singapore, Austin, Chicago, and the Cayman Islands."

With around $40bn in assets under management back in 2013, Brevan Howard was then reported to be Europe's largest hedge fund. But weak returns over the next few years saw its assets decline to $7bn by 2016. By the end of 2021, it had recovered to $16bn, a similar level to Third Point and Pershing Square but still a long way behind hedge fund giants like Bridgewater Associates, Renaissance Technologies, TCI, and Citadel.

The Master Fund, BH Macro's sole investment, is Brevan Howard's largest fund and had net assets of $9.8bn as of June 2022. BH Macro's stake in the Master Fund was worth $1.5bn suggesting it represents around 15% of the Master Fund's net assets.

Recent press reports have mentioned that Brevan Howard's total assets under management have climbed to $23bn, with credit trading and digital assets being notable new areas of activity. Sky News reported in July that Brevan Howard is searching for a US-based chairman, sparking speculation that it could soon be seeking its own stock-market listing.

Key stats for BH Macro

- Launched: Mar 2007
- Domicile: Guernsey
- Management firm: Brevan Howard Capital Management
- Tickers: BHMG (sterling) and BHMU (US dollar)
- AIC Sector: Hedge Funds
- NAV return last 10 years: 105% (2nd out of 4)
- Recent price: 5,120p
- Indicated spread: 5,110p–5,130p (0.4%)
- Market cap: £1.5bn
- NAV per share: 4,157p (16 Sep 2022)
- NAV update frequency: Weekly and month-end
- Premium to NAV: 23%
- Charges: 2.4% OCF (3.1% including performance fee) and 3.8% KID
- Management fee: 2.0% of NAV (including 0.5% within the Master Fund)
- Performance fee: 20% of NAV appreciation each year, subject to exceeding previous high watermark
- Discount control: Combination of share buybacks, tender offers, and capital returns when trading at a discount. Shares issued when at a premium
- Continuation vote: Yes, if the quarter-end NAV falls below $300m
- Net cash: 0.3% (30 Jun 2022)
- Year-end: 31 Dec
- Results released: Mar (finals) and Sep (interims)
- Dividends: No dividends paid to date

Price and related data as of 23 Sep 2022 unless otherwise indicated

Investment style and policies

BH Macro acts as one of three feeder funds for the Brevan Howard Master Fund. The investment objective of the Master Fund is "the generation of consistent long-term appreciation through active leveraged trading and investment on a global basis," which isn't terribly enlightening. In practice, it invests predominantly in fixed-income securities and currencies.

A recent Kepler Trust Intelligence research report said: "Brevan Howard's traders try to exploit pricing anomalies and to provide investors with asymmetric pay-off profiles over defined periods in the future. These trades are typically leveraged (using margin) and might typically generate proportionately high returns if the trade works out, but should it not, then the maximum loss might be the cost of putting the trade on." The overall aim is to achieve a low correlation with both equities and bonds.

Kepler adds that "there are a variety of different styles of traders. Some concentrate on relative value (RV) trades – these are those that typically offer the prospect of small wins but have a relatively low probability of losses. Their trading activities typically generate more consistent returns and could essentially be seen as paying for the long gamma traders to make their big potential payoff trades. The long gamma traders are betting on events which have big payoffs if they come to pass but have relatively low losses if they don't."

You can see these occasional big payoffs in BH Macro's monthly returns, with one or two months often accounting for the majority of returns in any given year. For example, there were gains of 10.2% and 6.9% in Jan and Feb 2008, 5.2% in Jan 2009, 6.2% in Aug 2011, 8.2% in May 2018, 5.5% and 18.3% in Feb and Mar 2020, and 5.4% in Mar 2022.

Leverage is needed to drive these sorts of returns, but there's little information on exactly how much leverage is used. The Master Fund accounts listed gross assets of $12.3bn at the end of 2021 and net assets of $8.0bn but with its full list of investments including futures, options, swaps, forward rate agreements, and swaptions. There are substantial amounts invested in other Brevan Howard funds, which have their own leverage, so it's impossible to know what the overall leverage position is. Rather alarmingly, the Master Fund is said to have no limit on the amount of leverage it employs.

But we can examine BH Macro's track record to see how it has dealt with difficult markets in the past. There have been sterling NAV losses of 1% or more in 21 months out of 185 since the IPO (roughly one month in nine). Only seven months have seen losses of greater than 2%, with the largest single monthly loss being 3.4%.

These figures are reassuring, although a leap of faith is still needed to assume both that risk management processes will continue to be operated in the same way and that they will be sufficient to deal with any future events.

Brevan Howard's website distils its approach into three bullet points:

- Macro Thinking – global macro research serves as the backbone of the investment process.
- Trade Structuring – seeking to structure convex trades, where the upside potential significantly outweighs the downside.
- Risk Management – risk management processes that focus on maximising potential returns while protecting capital invested.

Kepler's report provides some extra detail on risk management. It says Brevan Howard has "a highly resourced risk team whose job it is to police the traders and ensure that losses are minimised, both at a trader level and also at a fund level. Traders run their own books within defined mandates and risk tolerances, and there is no house view." It adds that: "If the risk team observes a concentration of risk in the overall portfolio toward any particular exposure, they have the authority to neutralise some of the risks or bring it down to within acceptable limits."

BH Macro says that the Master Fund has the flexibility to invest in a wide range of instruments including but not limited to:

- debt securities and obligations (which may be below investment grade);
- bank loans;
- listed and unlisted equities;
- other collective investment schemes;
- currencies;
- commodities;
- futures, options, warrants, swaps and other derivative instruments;
- digital assets.

It adds that the underlying philosophy is to construct strategies, often contingent in nature, with superior risk/return profiles, whose outcome will often be crystallised by an expected event occurring within a pre-determined period of time. It focuses primarily on economic change and monetary policy, and market inefficiencies.

BH Macro has a borrowing limit of 20% of NAV but tends not to use it, given the underlying leverage in the Master Fund. Although the trust can issue shares and buy them back to manage its rating, there are some restrictions around this given that such transactions need to result in a smaller or larger position in the Master Fund.

The Master Fund has its own set of investment restrictions such as investing not more than 20% of gross assets in the securities of any one issuer, the creditworthiness or solvency of any one counterparty other than the Prime Brokers, or a single collective investment scheme. It also does not invest in property, limits physical commodities to 10% of gross assets, and will not take or seek to take legal or management control of any issuer in which it invests.

Portfolio

BH Macro's own balance sheet largely consists of its holding in the Master Fund plus a little working capital to pay its ongoing costs, which are mostly fees to Brevan Howard. However, both its monthly shareholder reports[*] and its accounts break down the Master Fund portfolio a little.

Currently, the Master Fund has around two-thirds of its assets invested in five other Brevan Howard funds with the balance in its own direct holdings, also known as the Core Portfolio Manager Team. This table shows the allocation to each fund and what they have contributed to overall returns in 2021 and so far in 2022:

FUND	ALLOCATION AS OF AUG 2022 (DEC 2021)	ATTRIBUTION TO AUG 2022 (2021)	STYLE
Alpha Strategies Master Fund	31.5% (26.7%)	+9.1% (+2.0%)	Relative value (RV) and directional strategies in developed and emerging fixed income and FX markets
AS Macro Master Fund	9.7% (5.6%)	+1.5% (−0.2%)	Macro/RV strategies in developed market interest rate markets
FG Macro Master Fund	9.8% (7.2%)	+1.9% (−0.9%)	Multi-asset class macro trading
MB Macro Master Fund	9.8% (7.4%)	+1.8% (+0.2%)	Macro/RV strategies in Asia-focused interest rate and FX markets
Global Volatility Master Fund	6.7% (3.9%)	+1.1% (−0.1%)	Long volatility in multiple asset classes
Core Portfolio Manager Team	32.5% (49.2%)	+8.2% (+3.5%)	Multi-asset class macro, systematic, and RV trading

---

[*]   www.bhmacro.com/reporting/monthly-shareholder-report

Alpha Strategies and the Core Portfolio have driven the bulk of recent returns, which is not surprising given their larger position size. My impression is that the other funds are more volatile – they have all made returns of around 20% so far in 2022 but three of them made losses in 2021, with the FG Macro Master Fund losing nearly 10%.

This listing from the prospectus that accompanied the 2021 merger of BH Macro and BH Global shows an alternative way of analysing the portfolio. Although the information is now quite dated, it seems that the current percentages aren't significantly different:

- Rates: developed interest rates market – 36.4%
- Macro: multi-asset global markets, mainly directional – 42.9%
- EMG: global emerging markets – 4.0%
- FX: forwards and options – 3.9%
- Equities: global equity markets including indices and other derivatives – 0.4%
- Credit: corporate and asset-backed indices, bonds, and credit default swaps – 2.5%
- Commodities: futures and options – 1.7%
- Systematic: rules-based futures trading – 7.5%
- Digital assets: cryptocurrencies – 0.7%

BH Macro has also broken down its returns into asset class types in the last few years. These don't match up precisely with the strategy groups listed above but they illustrate the importance of interest rate movements to overall returns. Commodities and credit have made smaller positive returns while currencies and equities have been largely neutral.

ASSET CLASS	2019	2020	2021	2022 (TO 31 AUG)
Rates	11.4	19.7	2.5	17.2
FX	−1.4	1.4	−1.2	2.6
Commodities	0.1	1.6	0.2	0.4
Credit	−0.0	2.2	0.3	−0.2
Equity	−0.5	2.9	0.2	−1.3
Digital assets	-	-	0.6	0.0
Discount management	0.0	0.1	0.0	−0.8
Total	**9.5**	**27.8**	**2.7**	**18.0**

"WHILE IT'S A POPULAR TRUST TODAY, THAT'S A RELATIVELY RECENT PHENOMENON. BH MACRO FLITTED BETWEEN A PREMIUM AND DISCOUNT IN ITS EARLY YEARS, DESPITE ITS GREAT PERFORMANCE AT THAT TIME."

STUART WATSON

The annual and interim accounts only contain limited commentary on the Master Fund's performance. The 2021 accounts noted that: "Relative value strategies and trading in inflation, volatility, and some minor markets performed well, as did the capital deployed early in the year to digital assets, however, given that the overall environment was more difficult for traditional macro trading, it was a year of mixed results. The Master Fund ended 2021 with modest gains."

The 2022 interims said the Master Fund profited broadly from the Fed's "expeditious" pace of rate hikes, mortgage rate rises, the fall in equities, and the appreciation of the US dollar. Given the volatility in markets seen so far in 2022, you would have thought conditions have been ideal for BH Macro, and the 18.0% return up to August 2022 seems to bear that out.

Performance

BH Macro's performance is shown in detail in its monthly factsheet[*] across a series of three charts. These are a little small to reproduce here, so I'll describe what they show.

The first shows BH Macro's returns against two major hedge fund indices and global equity markets with two periods of strong performance from 2007 to 2011 and from 2018 onwards, with the lacklustre returns in between. The comparison against global equity markets is flattered by the fortunate starting point of just before the financial crisis. I suspect a chart that started in 2003, when the Master Fund was launched, would show the two are much more evenly matched.

The chart in the July 2022 factsheet shows BH Macro returning 300% since its IPO and the two hedge fund indices returning about 65% and 85%. So BH Macro would seem to be well ahead of its competition. These indices only include funds with assets over $500m that are open to new investment, so it's difficult to know how representative they are of all hedge fund returns.

Compared to (what's left of) the AIC hedge fund sector, on a NAV total return basis, BH Macro leads Third Point and Boussard & Gavaudan over one, three, and five years, and also since 2007. However, it trails Third Point over the last 10 years. Third Point has more direct equity exposure and its pattern of returns over time would seem to reflect that. Bill Ackman's Pershing Square, which is listed in the AIC's North America sector rather than hedge funds, also has a better long-term NAV record than BH Macro, although its London listing only dates back to 2014 and it has seen its discount widen substantially in recent years. Like Third Point, its style is much more direct equity investment.

---

[*] www.bhmacro.com/reporting/monthly-factsheet

BH Macro's second monthly factsheet chart is perhaps the most interesting and shows how BH Macro has performed in the 20 worst months for the S&P 500 since 2007. These range from −17% in October 2008 to −5% in July 2010. BH Macro produced negative returns in only three out of these 20 months. In five of them, it generated positive returns of 5% or more. If you are looking for a trust that appears to be negatively correlated to equity returns, BH Macro would seem to fit the bill, perhaps even more so than the three more traditional defensive trusts (Personal Assets, Capital Gearing, and Ruffer).

The third factsheet chart shows the monthly returns for BH Macro's sterling and dollar shares since its IPO. The two share classes have performed similarly over time, although the AIC's charts suggest the dollar shares are slightly ahead at +435% as of 23 September 2022 versus +410% for the sterling shares.

The sterling shares have only had two negative calendar years, being −0.9% in 2015 and −4.4% in 2017. Their best years have been when the market is in turmoil, such as 2007 through to 2009, 2011, 2018, 2020, and 2022. There have been plenty of negative months, of course, although the worst and best individual months are often in fairly close proximity, as markets that are experiencing large drawdowns are usually the most volatile.

Rating

While it's a popular trust today, that's a relatively recent phenomenon. BH Macro flitted between a premium and discount in its early years, despite its great performance at that time, and there was a persistent discount from 2013 to 2018. Since then, the trust has mostly enjoyed a premium rating, although it has slipped to a discount a few times, most notably for a few months after the fee increase was demanded and before the BH Global merger was completed.

The discount has rarely been greater than 5% for any extended period as BH Macro has been pretty good at managing the demand for its shares via a combination of capital returns, share buybacks, and tender offers. What's more, it says that if a class of shares trades at an average discount at or in excess of 8% of its monthly NAV in any calendar year, it will hold a class closure vote.

The average premium was just over 2% in 2021 but it's been around 10% so far in 2022 and climbed to around 20% near the end of September 2022. BH Macro has been issuing plenty of new shares over the past year, but its issuance is constrained by what the Master Fund can absorb.

Brevan Howard says it will issue more units in the Master Fund for up to 10% of any share count increase and use its "best endeavours" above that level. The number of sterling shares has increased by 20% over the past 12 months but that still hasn't been enough to keep the premium from getting ever wider. Kepler notes that the Master Fund is currently soft closed to new money, so buying shares in BH Macro is effectively the only route in for most investors. However, there's clearly a risk that BH Macro's rating could decline from its current level if the Master Fund has another period of lower returns.

Directors, managers, and major shareholders

Whenever a trust is so closely associated with its management firm, there are always questions about how independent its board is. Clearly, last year's fee increase put BH Macro's directors in a very difficult situation, but the ensuing merger with BH Global and the trust's performance since then seems to have vindicated the decisions they made. Of course, BH Macro's board also negotiated a reduction in fees several years ago, and many of its current members have extensive experience on the boards of other trusts.

Richard Horlick has served since 2019 and has been Chairman since early 2021. The other directors were appointed in 2014, 2016, 2020, and 2021 (the last of these was a transfer from BH Global). Their collective shareholding is 28,600 sterling shares worth around £1.5m. The directors don't hold any dollar shares.

I couldn't find any useful information in terms of who has overall responsibility for the Master Fund on a day-to-day basis. Similarly, there are no BH Macro presentations on YouTube or on BH Macro's own website, and I couldn't see any podcast interviews either. That's pretty unusual but, given the trust's high premium rating, there's little need for marketing right now.

The largest holders of the sterling shares are Ferlim Nominees (17.5%), Rathbone Nominees (10.1%), Smith & Williamson Nominees (8.0%), Cheviot Capital Nominees (6.7%), Pershing Nominees Limited (4.9%), and Lion Nominees (4.1%). Ferlim appears to be a holding company for Investec, the firm which pushed for the merger of BH Macro and BH Global.

Dividends

The Master Fund pays no dividends, so BH Macro hasn't paid any to date either. The directors don't entirely rule the possibility out, saying they would consider it "if appropriate". Although BH Macro would be liable to pay a dividend under the usual investment trust rules (having to pay out 85% of its net income), its high charges mean this is highly unlikely to occur in practice.

Charges

I've touched on fees already, but clearly the standard hedge fund arrangement of 2 and 20 (i.e., a 2% annual fee plus a 20% performance fee) is astronomically high compared to most other trusts. Both Third Point and Boussard & Gavaudan have the same 20% performance element although their annual fees are a little lower at 1.25% and 1.5% respectively. Pershing Square is 1.5% annual and 16% performance.

Gearing

There is no gearing at the trust level to worry about, and there are no unused borrowing facilities mentioned in the annual report. As mentioned earlier, there is an unspecified amount of leverage within the Master Fund.

Closing thoughts

BH Macro offers something radically different to every other trust on the London market. The three wealth-preserving trusts come closest but don't appear to have the same negative correlation to global equities and fixed income.

The high charges will no doubt put off many investors, but I think you could make a case for them being worth paying in this instance. Of course, you would need to put a fairly substantial part of your portfolio into this trust in order for it to smooth your overall returns.

The unknown amount of leverage within the Master Fund is worth highlighting again and the fact its underlying positions are essentially unknowable. Even after 15 years of no obvious disasters, it might only take a few missteps to cause a major price decline. Likewise, the high premium rating that exists right now could also dampen investor returns over the long term.

This is a shortened and updated version of an article that appeared on the Money Makers *website in early September 2022.*

MONEY MAKERS

You can read Stuart Watson's fund profiles and access much more exclusive investment trust analysis and information by becoming a member of the *Money Makers circle*. Just go to money-makers.co/membership-join for full details of how to sign up.

The aim of the fund profiles is to cover a wide range of trusts that invest both in equities and alternative assets, providing a long-term perspective on what drives their performance and setting out key points potential investors need to know. Over 70 profiles have been published to date and new ones appear on a weekly basis. Some of the most recent trusts that have been featured are:

- 3i Group
- AVI Global Trust
- Caledonia Investments
- CT Global Managed Portfolio
- HarbourVest Global Private Equity
- Literacy Capital
- Murray International
- Pershing Square Holdings
- Round Hill Music Royalty
- Scottish American

- AEW UK REIT
- BBGI Global Infrastructure
- Cordiant Digital Infrastructure
- Diverse Income Trust
- Impax Environmental Markets
- Mobius Investment Trust
- North Atlantic Smaller Companies
- PRS REIT
- Ruffer Investment Company
- Value And Indexed Property

Stuart has been investing in trusts for over 25 years and his top 10 personal holdings currently include:

- Bellevue Healthcare
- Gresham House Energy Storage
- JPMorgan Global Growth & Income
- Lindsell Train Global Equity
- Vanguard FTSE All-World ETF

- Fundsmith Equity
- HgCapital Trust
- Keystone Positive Change
- RIT Capital Partners
- Worldwide Healthcare Trust

ANALYSING INVESTMENT TRUSTS

by JONATHAN DAVIS

TRUST BASICS

For first-time investors in trusts, here is an overview of investment trusts – what they are and how they invest – from editor JONATHAN DAVIS.

What is an investment trust?

INVESTMENT TRUSTS, ALSO known as investment companies, are a type of collective investment fund. All types of fund pool the money of a large number of different investors and delegate the investment of their pooled assets, typically to a professional fund manager. The idea is that this enables shareholders in the trust to spread their risks and benefit from the professional skills and economies of scale available to an investment management firm. Funds are able to buy and sell investments without paying tax on realised gains.

Collective funds have been a simple and popular way for individual investors to invest their savings for many years, and investment trusts have shared in that success. Today more than £250bn of savers' assets are invested in investment trusts. The first investment trust was launched as long ago as 1868, so they have a long history. Sales of open-ended funds (unit trusts, OEICs and UCITs funds) have grown faster, but investment trust performance has generally been superior.

How do they differ from unit trusts and open-ended funds?

There are several differences. The most important ones are that shares in investment companies are traded on a stock exchange and are overseen by an independent board of directors, like any other listed company. Shareholders have the right to vote at annual general meetings (AGMs) on a range of things, including the election of directors, changes in investment policy and share issuance. Trusts can also, unlike most open-ended funds, borrow money in order to enhance returns. Whereas the number of units in a unit trust rises and falls from day to day in response to supply and demand, an investment trust is able to deploy permanent capital.

What are discounts?

Because shares in investment trusts are traded on a stock exchange, the share price will fluctuate from day to day in response to supply and demand. Sometimes the shares will change hands for less than the net asset value (NAV) per share of the company. At other times they will change hands for more than the NAV per share. The difference between the share price and the NAV per share is calculated as a percentage of the NAV and is called a discount if the share price is below the equivalent NAV and a premium if it is above the NAV.

What is gearing?

In investment, gearing refers to the ability of an investor to borrow money in an attempt to enhance the returns that flow from his or her investment decisions. If investments rise more rapidly than the cost of the borrowing, this has the effect of producing higher returns. The reverse is also true, meaning that gains and losses are magnified. Investment trusts typically borrow around 5–10% of their assets, although this figure varies widely from one trust to another.

What are the main advantages of investing in an investment trust?

Because the capital is largely fixed, the managers of an investment trust can buy and sell the trust's investments whenever they need, rather than having to buy and sell simply because money is flowing in or out of the fund, as unit trust managers are required to do. The ability to gear, or use borrowed money, can also potentially produce better returns. The fact that the board of an investment trust is directly accountable to the shareholders is important. So too is the ability of boards to smooth the payment of dividend income by putting aside surplus revenue as reserves.

Because their capital base is permanent, investment companies are free to invest in a much wider range of investments than other types of fund. In fact, they can invest in almost anything. Although many of the largest trusts invest in listed stocks and bonds, the biggest growth in recent years has been in a range of more specialist areas, such as renewable energy, infrastructure, debt securities, music royalties and private equity. Investment trusts offer fund investors a broader choice and greater scope for diversification, in other words.

And what are the disadvantages?

The two main disadvantages are share price volatility and potential loss of liquidity. Because investment trusts can trade at a discount to the value of their assets, an investor who sells at the wrong moment may not receive the full asset value for their shares at that point. The day-to-day value of the investment will also fluctuate more than an equivalent open-ended fund. In the case of more specialist trusts, it may not always be possible to buy or sell shares in a trust at a good price because of a lack of liquidity in the market. Investors need to make sure they understand these features before investing.

How many trusts are there?

According to the industry trade body, the Association of Investment Companies, there were just over 380 investment trusts with more than £260bn in assets (as at the end of August 2022). They are split between a number of different sectors, reflecting the regions or type of investments in which they invest. Scottish Mortgage, the largest trust, has approximately £14bn in assets.

What are alternative assets?

While investment trusts have traditionally invested primarily in publicly listed stocks and shares, whose values are known every day, the last decade has seen significant growth in so-called alternative assets. These are trusts which invest in longer term assets which are mostly not traded daily and therefore can be valued only at less frequent intervals. Examples include commercial property, renewable energy, infrastructure and private equity. Many of these alternative trusts are popular because of their ability to pay higher levels of income.

How are they regulated?

All investment companies are regulated by the Financial Conduct Authority. So too are the managers the board appoints to manage the trust's investments. Investment trusts are also subject to the Listing Rules of the stock exchange on which they are listed. The board of directors is accountable to shareholders and regulators for the performance of the trust and the appointment of the manager and are legally bound by the requirements of successive Companies Acts.

How do I invest in an investment trust?

There are a number of different ways. You can buy them directly through a stockbroker or via an online platform. A few larger investment trusts also have monthly savings schemes where you can transfer a fixed sum every month to the company, which then invests it into its shares on your behalf. If you have a financial adviser, or a portfolio manager, they can arrange the investment for you.

What do investment trusts cost?

As with any share, investors in investment trusts will need to pay brokerage commission when buying or selling shares in an investment trust, and also stamp duty on purchases. The managers appointed by the trust's directors to make its investments charge an annual management fee which is paid automatically, together with dealing and administration costs, out of the trust's assets. These management fees typically range from as little as 0.3% to 2.0% or more of the trust's assets.

What are tax wrappers?

Tax wrappers are schemes which allow individual investors, if they comply with the rules set by the government, to avoid tax on part or all of their investments. The two most important tax wrappers are the Individual Savings Account (ISA) and the

Self-Invested Personal Pension (SIPP). The majority of investment trusts can be held in an ISA or SIPP. There are annual limits on the amounts that can be invested each year (currently £20,000 for an ISA). Venture capital trusts (VCTs) are a specialist type of investment trust which also have a number of tax advantages, reflecting their higher risk. VCTs invest in start up and early stage businesses.

Who owns investment trusts?

Twenty-five years ago life insurance companies were the biggest investors in investment trusts, which they used to manage their client funds and pensions. These days such institutional investors mostly manage their own investments directly. Other than some specialist types of trust, the largest investors in trusts today are wealth management firms (formerly stockbroking firms), other types of intermediary and, increasingly, private investors. The growing number of individual investors reflects the growing influence of online platforms, which give individual investors the ability to choose their own investments for ISAs, SIPPs and taxable share/fund accounts.

Are they as difficult to understand as some people say?

Investment trusts are a little more complex than a simple open-ended fund, but no more difficult to understand than most types of listed company. It is important to understand the concept of discounts and premiums before you start to invest, but buying, selling and following the fortunes of your investment could not be easier. If you like the idea of making the connoisseur's choice when investing, you will find the effort of understanding investment trusts worthwhile.

Key terms explained

Investment trusts (aka investment companies) pool the money of individual and professional investors and invest it for them in order to generate capital gains, dividend income, or both. These are the most important factors that determine how good an investment they are:

SHARE PRICE
The price (typically in pence) you will be asked to pay to buy or sell shares in any investment company. Your interest is to see it go up, not down.

SPREAD
The difference between the price per share to pay if you want to buy and that you will be offered if you wish to sell – can be anything from 0% (good) to 5% or more (bad). The bigger the trust, the tighter the spread should be.

MARKET CAPITALISATION

The aggregate current value of all the shares a trust has issued – in essence, therefore, what the market in its wisdom thinks the investment company is worth today. (The market is not always wise and would be a duller and less interesting place if it were.)

NET ASSET VALUE (NAV)

The value of the company's investments less running costs at the most recent valuation point – typically (and ideally) that will be yesterday's quoted market price, but for some types of investment trust, whose assets are not traded on a daily basis, it might be one or more months ago.

NET ASSET VALUE PER SHARE

This is calculated, not surprisingly, by dividing the NAV (see above) by the number of shares in issue. You can compare it directly with the share price to find the discount or premium.

DISCOUNT/PREMIUM

When the share price is below the investment company's net asset value per share it is said to be trading 'at a discount'; if it trades above the NAV per share, then the trust is selling 'at a premium'.

DIVIDEND YIELD

How much a trust pays out as income each year to its shareholders, expressed as a percentage of its share price. The usual figure quoted is based on the dividends a company has paid in the previous 12 months. Over time you hope to see the dividend increasing at least in line with inflation.

DIVIDEND HERO

A catchy term invented by the industry trade body to describe trusts which have increased their dividend every year for more than 20 consecutive years (see the data section for a full list).

THE FUND MANAGER

The person (or team) responsible for choosing and managing the investment trust's capital. Will typically be professionally qualified and highly paid. How much value he or she really adds is a lively source of debate.

THE BOARD

Investment companies are listed companies, so they must comply with stock exchange rules and appoint a board of independent directors who are legally responsible for overseeing the company and protecting the interests of its shareholders, which ultimately means replacing the manager or closing down the trust if results are not good.

GEARING

A fancy word for borrowing money in order to try and boost the performance of a company's shares – a case of more risk for potentially more reward. A number of different types of borrowing (e.g., with fixed or variable interest rates) can be used.

FEES AND CHARGES

What it costs to own shares in an investment trust – a figure that (confusingly) can be calculated in several different ways. More important than it sounds on first hearing.

OCR

Short for Ongoing Charge Ratio, one of the most commonly used formulas used to measure the annual cost of owning a trust. Expressed as a percentage of the NAV.

SECTORS

Investment trusts come in many shapes and sizes, so for convenience are categorised into one of a number of different sectors, based on the kind of things that they invest in.

PERFORMANCE

A popular and over-used term which tells you how much money an investment trust has made for its shareholders over any given period of time – by definition, a backward-looking measurement. It does not guarantee future performance will be as good.

BENCHMARK

The outcome against which a trust and its shareholders have agreed to measure its performance. This is typically a stock market index relevant to the area or style in which the portfolio is being invested (e.g., the FTSE All-Share index for trusts investing in UK equity markets).

TOTAL RETURN

A way of combining the income a trust pays with the capital gains it also generates (you hope) over time, so as to allow fair comparisons with other trusts and funds. Shown either as a simple percentage gain over the period or as an annualised gain, the compound rate of return per annum.

RISK AND RETURN

Riskier investments tend to produce higher returns over time, typically at the cost of doing less well when market conditions are unfavourable and better when they are more helpful. Risk comes in many (dis)guises, however – some more visible than others.

BETA

This is a term used in financial economics to measure the extent to which the shares of a company rise or fall relative to the stock market as a whole. The stock market has a beta of 1.0, so if the market rises 10%, then a trust with a beta of 1.2 is expected to rise by 12% (=10 × 1.2). If it falls by 10%, the shares should fall by 12%.

ALPHA

A statistical measure of the additional returns that a trust has made after adjusting for the relative risk of its portfolio. It is often used (not entirely accurately) as shorthand for fund manager skill.

ACTIVE MANAGEMENT

What is going on when the investment manager of a trust makes a conscious decision not to include in its portfolio all the stocks or shares that make up its benchmark index. The latter can be easily and much more cheaply replicated by a computer – what is known as passive management. All investment trusts are actively managed.

INVESTMENT STYLE

An attempt to characterise the way in which the manager of a trust chooses to invest. One common distinction is between value and growth. The former style aims to find companies whose shares are cheap relative to their competitors or historic price. The latter concentrates on finding companies with above average sales and profit growth prospects.

IS THERE ANY DIFFERENCE BETWEEN AN INVESTMENT COMPANY AND INVESTMENT TRUST?

Basically no. Strictly speaking, investment trusts are investment companies but not all investment companies are investment trusts. Feel free to use either term interchangeably, without fear of embarrassment.

CLOSED-END FUNDS

Investment trusts are an example of what is called a 'closed-end fund', meaning that its capital base is intended to be fixed and permanent (unlike unit trusts, OEICs and horribly named UCITs 3 funds, which take in and return money to investors on a daily basis and are therefore called open-ended). The distinction is no longer quite as important as it was, as it has become somewhat easier for successful investment companies to raise new money through regular share issues.

USEFUL SOURCES OF INFORMATION

Industry information

The Association of Investment Companies | www.theaic.co.uk

Data, news and research

Money Makers | www.money-makers.co

Morningstar | www.morningstar.co.uk

Trustnet | www.trustnet.com

Citywire | www.citywire.co.uk

Platforms

Interactive Investor | www.iii.co.uk

Hargreaves Lansdown | www.hl.co.uk

A.J.Bell | www.ajbell.co.uk

Fidelity International | www.fidelity.co.uk

News and sponsored research

Edison | www.edisoninvestmentresearch.com

QuotedData | www.quoteddata.com

Trust Intelligence (Kepler Partners) | www.trustintelligence.co.uk

Specialist publications

Investment Trusts Newsletter (McHattie Group) | www.tipsheets.co.uk

Investment Trust Insider (Citywire) | www.citywire.co.uk

Publications that regularly feature investment trusts

Financial Times | www.ft.com

Investors Chronicle | www.investorschronicle.co.uk

Money Makers newsletter | www.money-makers.co

MoneyWeek | www.moneyweek.com

The Telegraph | www.telegraph.co.uk

INCOME PORTFOLIOS

How to create and track them, by JONATHAN DAVIS

The lure of income

INVESTING FOR INCOME has always been one of the strong selling features of the investment trust sector. The ability to put aside up to 15% of a trust's annual income in any year as reserves and draw on those reserves to sustain dividend payments in years when markets fall gives their yields a stability that other types of fund cannot match. The rapidly growing number of alternative asset trusts since the global financial crisis, most of which are sold primarily on the basis of their attractive dividend-paying potential, has brought in yet more income-seeking investors in the last 15 years.

The following table summarises the yields that are available in some of the most important sectors of the investment trust universe, as at 30 September 2022. A year earlier, before discounts widened, these figures were uniformly lower. That underlines how, other things being equal, falling share prices have the effect of increasing the dividend yield on offer to shareholders. This is one of the silver linings of bear markets and a potential opportunity for income investors.

	DIVIDEND YIELD	DISCOUNT	SHARE PRICE TOTAL RETURN				
	(%)	(%)	YEAR TO DATE (%)	1-YEAR (%)	3-YEAR (%)	5-YEAR (%)	10-YEAR (%)
Debt	8.4	-15.6		-6.9	1.7	7.0	49.4
Property	7.3	-38.8	-30.6	-25.9	-16.9	-4.1	79.7
Infrastructure	5.3	-12.9	-7.8	-2.5	6.6	30.8	133.7
Emerging Markets	3.9	-19.8	-18.5	-17.6	5.4	24.7	48.7
Specialist Alternatives	3.9	-24.6	4.0	8.1	116.9	-12.3	76.6
UK	3.9	-8.7	-23.7	-20.1	-2.1	-1.0	97.5
Private Equity	3.2	-33.7	-30.9	-21.8	11.3	32.9	393
Specialist Equity	2.9	-8.1	-24.1	-19.3	20.7	30.8	193.1
Europe	2.5	-12.4	-31.2	-26.4	4.8	6.4	164.8
Asia Pacific	2.2	-12.5	-16.2	-15.9	18.7	18.0	157.5
Global	1.8	-14.7	-27.8	-25.8	17.3	31.6	188.3
North America	1.5	-8.4	-18.2	-13.4	33.4	63.7	164.7
Japan	1.5	-10.4	-27.0	-26.7	-5.4	6.0	205.4
Hedge Funds	1.2	-24.4	-6.6	0.1	73.3	126	132.1

Of course it remains the case that dividends are never guaranteed. While trusts in the infrastructure business typically have long-term contracts which in practice effectively underwrite the certainty of their future cash flows, for equity investment trusts the ability to sustain their dividend income is always vulnerable during times of economic stress or hardship. The pandemic, during which the value of dividends paid by UK listed companies fell by 40% (and those of commercial property trusts, investing in offices, factories and shops, by even more) was a classic example.

Yet the fact that trusts such as City of London have been able to increase their dividends each year for more than 50 years, through good times and bad, is testament to the potential resilience of the income that many investment trusts, by being able to draw on their reserves, are able to pay out as dividends. If, as seems likely, most developed economies are facing a recession as we move into 2023, this resilience is sure to be tested again.

In this section I take a look at the way in which the AIC's website enables shareholders in investment trusts to track the income from their portfolios and assess the sustainability of the dividends on which they may be relying. Elsewhere in this section we include for the first time a list of those trusts which are pursuing a different approach to managing their dividends (a so-called enhanced income policy) and those which have the authority to pay income out of capital as well as out of their revenue reserves.

Setting up a portfolio

The Income Finder feature on the AIC's website is a useful starting point for managing a portfolio of investment trusts that are held for income. As an illustration I have used the example of the *Money Makers* income portfolio, one of four portfolios which I track for subscribers to the *Money Makers Circle*, my subscription service for investment trust investors.

The Income Finder function is found in a dropdown menu under the <u>Research tools</u> tab on the main page of the AIC's recently revamped website. Once you have done that you will face a page that looks as follows. There are five tabs above the blank chart space: Income Builder, Dividend Diary, My Income Portfolios, Guides and Glossary and Dividend Heroes.

It is important to say at the outset that you can use the Income Builder feature in more than one way. One is to track the performance of a real-life portfolio you already have. The second is to use it as a research tool, experimenting with different combinations of trusts to work out the potential income returns and month-by-month payment profile of different options.

Either way, the first step is to create a new portfolio, by clicking the + Add new portfolio function, and give it a name. You can create as many portfolios as you like. Then, staying on the Income Builder tab (like the other tabs, highlighted in red when it is active), you will use the list of investment trusts listed, in alphabetical order, down the right hand side of the page to create your portfolio.

The only trusts listed here are those that pay a dividend, so if you cannot find a trust it means that it is not yet a dividend-payer. You can narrow the list of choices by choosing a specific AIC sector or the Dividend pay month, meaning the month in which the trust pays a dividend.

Every time you choose the name of a specific trust (by clicking the + sign next to the name of the trust) that you want, you will be asked to input one of two values. The first is a number of shares, the second the value of a holding (in £). The algorithm will then automatically calculate the other value by reference to the current price of the shares.

For example, if you input (say) the name of Murray Income, a popular trust in the UK equity income sector, you will see a screen that looks like this:

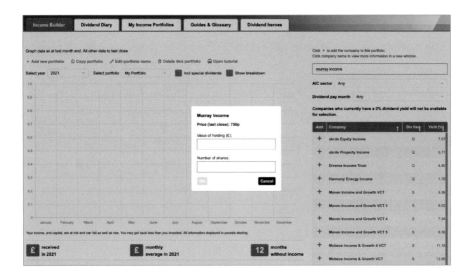

Enter the figure of 5,000 shares and you will then see the current value calculated. Alternatively, if you enter the amount you are looking to invest, say £5,000, it will give you the number of shares you can buy for that amount.

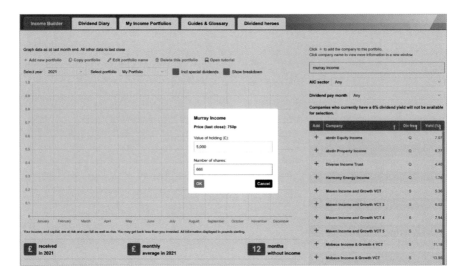

Click on <u>OK</u> and the page will be repopulated with a chart and underneath some basic information about the dividend income paid by the trust you have entered.

By default the chart shows you the payment profile for the last full calendar year – 2021 at the time this was written – but you can also use another dropdown menu to show the same information for any of the last five calendar years, or the equivalent data for just the last 12 months. Income Builder also shows you in which month the dividends have been paid and what the total equates to as a monthly average. Note that the payment dates shown in the chart are the date the dividend is paid, not the day that it is declared.

Populating the portfolio

The next step then is to populate the rest of your portfolio. If it is a real portfolio it is obviously important to check that the figures are correct (share splits can occasionally produce some obviously anomalous results and you will have to adjust the number of shares manually). If it is a portfolio you are putting together for research purposes, you can easily chop and change the inputs by using a combination of the + sign and the bin icon.

One thing that will immediately become clear from the chart is how regular the income profile of your portfolio is likely to be. If a reasonably consistent dividend income every month is important to you, you can adjust your portfolio to help achieve that, although this may involve some trade-offs which reduce your total income over the whole 12 months.

If you tick the <u>show breakdown</u> option above and to the right of the chart, the columns in the chart will also give you the precise value of the dividend payments from each company, allowing you to visualise what proportion of the month's total each dividend represents. Clicking on the columns will show you the precise amounts each trust paid each month.

Once you have completed experimenting and have input your final choices, you will have a clear picture of the whole portfolio. The table below the chart will list the current dividend yield and the frequency with which each company disperses dividends.

It is a matter of choice by the board of directors whether investment trusts pay dividends monthly, quarterly, bi-annually or just once a year. They also have the option of paying a one-off <u>special dividend</u>.

An example portfolio

The next chart shows how the figures for the *Money Makers* income portfolio looked in the first week of October 2022. The portfolio was created with £100,000 on 1 January 2017, originally split between 20 holdings of £5,000, a mixture of equity and alternative asset trusts. I have made only a few changes to it since then, in line with the general principle that buy and hold (or buy and forget) is frequently the best default option for those with a medium to longer term investment objective.

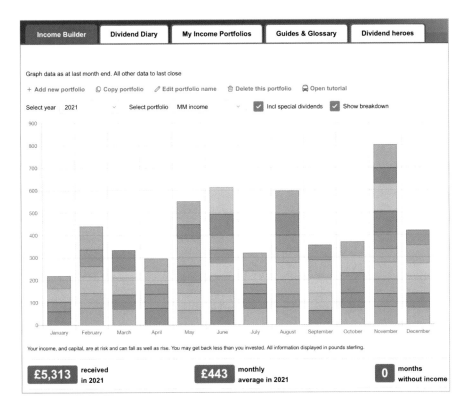

In 2021, the data shows, the portfolio produced an annual income of £5,313, or £443 a month. By clicking on the <u>select year</u> box to the top left of the chart I can see that over the last 12 months the income has been £5,836, or £486 a month. This tells me that the dividend income from the portfolio companies has continued to grow from last year to this, as you would expect in normal market conditions if your original choices were soundly based.

Using the same <u>select year</u> dropdown menu tells me that the total dividend income in 2017, the first year of the portfolio, was £3,747. A further option, important if your holdings in the portfolio are outside a tax wrapper (ISA), will show you what the total income received was in the last tax year (2021–2022: £5,393). This will be a figure that you will need to check and then include in your annual tax return if it is outside an ISA.*

All the data shown on the Income Builder page can be downloaded to a spreadsheet and analysed if needed. Looking back, for example, the first year yield on the original £100,000 invested, according to the website, was 3.7% (but see my later

---

* If you have invested in a venture capital trust, the dividends do not need to be included in your tax return.

note on the limitations of this function). The current capital value of the portfolio is not shown in Income Builder, but I monitor it separately and can calculate the current trailing 12-month yield (the last 12 months of dividend income expressed as a percentage of its current value). At the time of writing it is now 5.2%.

What the figures show is that, despite both the pandemic and this year's fall in equity markets, the amount of dividend income received has grown by 55% since year one of this portfolio. The dividend yield of the component companies at the time of writing ranges from 8.6% to 2.2%. While the portfolio receives dividend payments every month, I have not chosen to spread them more evenly across the calendar year, but it would be possible to do so. All but two of the trusts in the portfolio pay quarterly dividends.

The art of managing an income portfolio is to balance the level of dividend income against the potential for capital growth. For the longer-term investor, the initial yield is not necessarily the most important number. The ability of a trust to grow its dividend is just as important as the starting yield. The income from a trust with a fast rate of dividend growth will surprisingly quickly exceed that of a trust which has a higher starting yield but grows more sedately.

The value of Income Builder

There is no doubt that the Income Builder function is a valuable tool for any investor looking to use investment trusts for regular dividend income. It is simple and fast to use, once you have mastered the basic idea. Having used it a fair deal, I can think of some minor improvements. When building a portfolio for the first time, for example, it would be helpful to be able to rank and sort the component trusts in a portfolio by name, yield and amounts paid.

You can do this later, once the portfolio has been created, by clicking on the relevant portfolio's name under the My Income Portfolios tab, but not during the process of construction. A minor irritation is that you can download the data into a spreadsheet from the Income Builder page, but not from the portfolio tab under the My Income Portfolios tab. That means you cannot download the five-year dividend growth figure, which only appears on the latter page.

The biggest issue that will confront most users is that the historical comparisons between this year and past years are limited by the fact that the prior year comparisons assume that what you own today is the same as what you owned at the outset. If you have made changes to the portfolio since the start of the exercise, the comparable numbers will not be accurate. They only show you what this year's portfolio would have been worth – and what the income would have been – five years ago if you had owned exactly the same things then as you do now.

What is in the Income Portfolio?

Dividend frequency:	A Annual	S Semi-annual	Q Quarterly	M Monthly		

Company	AIC sector	Income received (£) in 2021	# Shares held	Div freq	Yield (%)	
LXI REIT	Property - UK Commercial	295.00	5,000	Q	5.15	✏ 🗑
HICL Infrastructure	Infrastructure	250.39	3,035	Q	5.14	✏ 🗑
Renewables Infrastructure Group	Renewable Energy Infrastructure	309.61	4,580	Q	5.34	✏ 🗑
Impact Healthcare REIT	Property - UK Healthcare	310.71	4,870	Q	6.53	✏ 🗑
Murray Income	UK Equity Income	208.08	689	Q	4.80	✏ 🗑
Law Debenture Corporation	UK Equity Income	265.55	940	Q	4.21	✏ 🗑
Tritax Big Box REIT	Property - UK Logistics	236.40	3,630	Q	5.00	✏ 🗑
Hipgnosis Songs	Royalties	262.50	5,000	Q	6.08	✏ 🗑
Greencoat UK Wind	Renewable Energy Infrastructure	298.57	4,170	Q	5.02	✏ 🗑
JPMorgan Global Emerging Markets Income	Global Emerging Markets	220.32	4,320	Q	4.34	✏ 🗑
Diverse Income Trust	UK Equity Income	203.81	5,435	Q	4.40	✏ 🗑
Supermarket Income REIT	Property - UK Commercial	294.00	5,000	Q	5.66	✏ 🗑
BlackRock World Mining	Commodities & Natural Resources	352.24	1,480	Q	7.30	✏ 🗑
Bluefield Solar Income Fund	Renewable Energy Infrastructure	376.00	4,700	Q	6.14	✏ 🗑
JPMorgan Global Growth & Income	Global Equity Income	253.98	1,800	Q	4.01	✏ 🗑
CT Global Managed Portfolio Income	Flexible Investment	254.00	4,000	Q	5.59	✏ 🗑
International Public Partnerships	Infrastructure	242.45	3,250	S	5.07	✏ 🗑
Finsbury Growth & Income	UK Equity Income	131.16	767	S	2.21	✏ 🗑
Digital 9 Infrastructure	Infrastructure	132.00	4,400	Q	5.75	✏ 🗑
AEW UK REIT	Property - UK Commercial	416.00	5,200	Q	8.65	✏ 🗑

The income builder tool cannot make adjustments to the # Shares held. Therefore, if your chosen investment company undergoes a share split, please edit the record to reflect the new number of shares you currently hold.

Please note. All values are based on actual dividend payment dates. On occasion this can lead to irregular payment schedules.

Companies that now show 0% yield would previously have paid dividends but currently do not.

That is not without its value, but it is only accurate for an investor who never changes his or her portfolio. It is certainly not a substitute for a comprehensive portfolio tracking and measurement system. The way that I get around that is by making a point of saving the relevant totals in a spreadsheet every time I make a change to the income portfolio. That is rather cumbersome, but manageable.

What this means is that, for the example I am using, the figures I gave earlier for past-year income are not 100% accurate, because of the changes I have made subsequently. I used them earlier merely as an illustration of the information which Income Builder is able to show you. The amount the income portfolio produced in its first year was actually £3,914, not the £3,747 I quoted previously. My original target was to look for a yield of around 4.0%, but I have since sold two or three trusts and replaced them with others.

What I can do, armed with the dividend information, is to work out the total return on the income portfolio since launch by adding the total dividends actually received to the gain in capital value over the same period. In the case of the *Money Makers* income portfolio, it shows me that the portfolio has paid out more than £28,000 in dividends since it began, in addition to capital gains of more than £13,000.

Taken with the current market value, I can calculate that the total return since launch of the income portfolio has ranged between 7% and 10% per annum, depending on the price of the shares at the point of calculation. After the stock market declines of the first nine months of the year, the figure is currently towards the lower end of the range, offset in part by now having a higher dividend yield.

What about the other tabs?

Most of the other tabs on the Income Finder page are largely self-explanatory. The Dividend Diary lays out in calendar format the specific days within each month that individual trusts have paid their dividends. Because dividend payment days are declared several weeks in advance, it is possible to look a few weeks ahead to see which trusts are scheduled to pay dividends on specific future dates. It is important to remember however that dividends are only paid to shareholders who are on the register on the ex-dividend date, which is typically a few weeks before the payment date.

The My Income portfolios tab gives you access to more details of other portfolios that you have created, including the five-year dividend growth figures. As mentioned above, while on the Income Builder tab, there is an Export current portfolio button at the bottom of the page, allowing you to download all the details in .csv format, one that can be easily opened by Excel, Numbers and most spreadsheet software, that is not possible from the My Income Portfolios page. You can also view the dividend cover here. This is calculated to show the extent to which the expected annual dividend payment for each trust is covered by the most recently reported revenue reserves for each trust. It is measured in years. So, if it costs £10m to service the entire dividend of the trust and its most recently reported revenue reserve figure is £15m, the dividend cover is 1.5 years. A cover of less than 1 implies that the company would not be able to maintain its dividend pay-out rate solely using its reserves. Of course, even in times of stress, the trust's own income levels are unlikely to drop to 0, so a cover of less than 1 does not automatically lead to a reduced dividend pay-out.

The Guides & Glossary tab is a help page, while the final tab is a useful summary of those trusts which have earned the AIC's 'dividend hero' status, meaning that they have increased their dividend every year for at least 20 years in succession (you can see the results a few pages on in this *Handbook*). There you will also find a list of Next Generation Dividend Heroes, those trusts which have increased their dividend every year for at least 10 years, but not yet achieved the 20-year track record needed for the original list.

Looking through the list of dividend heroes, it is evident that there is, on average, an inverse correlation between the dividend yield and the rate of historic dividend growth. The higher the current yield, the lower the rate of dividend growth, and vice versa. There are exceptions however, including this year some commercial property trusts which appear close to the top of the list on both measures. It is a warning that those future dividends may be threatened by rising interest rates and the risk of a recession.

It is a reminder that however useful the data may be, for an income investor the challenge is always to look deeper than the headline numbers in order to understand what the potential payouts and risks are for each individual trust they look at. In an inflationary environment, it is more important than ever to assess how likely a trust will be able to achieve dividend increases which can at least match the rate of inflation over 3–5 years, if not every year.

Income Builder is not a substitute for closely monitoring the performance of a real-life portfolio, but it is still a handy resource both for researching a potential income portfolio and tracking the actual and potential income that any such portfolio will produce. As such it certainly deserves a place in the toolkit of resources that any investment trust investor can call on.

The Income Portfolio ranked by yield

Company	AIC sector	Dividend yield (%)	5yr dividend growth (%) p.a.	Dividend cover	Dividend frequency
AEW UK REIT	Property - UK Commercial	8.65	0.00	0.00	Quarterly
BlackRock World Mining	Commodities & Natural Resources	7.30	26.73	0.90	Quarterly
Impact Healthcare REIT	Property - UK Healthcare	6.53	N/A	0.00	Quarterly
Bluefield Solar Income Fund	Renewable Energy Infrastructure	6.14	2.49	0.00	Four times a year
Hipgnosis Songs	Royalties	6.08	N/A	0.00	Quarterly
Digital 9 Infrastructure	Infrastructure	5.75	N/A	N/A	Quarterly
Supermarket Income REIT	Property - UK Commercial	5.66	N/A	0.00	Quarterly
CT Global Managed Portfolio Income	Flexible Investment	5.59	4.06	0.97	Quarterly
Renewables Infrastructure Group	Renewable Energy Infrastructure	5.34	1.58	0.00	Quarterly
LXI REIT	Property - UK Commercial	5.15	N/A	0.00	Quarterly
HICL Infrastructure	Infrastructure	5.14	1.52	11.89	Quarterly
International Public Partnerships	Infrastructure	5.07	2.57	0.00	Semi-Annually
Greencoat UK Wind	Renewable Energy Infrastructure	5.02	2.52	0.00	Quarterly
Tritax Big Box REIT	Property - UK Logistics	5.00	1.56	N/A	Four times a year
Murray Income	UK Equity Income	4.80	1.91	0.80	Quarterly
Diverse Income Trust	UK Equity Income	4.40	5.39	1.15	Quarterly
JPMorgan Global Emerging Markets Income	Global Emerging Markets	4.34	1.20	0.95	Quarterly
Law Debenture Corporation	UK Equity Income	4.21	11.67	1.14	Quarterly
JPMorgan Global Growth & Income	Global Equity Income	4.01	20.77	0.00	Quarterly
Finsbury Growth & Income	UK Equity Income	2.21	4.97	1.26	Semi-Annually

Source for all charts: AIC website. Note that this table can be sorted by column

EXPLAINING DISCOUNTS

Understanding discounts and premiums is key to knowing how investment trusts behave, as EMMA BIRD, *head of research at Winterflood Securities, explains in this Q&A.*

1. What do we mean by a discount/premium?

A discount or premium shows the relationship between an investment trust's net asset value (NAV) and its share price. If a trust's share price is higher than its NAV per share then it is said to be trading at a premium, while a trust is said to be trading on a discount if its share price is below its NAV per share.

2. How are they calculated?

A discount or premium is calculated by dividing the share price by the NAV per share and taking away 1 to give a percentage figure. A positive number gives a premium and a negative number gives a discount. For example, as at 30 September 2022, Alliance Trust's share price was 920.00p and its NAV per share was 969.60p, meaning that it was trading on a 5.1% discount (920.00 ÷ 969.60 − 1 = −0.051 = −5.1%).

3. How often do NAVs get published?

The frequency of NAV publications varies depending on an investment trust's underlying asset class. Long-only equity funds and those investing in publicly traded bonds will generally publish daily announcements of their NAVs as at the close of the previous business day. In contrast, funds investing in illiquid asset classes that are not publicly traded, such as property, private equity or infrastructure, tend to publish monthly or quarterly NAVs, with a time lag of about a month.

4. How reliable are NAV calculations?

For long-only equity investment trusts, NAV calculations can be expected to be very reliable, as they are based on the publicly available closing share prices of the underlying shares. For alternative assets without a set market price, valuations are usually produced or validated by third-party specialists. However, by the time these NAVs are published, they are already out of date, and the rating is therefore likely to reflect the market's expectation of the current asset valuations rather than the last published NAV.

5. Why do different sources sometimes give different figures?

Discount figures can vary from different sources if they use different NAVs in the calculation. Some data providers use the NAV including income (cum-income), while others use a figure excluding income (ex-income). In addition, if an investment trust has long-term debt, this can either be reflected in the NAV at par value (the amount of money that the fund will repay at the maturity date of the bond) or at fair value (the market price an investor would currently be willing to buy the debt for).

For example, Alliance Trust's cum-income NAV with debt valued at fair value was 969.60p at 30 September, resulting in a 5.1% discount when compared to share price of 920.00p. However, its ex-income NAV with debt valued at par was 951.40p, giving a discount of 3.3%. When looking at discount figures you need to look carefully at the basis on which they have been calculated. The industry standard is to use the cum-income NAV with debt at fair value.

6. What are the main factors that drive discounts/premiums?

Discounts and premiums are driven by both an investment trust's share price, which rises or falls depending on the amount of demand for the shares, and its NAV, which reflects the performance of the underlying portfolio of assets. In addition, investment trust boards can choose to intervene in the market to buy back shares to help narrow the discount, or issue new shares in order to stop the premium extending too far.

7. How common are zero discount policies?

Some investment trusts have a zero discount policy, committing to buy back shares at a discount and issue shares at a premium, in an attempt to maintain the share price very close to the underlying NAV per share. However, these are relatively rare, with only a handful of trusts committing to this mechanism. Of these the best known is probably Personal Assets Trust, which has been successfully implementing a zero-discount policy for many years.

8. How many trusts have hard discount controls?

While zero-discount policies are reasonably uncommon, numerous investment trusts have stated discount control mechanisms committing to maintain the discount at narrower than a certain level, say 5% or 10%, through the use of share buybacks. We estimate that approximately 45 trusts, or around 15% of the investment trust universe, have a firm discount target.

9. How effective are share buybacks at controlling discounts?

Share buybacks can help to control discounts by reducing the number of shares in issue and increasing the share price. A proven commitment by a board to repurchase shares if the discount widens past a certain level can also help to provide a natural floor. However, if underlying demand for the fund's shares remains weak, buybacks are unlikely to provide a long-term solution. Large and regular share buyback programmes will also cause the fund to shrink in size, which in turn may make it less appealing to a number of investors and therefore exacerbate the problem.

10. What are the arguments for controlling premiums if you are an investment company?

Excessive premiums can make an investment company less appealing to new investors, as they would be knowingly paying significantly more per share than the underlying portfolio is worth. Issuing shares to prevent the premium from extending too far can therefore help to ensure new investors remain willing to invest. Furthermore, issuing shares at a premium adds to the NAV per share for existing investors as the fund raises new money at the prevailing share price and reinvests it in the portfolio at cheaper valuations.

11. Why do big discounts persist (for years in some cases)?

Large discounts can persist for prolonged periods if the fund, or the asset class in which it invests, is out of favour with investors. Boards may choose not to intervene if they believe that natural demand remains weak and share buybacks will therefore not lead to any significant re-rating. However, some boards may propose tender offers, a mechanism that allows a certain proportion of shareholdings to be redeemed closer to NAV, or suggest an orderly wind-up of the fund, if the ingrained discount is thought to reflect a sustained or permanent lack of demand for the offering.

12. How quickly can discounts move to premiums and vice versa?

Investment trusts can move from trading on a discount to a premium, and vice versa, depending on the level of demand for the vehicle. Catalysts for a re-rating are often a change of investment objective, strategy or manager. The move from a discount to a premium can either be fairly quick in reaction to an announcement of an upcoming change, or can be steady over a longer period of time as a fund's shareholder base evolves.

13. How should shareholders think about discount/premiums when contemplating portfolio moves?

On the face of it, buying an investment trust at a discount means you are accessing it cheaply, while buying at a premium implies paying more than the underlying portfolio is worth. However, shareholders only receive the share price return and so buying at a discount does not guarantee a successful investment, for example if the discount widens further. One way to identify potentially attractive value opportunities is to look at the current rating compared with the fund's own historical discount or premium, as well as compared with its peer group.

The presence, or lack thereof, of discount control mechanisms can also give an idea of the amount of potential downside discount risk. With some specialist trusts where the NAVs are reported with a lag, and therefore out of date, an investor may decide that paying a premium is justified when set against the estimated current NAV.

14. Discounts generally have narrowed in recent years – why?

The investment trust sector average discount has been narrowing over recent years and indeed decades. This reflects the prevalence of buybacks since April 1999 (when the tax rules changed to make them a practical reality), increased corporate activity and strong performance records. All these trends have attracted new buyers to the sector. In addition, the low interest rate environment that had persisted since the global financial crisis coincided with a wave of new investment trust launches focusing on alternative income. The demand for this income led to these types of funds often trading on premiums, or at worst small discounts, which helped to narrow the overall sector average discount.

Investment trust sector (ex 3i) average discount since the start of 2020

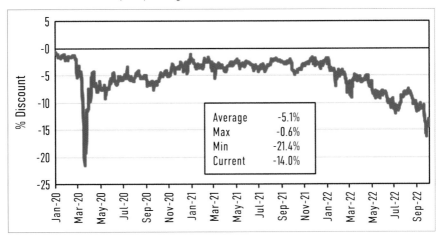

Source: Winterflood Securities, 30 September 2022

15. They have widened dramatically in the last year however – what is behind that?

Discounts across the investment trust sector have widened dramatically over the last year, which can be at least partially attributed to the prevailing investor uncertainty and negative market sentiment, which is leading to reduced demand. In addition, the environment of rising interest rate and inflation expectations has hurt the investment trust sector as growth equities and alternative income assets have fallen out of favour.

Relative discounts

16. Which sectors have been worst affected?

The worst affected sub-sectors include commercial property and private equity/ growth capital. Higher interest rates will mean that debt, which is often used to partially fund property purchases, will become more expensive and therefore reduce demand for real estate, putting downward pressure on valuations. In addition, a higher 'risk-free' rate lowers the comparative yield advantage of property investment companies, while there are also some investor concerns around the cost of debt financing at the fund level. Private equity and growth capital investment trusts have seen a sell-off as the rising interest rate environment has led to a reversal in market leadership, from growth to value, and discounts have widened as investors started to price in expectations of future valuation declines.

17. What will it take for the trend in discounts to reverse? Is this a buying opportunity?

I expect that a reversal in market sentiment is required before discounts tighten notably from their current levels. This, in turn, is likely to be caused by evidence of inflation peaking and reduced fears of further interest rate rises, while positive economic growth forecasts may also be key. Market conditions may remain volatile in the near term against the current uncertain backdrop, but the historically wide discount levels, particularly in asset classes that have seen the most dramatic de-ratings, offer an attractive opportunity for patient investors, in my view.

A year of discount moves

Fund	Ticker	Now	Previous	Change	Fund	Ticker	Now	Previous	Change
Doric Nimrod Air Three	DNA3	108.1%	22.1%	86.1%	Molten Ventures	GROW	-67.6%	17.7%	-85.3%
JPMorgan Russian	JRS	54.8%	-9.6%	64.4%	Chrysalis Investments	CHRY	-61.4%	10.9%	-72.3%
Doric Nimrod Air One	DNA	4.6%	-47.3%	51.9%	Seraphim Space	SSIT	-38.7%	24.0%	-62.8%
ASIA Strategic Holdings	ASIA	-29.2%	-72.4%	43.2%	Augmentum Fintech	AUGM	-40.7%	12.7%	-53.5%
Gabelli Merger Plus	GMP	-3.4%	-39.2%	35.8%	Tritax Big Box REIT	BBOX	-38.8%	14.5%	-53.2%
Doric Nimrod Air Two	DNA2	4.2%	-29.5%	33.7%	Taylor Maritime Investments	TMI	-35.9%	14.5%	-50.4%
Chelverton UK Dividend	SDV	12.4%	-6.1%	18.5%	Tritax Eurobox	EBOX	-51.6%	-2.9%	-48.8%
ICG Longbow Senior Secured UK Pro	LBOW	-21.2%	-38.8%	17.6%	Industrials REIT	MLI	-24.8%	23.8%	-48.5%
Trian Investors 1	TI1	-7.5%	-24.2%	16.7%	Warehouse REIT	WHR	-37.8%	9.0%	-46.8%
Athelney Trust	ATY	-2.0%	-13.6%	11.5%	Schiehallion Fund C	MNTC	-19.0%	27.1%	-46.1%
Independent IT	IIT	-3.5%	-13.4%	10.0%	Petershill Partners	PHLL	-48.4%	-3.9%	-44.5%
Marble Point Loan Financing	MPLF	-6.8%	-15.5%	8.7%	Urban Logistics REIT	SHED	-31.3%	10.5%	-41.8%
Middlefield Canadian Income	MCT	-7.9%	-16.5%	8.6%	3i Group	III	-23.1%	17.0%	-40.2%
DP Aircraft	DPA	-76.1%	-84.6%	8.6%	Primary Health Properties	PHP	-7.2%	31.2%	-38.4%
Gulf Investment Fund	GIF	3.3%	-5.2%	8.4%	Unite Group	UTG	-8.7%	29.4%	-38.1%

The table shows the biggest change in discounts over the 12 months to 30 September 2022. If the change is positive it means the discount on the shares has narrowed or gone from a discount to a premium. If it is negative it means that the discount has widened or moved from a premium to a discount. Source: Numis Securities

The largest equity sectors

AIC SECTOR	NET ASSETS (£M)	MARKET CAP (£M)	MARKET CAP (£M) 2017	# COMPANIES	% INDUSTRY NET ASSETS	5 YR MARKET CAP % GROWTH	AVERAGE GEARING %
Global	28,645	26,118	22,941	16	11.9%	13.9%	8.3%
Flexible Investment	15,567	11,542	8,229	21	6.5%	40.3%	11.0%
North America*	12,520	9,016	2,534	7	5.2%	387.7%	4.9%
UK Equity Income	10,448	10,065	10,092	21	4.3%	-0.3%	9.4%
Global Smaller Companies**	5,893	4,911	273	5	2.4%	1699.7%	3.3%
Global Emerging Markets	5,671	5,008	5,889	10	2.4%	-15.0%	2.8%
UK Smaller Companies	5,204	4,497	4,580	24	2.2%	-1.8%	4.1%
Global Equity Income	4,408	4,179	3,104	6	1.8%	34.6%	8.1%
Europe	3,753	3,288	3,307	7	1.6%	-0.6%	6.4%
UK All Companies	3,581	3,177	4,758	9	1.5%	-33.2%	8.4%
Asia Pacific	3,263	2,947	2,368	6	1.4%	24.5%	4.6%
Country Specialist	2,870	2,318	1,897	5	1.2%	22.2%	0.0%
Japan	2,250	2,053	1,660	6	0.9%	23.7%	16.8%
Asia Pacific Equity Income	2,057	1,926	1,963	5	0.9%	-1.9%	4.2%
China / Greater China	1,966	1,771	1,400	4	0.8%	26.5%	12.9%
European Smaller Companies	1,817	1,560	1,772	4	0.8%	-12.0%	4.1%
India	1,585	1,318	1,117	4	0.7%	18.1%	2.9%
Asia Pacific Smaller Companies	1,143	1,019	1,231	3	0.5%	-17.2%	6.2%
Japanese Smaller Companies	1,105	1,012	778	5	0.5%	30.0%	5.7%
Financials	503	457	358	1	0.2%	27.6%	0.9%
North American Smaller Companies	431	379	686	2	0.2%	-44.7%	4.3%
UK Equity & Bond Income	191	187	1,010	1	0.1%	-81.5%	23.3%
Latin America	164	143	237	2	0.1%	-39.8%	9.4%

Source: AIC/Morningstar, all figures to 30/09/22 unless otherwise stated

*Please note Pershing Square holdings which has a current market cap of £6bn, moved from Hedge Fund to North American sector in January 2022

** Smithson and Herald are two large companies moving into this space after 2017 (IPO and sector change respectively)

There are no fixed rules for what an investment trust can invest in. The trust's strategy does, however, have to be outlined in a prospectus and approved by shareholders if, as does happen, the board wishes to change that objective at a later date. For convenience, and to help comparative analysis, trusts are grouped into a number of different sectors, based primarily on their investment focus. These are listed here and on the following three spreads. It has become conventional to list highly specialised investment trusts in separate categories.

The majority of the sector categories are self-explanatory. It is worth noting, however, that individual trusts within each broad sector category will often have somewhat different investment objectives and benchmarks. The 'flexible investment' sector is a relatively new one that includes a number of trusts which invest across a broad range of asset classes, not just equities. Most of these were previously included in the global sector.

These sectoral classifications are reviewed at regular intervals by a committee of the Association of Investment Companies. In 2019 the AIC introduced a number of changes to its categorisation of Asian trusts and specialist trusts in particular. In 2020 utilities was changed to infrastructure securities. By tradition the sectoral breakdown distinguishes between trusts that invest primarily in large cap stocks and those that focus on mid and smaller companies, whatever their regional focus.

The table on this page summarises the sectors which, together with healthcare, financials and technology, are normally described as conventional equity trusts, to distinguish them from so-called 'alternative assets', such as infrastructure, commercial property and private equity. With the latter proving very popular in recent years, conventional trusts today account for about 50% of the industry's total assets. Before the global financial crisis, it was notably higher.

A notable feature of the table is that only around 20% of these conventional equity trusts have the UK as their primary investment focus. Investment trusts from the very earliest days have always had a bias towards investment outside the UK. The aim of the very first trust to be launched, Foreign & Colonial (now known simply as F&C), was to enable its shareholders to diversify their portfolios by investing in bonds issued by companies outside the UK.

An overseas focus is one reason why investment trusts have on average performed significantly better than the FTSE All-Share index over recent years. Since November 2020 however, with Brexit uncertainty eliminated, the UK's successful vaccination programme reviving the economy, and many UK stocks cheap by comparison to international peers, that pattern has reversed. The investment trust sector index has lagged the UK equity market in 2022 by a significant margin, although the strength of the UK market has been mostly confined to the FTSE 100 index of large cap names, with the midcap (250), small cap and AIM indices down by 20–30% in the first nine months of the year. ■

Specialist sectors

AIC SECTOR	NET ASSETS (£M)	MARKET CAP (£M)	MARKET CAP (£M) 2017	# COMPANIES	% INDUSTRY NET ASSETS	5 YR MARKET CAP % GROWTH	AVERAGE GEARING %
Private Equity	29,566	20,301	16,908	16	12.3%	20.1%	2.0%
Renewable Energy Infrastructure	16,875	16,311	4,113	22	7.0%	296.6%	2.8%
Infrastructure	14,915	14,361	10,719	9	6.2%	34.0%	1.4%
Growth Capital	6,785	3,952	n/a	6	2.8%	n/a	0.0%
Biotechnology & Healthcare	6,084	5,518	2,459	7	2.5%	124.4%	4.8%
Technology & Media	4,110	3,558	2,441	5	1.7%	45.8%	0.0%
Debt - Direct Lending	2,713	2,327	n/a	8	1.1%	n/a	9.4%
Hedge Funds	2,524	2,444	4,360	6	1.0%	-43.9%	0.0%
Commodities & Natural Resources	2,216	1,824	1,965	8	0.9%	-7.1%	5.6%
Royalties	2,187	1,424	n/a	2	0.9%	n/a	12.7%
Debt - Structured Finance	1,996	1,673	n/a	7	0.8%	n/a	3.4%
Debt - Loans & Bonds	1,530	1,430	n/a	9	0.6%	n/a	3.8%
Leasing	1,675	1,160	1,353	7	0.7%	-14.3%	99.2%
Environmental	1,397	1,320	527	3	0.6%	150.6%	1.0%
Infrastructure Securities	271	275	189	2	0.1%	45.8%	17.9%
Farmland & Forestry	179	182	181	1	0.1%	0.8%	0.0%
Other (Insurance & Reinsurance Strategies and Leasing)	136	94	458	3	0.1%	-79.4%	1.9%
TOTAL	**95,159**	**78,156**	**45,671**	**121**	**39.5%**	**71.1%**	

Source: AIC/Morningstar, all figures to 30/09/22 unless otherwise stated

The specialist sectors are also clearly identified by their name. Unlike the conventional trusts, which are mainly defined by their regional focus, the specialist sectors are mostly grouped by industry. The specialist sector is worth looking at in more detail to get a flavour of the wide (and expanding) range of investment strategies which are available once you look beyond the conventional equity trusts.

The market value of private equity, infrastructure and renewable energy trusts has grown by 50% over the last five years, thanks to good performance, the arrival of new entrants and considerable secondary share issuance. Together with commercial property, they make up the majority of the so-called alternative asset sector.

The biotechnology and healthcare sector has also seen a significant expansion. Along with technology, they qualify as specialist trusts by virtue of being narrowly focused on one particular sector of the listed equity market. Unlike alternatives, their appeal lies mainly in the potential for capital growth rather than their ability to generate solid and reliable dividend income streams.

A number of new specialist sectors have appeared in the last few years. One is music royalties. Another is growth capital, a category consisting of six trusts which invest their capital in growing but not yet mature private companies. The three biggest are Schroder UK Public Private (SUPP), Schiehallion (MNTN) and Chrysalis (CHRY). Being riskier than conventional private equity, they have sold off dramatically in 2022 after very strong performance earlier.

The way the universe of listed trusts looks can change significantly from decade to decade, reflecting the changing market environment and investor appetite. Investment trusts run by hedge fund managers were popular before the global financial crisis, but with notable exceptions (Pershing Square, Third Point and BH Macro) have mostly disappeared. Trusts investing in debt and insurance are also in retreat after underperforming. Newcomers include trusts that invest in the space industry, shipping, farmland, digital infrastructure, battery storage and energy efficiency. ■

Property sectors

AIC SECTOR	NET ASSETS (£M)	MARKET CAP (£M)	MARKET CAP (£M) 2017
Property - UK Commercial	9,723	6,898	5,298
Property - UK Logistics	6,135	3,608	2,110
Property - UK Residential	2,979	2,174	1,944
Property - Europe	2,194	1,332	678
Property Securities	1,011	941	1,152
Property - UK Healthcare	1,167	983	n/a
Property - Debt	976	844	n/a
Property - Rest of World	213	100	364

Top 15

COMPANY NAME	TICKER	AIC SECTOR	MANAGEMENT GROUP
Tritax Big Box REIT	BBOX	Property - UK Logistics	Tritax Management
LXI REIT	LXI	Property - UK Commercial	LJ Capital
Supermarket Income REIT	SUPR	Property - UK Commercial	Atrato Capital
UK Commercial Property REIT	UKCM	Property - UK Commercial	abrdn
Tritax Eurobox	BOXE	Property - Europe	Tritax Management
Balanced Commercial Property	BCPT	Property - UK Commercial	Columbia Threadneedle
TR Property	TRY	Property Securities	Columbia Threadneedle
Home REIT	HOME	Property - UK Residential	Alvarium Home REIT Advisors
Urban Logistics REIT	SHED	Property - UK Logistics	Pacific Capital Partners
Civitas Social Housing	CSH	Property - UK Residential	Civitas Investment Management
PRS REIT	PRSR	Property - UK Residential	Sigma Capital
Warehouse REIT	WHR	Property - UK Logistics	Tilstone Partners
Target Healthcare REIT	THRL	Property - UK Healthcare	Target Fund Managers
Regional REIT	RGL	Property - UK Commercial	Toscafund Asset Management
Phoenix Spree Deutschland	PSDL	Property - Europe	QSix

Source: AIC/Morningstar, all figures to 30/09/22 unless otherwise stated

	NUMBER OF COMPANIES	% INDUSTRY NET ASSETS	5 YEAR MARKET CAP % GROWTH	AVERAGE GEARING %
	15	4.0%	30.2%	26.0%
	3	2.5%	71.0%	21.3%
	6	1.2%	11.9%	35.2%
	4	0.9%	96.3%	18.0%
	1	0.4%	-18.3%	15.2%
	2	0.5%	n/a	16.7%
	5	0.4%	n/a	3.6%
	2	0.1%	-72.6%	56.7%

% YIELD	% 5 YEAR DIVIDEND GROWTH	GEARING (%)	ONGOING CHARGE %	% 5YR SHARE PRICE TOTAL RETURN	% 5 YEAR NAV TOTAL RETURN	TOTAL ASSETS (£M)	NET ASSETS (£M)
4.9%	1.6%	27.44%	0.79%	16.9%	123.0%	5,853	4,508
5.1%		5.31%	1.00%	48.5%	73.3%	2,652	2,465
5.6%		26.11%		40.1%	57.8%	1,852	1,441
5.6%	-6.1%	10.59%	0.80%	-18.2%	50.8%	1,716	1,467
6.9%		7.78%				1,630	1,138
6.0%	-6.2%	15.50%	0.90%	-33.0%	27.2%	1,352	1,043
4.9%	11.2%	15.16%	0.58%	-3.4%	-2.8%	1,258	1,011
6.1%		9.31%	1.41%			1,165	919
5.9%	4.1%	11.32%		36.1%	110.0%	1,089	890
8.7%		38.96%		-23.9%	37.6%	1,030	679
4.3%		41.25%		15.2%	48.5%	993	637
5.9%		25.04%	1.20%	34.8%	127.2%	957	737
7.4%	1.5%	23.74%	1.55%	4.7%	48.2%	916	697
10.3%	-3.2%	56.66%	4.60%	-9.6%	37.6%	909	526
2.2%	3.6%	43.67%		-2.5%	82.9%	705	453

An important distinction in the property sector table is between trusts that invest directly in property (that is, buy, sell and lease out the bricks and mortar themselves) and those that invest primarily in the shares or debt of other listed property companies. The former by their nature are less liquid than the latter. Buildings such as offices, shops and factories can take many months to purchase and cannot be sold in a hurry, whereas shares in a property company can be bought and sold within minutes.

The two types of property investment trust therefore have very different characteristics as investments. TR Property is the last remaining example of a trust that invests almost exclusively in the shares of other property companies (in its case scattered across the whole of Europe). The trust's shares therefore trade very much like other types of share, rising and falling much more markedly from day to day than those of trusts which invest directly in their own property assets.

Until a few years ago most of the biggest trusts in the property sector were so-called generalist commercial property trusts, the likes of BMO Commercial Property and Standard Life Property Income, funds managed by the big fund management companies. They own a well diversified portfolio of assets in all three of the main property categories, shops, offices and industrial buildings. They have been supplanted in popularity more recently by a range of trusts that specialise in smaller, niche sectors of the market, such as social housing, doctors' surgeries and warehouses.

That trend can be seen in the table of the 15 largest property trusts. Tritax Big Box, which invests in the huge distribution warehouses used by Amazon and other retailers to move products around the country, only came to the market in 2013 but is now, through good performance and multiple issues of new shares, the single largest trust in the sector. Its sister company Tritax Eurobox did not exist until five years ago.

For some time many of these new-look property companies traded on premiums to net asset value, reflecting the appeal in a low interest rate environment of above average dividend yields and long term, often wholly or partially inflation-linked income streams. 2022 has seen a change in that respect. Aggressive moves by the Federal Reserve and other central banks to raise interest rates and head off rising inflation, combined with fears of a recession, prompted a sharp derating across nearly every property sub-sector.

For example the shares in Tritax Big Box have moved in just nine months from trading around NAV to a discount of more than 40%, more than offsetting a further gain in net asset value. Trusts operating in the social housing sector have similarly sold off, although this in part reflects regulatory concerns about the durability of their business models. Even the largest and most popular specialist trusts, such as LXI REIT and Supermarket Income REIT, have also derated suddenly.

The story across the generalist commercial property sector is slightly more nuanced. Many of these trusts have yet to recover fully from the pandemic in 2020, when all but one of the trusts in the mainstream commercial property group were forced to cut their dividends as lockdowns left many of their tenants struggling to pay their rents.

Since then they have slowly been rebuilding their income and NAVs have recovered, but discounts have remained wide by historical standards. The interest rate rises that have adversely affected specialist property trusts have also stopped the share price recovery of UK commerical property in its tracks. AEW REIT, for example, the only trust to have maintained its dividend through the pandemic, was one of the few to be trading at a premium in June 2022, but three months later was sitting on a discount of more than 25%. Many of the larger generalists had discounts more than double that.

While the outlook for commercial property remains clouded by the uncertain outlook for interest rates and economic activity, the effect of the derating in both generalist and specialist property trusts has been to produce more attractive dividend yields. The average yield in the generalist sector stood at 5.8% at the start of October 2022, 5.0% in specialist healthcare and more than 6.5% in the logistics and warehouse sector. ■

VCT sectors

AIC SECTOR	NET ASSETS (£M)	MARKET CAP (£M)
VCT Generalist	5,075	4,746
VCT AIM Quoted	862	797
VCT Generalist: Pre-qualifying	104	102
VCT Specialist: Environmental	93	83
VCT Specialist: Healthcare & Biotechnology	19	19
VCT Specialist: Environmental Pre Qualifying	18	19
VCT Specialist: Technology Pre Qualifying	18	17
VCT Specialist: Media, Leisure & Events	12	8
VCT Specialist: Technology	9	7
VCT AIM Quoted: Pre-qualifying	3	3

Top VCTs

COMPANY NAME	MANAGEMENT GROUP	AIC SECTOR	
Octopus Titan VCT	Octopus Investments	VCT Generalist	
Octopus Apollo VCT	Octopus Investments	VCT Generalist	
Unicorn AIM VCT	Unicorn Asset Management	VCT AIM Quoted	
Baronsmead Second Venture Trust	Gresham House	VCT Generalist	
Amati AIM VCT	Amati Global Investors	VCT AIM Quoted	
Baronsmead Venture Trust	Gresham House	VCT Generalist	
Pembroke VCT B shares	Oakley Capital Investments	VCT Generalist	
Foresight VCT	Foresight Group	VCT Generalist	
ProVen Growth and Income VCT	Beringea	VCT Generalist	
Hargreave Hale AIM VCT	Canaccord Genuity	VCT AIM Quoted	
ProVen VCT	Beringea	VCT Generalist	
British Smaller Companies VCT	YFM Private Equity	VCT Generalist	
Octopus AIM VCT	Octopus Investments	VCT AIM Quoted	
Foresight Enterprise VCT	Foresight Group	VCT Generalist	
Albion Technology & General VCT	Albion Capital Group	VCT Generalist	
Northern 3 VCT	Mercia Asset Management	VCT Generalist	
Northern 2 VCT	Mercia Asset Management	VCT Generalist	
Molten Ventures VCT	Molten Ventures	VCT Generalist	
Albion Enterprise VCT	Albion Capital Group	VCT Generalist	
Albion Development VCT	Albion Capital Group	VCT Generalist	
Kings Arms Yard VCT	Albion Capital Group	VCT Generalist	
British Smaller Companies VCT 2	YFM Private Equity	VCT Generalist	
The Income & Growth VCT	Gresham House	VCT Generalist	
Northern Venture Trust	Mercia Asset Management	VCT Generalist	

	MARKET CAP (£M) 2017		# COMPANIES	% VCT INDUSTRY NET ASSETS	5 YEAR MARKET CAP % GROWTH
	2,541		34	81.7%	86.8%
	596		7	13.9%	33.7%
	156		2	1.7%	-34.6%
	164		3	1.5%	-49.3%
	4		1	0.3%	397.9%
	6		-	0.3%	232.9%
	n/a		1	0.3%	n/a
	26		1	0.2%	-67.9%
	11		1	0.1%	-30.7%
	n/a		1	0.0%	n/a

	TOTAL ASSETS (£M)	MARKET CAP (£M)	NET ASSETS (£M)	NET ASSETS 2017 (£M)	LAUNCH DATE	YIELD %	% SPREAD
	1,196	1,137	1,196	419	28/12/2007	5.7%	2.3%
	303	285	303	155	17/10/2006	5.3%	4.1%
	225	207	225	175	11/04/2007	0.0%	0.0%
	224	213	224	185	30/01/2001	0.0%	0.0%
	221	196	221	55	22/02/2001	6.9%	0.0%
	203	194	203	158	03/04/1998	0.0%	0.0%
	198	180	198	26	01/04/2015	2.8%	0.0%
	196	170	196	140	02/11/1999	5.8%	3.9%
	178	171	178	112	31/05/2001	5.1%	0.0%
	175	167	175	66	29/10/2004	0.0%	0.0%
	173	159	173	103	10/04/2000	0.0%	0.0%
	158	146	158	84	04/04/1996	11.5%	0.0%
	136	128	136	119	17/03/2004	6.9%	0.0%
	135	125	135	67	16/03/1998	5.6%	4.8%
	127	121	127	69	16/01/2001	5.3%	0.0%
	117	111	117	74	17/12/2001	5.6%	0.0%
	115	109	115	77	21/04/1999	6.2%	0.0%
	114	103	114	37	18/05/1998	5.5%	3.7%
	114	108	114	51	05/04/2007	5.1%	0.0%
	114	107	114	47	27/01/1999	5.0%	0.0%
	112	99	112	59	04/04/1996	5.7%	0.0%
	110	101	110	58	12/04/2001	14.4%	0.0%
	110	100	110	61	15/11/2000	10.3%	0.0%
	108	103	108	74	01/11/1995	6.5%	0.0%

COMPANY NAME	MANAGEMENT GROUP	AIC SECTOR	
Thames Ventures VCT 1	Downing	VCT Generalist	
Mobeus Income & Growth VCT	Gresham House	VCT Generalist	
Octopus AIM VCT 2	Octopus Investments	VCT AIM Quoted	
Crown Place VCT	Albion Capital Group	VCT Generalist	
Maven Income and Growth VCT 4	Maven Capital Partners	VCT Generalist	
Mobeus Income & Growth 4 VCT	Gresham House	VCT Generalist	
Puma VCT 13	Puma Investments	VCT Generalist	
Mobeus Income & Growth 2 VCT	Gresham House	VCT Generalist	
Albion VCT	Albion Capital Group	VCT Generalist	
Maven Income and Growth VCT 5	Maven Capital Partners	VCT Generalist	
Maven Income and Growth VCT	Maven Capital Partners	VCT Generalist	
Maven Income and Growth VCT 3	Maven Capital Partners	VCT Generalist	

Source: AIC/Morningstar, all figures to 30/09/22 unless otherwise stated

Venture capital trusts are specialist investment companies that exist to support companies at an early stage of their development, in return for which shareholders in the VCTs are offered potentially attractive tax breaks. Most of these trusts will be investing in unlisted securities, although an exception are the AIM VCTs, which own mostly shares listed on the Alternative Investment Market.

By their nature, most VCTs are designed to be relatively small in size and are inherently riskier than conventional equity trusts. Some of the first VCTs to be launched have grown however to become substantial and mature businesses. Of these Octopus Titan is comfortably the largest and best known, having been early investors in at least four companies which have gone on to become so-called "unicorns", meaning companies which are valued at $1bn or more.

The trust was launched in 2007 and now itself has a market value of more than £1bn, while the Octopus management company has also subsequently followed up with a number of other VCTs and a renewable energy infrastructure trust. The AIC now breaks down VCTs into 10 different sub-sectors, reflecting the kind of business that they were set up to invest in. Many of these have yet to generate a five-year history.

Although the purpose behind giving tax breaks to investors in VCTs is to encourage the financing of early-stage businesses, many higher rate taxpayers in the first VCTs found the tax-free dividends a particularly strong attraction. The criteria VCTs must meet in order for their shareholders to qualify for the

TOTAL ASSETS (£M)	MARKET CAP (£M)	NET ASSETS (£M)	NET ASSETS 2017 (£M)	LAUNCH DATE	YIELD %	% SPREAD
108	103	108	90	30/04/1996	5.3%	3.5%
98	88	98	56	08/10/2004	14.0%	0.0%
96	90	96	79	25/01/2006	6.8%	0.0%
88	82	88	46	08/04/1998	0.0%	0.0%
87	82	87	30	17/02/2005	7.9%	3.2%
78	73	78	53	08/03/1999	11.2%	3.7%
75	72	75	n/a	02/07/2018	0.0%	10.9%
72	64	72	37	16/12/2005	0.0%	0.0%
64	59	64	63	01/04/1996	6.7%	0.0%
62	58	62	31	04/12/2000	6.4%	6.1%
60	56	60	32	06/04/2000	5.4%	0.0%
59	57	59	32	12/12/2001	8.8%	3.7%

tax benefits have subsequently been tightened to make sure that the majority of a VCT's investments are genuine higher risk, early-stage ventures. In September 2022 the Treasury announced that the tax regime for VCTs would continue after 2025, reflecting their significant contribution to funding technology and other businesses. Research by the AIC found that in the past five years VCTs have invested £1.7bn into 530 companies.

As the demand for VCTs shows however, the appeal of the tax-free dividends remains and several of the older trusts have also generated notable capital gains as well, as noted by Alex Davies in his annual review of the sector earlier in the *Handbook*. Inevitably, however, the value of some of the largest equity VCTs have been impacted by the decline in stock markets this year, particularly in the smaller companies sector and on AIM.

Looking at share price performance, Octopus Titan VCT is down around 10%. AIM VCTs are down by an average of 30% over the 12 months to 1 October 2022. Given that there is very little liquidity in VCT shares – most investors who own them tend to keep them indefinitely to avoid losing the tax breaks – the underlying value of these trusts may be lower than the reported numbers suggest.

The dividend yields on offer from the most mature VCTs have, however, increased as share prices have declined. In the generalist sector the average dividend yield is now more than 8.0%, although there is no guarantee that those levels of dividend will be sustained and shareholders need to be wary about the risks of venture capital and early-stage companies if we enter a recession. ∎

Largest management groups

MANAGEMENT GROUP	NUMBER OF COMPANIES	TOTAL ASSETS (£M)	NET ASSETS (£M)	MARKET CAP (£M)	AVG MARKET CAP (£M)	% TOTAL ASSETS 2022
Baillie Gifford	13	23,348	20,380	18,818	1,457	9.0%
3i Group	1	14,659	13,684	10,638	10,638	5.5%
J.P. Morgan Asset Management	20	12,093	10,990	9,970	453	4.5%
abrdn	22	11,810	10,599	8,359	380	4.4%
Columbia Threadneedle	10	10,486	9,105	8,083	815	4.0%
Pershing Square Capital Management	1	10,058	7,933	5,225	5,835	3.3%
Tritax Management	2	7,344	5,506	3,050	1,561	2.8%
Janus Henderson Investors	12	6,916	6,303	5,922	493	2.6%
InfraRed Capital Partners	2	6,649	6,649	6,436	3,218	2.5%
Greencoat Capital	2	5,817	4,666	4,650	2,406	2.2%
Fidelity	6	5,348	4,546	4,069	678	2.0%
Frostrow Capital	5	5,253	5,107	4,747	950	2.0%
RIT Capital Partners	1	4,364	3,944	3,252	3,253	1.6%
BlackRock Investment Management (UK)	9	4,067	3,578	3,311	368	1.5%
Goldman Sachs Asset Management, L.P.	1	3,976	3,976	2,117	2,118	1.5%
Polar Capital Holdings	3	3,818	3,673	3,315	1,105	1.4%
Schroder Investment Management	9	3,296	3,095	2,721	302	1.2%
HarbourVest Advisers L.P.	1	3,253	3,253	1,661	1,661	1.2%
Willis Towers Watson	1	3,078	2,827	2,707	2,708	1.2%
Pantheon Ventures	2	3,020	3,020	1,752	876	1.1%
Amber Infrastructure Group	1	2,971	2,971	2,901	2,901	1.1%
3i Investments	1	2,888	2,657	2,710	2,710	1.1%
Caledonia Investments	1	2,781	2,781	1,727	1,727	1.0%
Fundsmith	2	2,678	2,678	2,400	1,200	1.0%
Gresham House	12	2,309	2,123	2,167	181	0.9%
Tetragon Financial Management	1	2,303	2,303	756	843	1.0%
Foresight Group	8	2,293	2,293	2,172	272	0.9%
Allianz Global Investors	3	2,287	2,169	1,993	664	0.9%
Troy Asset Management	3	2,249	2,227	2,229	743	0.8%
Franklin Templeton Investments	1	2,022	1,872	1,638	1,638	0.8%

Source: AIC/Morningstar, all figures to 30/09/22 unless otherwise stated

TOTAL ASSETS 2017 (£M)	% TOTAL ASSETS 2017
10,126	5.9%
6,107	3.6%
11,251	6.6%
7,404	4.3%
9,068	5.3%
3,004	1.8%
2,160	1.3%
6,620	3.9%
3,560	2.1%
1,136	0.7%
4,183	2.4%
3,401	2.0%
3,212	1.9%
3,375	2.0%
-	-
2,002	1.2%
2,843	1.7%
1,188	0.7%
2,906	1.7%
1,404	0.8%
1,906	1.1%
1,724	1.0%
1,826	1.1%
278	0.2%
110	0.1%
1,439	0.8%
708	0.4%
1,397	0.8%
229	0.1%
2,457	1.4%

The management groups with the most trust mandates are listed here. The trust sector is a competitive one, in which no management group has a dominant position. There has, however, been some notable consolidation in the last few years. The 20 largest groups manage 60% of total industry assets, up from 47% five years ago, but still only six firms out of nearly 380 in total manage more than 10 trusts.

In 2018 Baillie Gifford, a private partnership based in Edinburgh, became the largest player in the investment trust sector for the first time, overtaking 3i and J.P. Morgan. After an exceptional year of performance in 2020–21, its style of investing has fallen out of favour in 2022. The total market value of its 13 trusts has fallen by a third, a dramatic change in fortunes. With notable exceptions, such as 3i, InfraRed Capital Partners and Schroders, most other management groups have seen the value of their investment trusts decline as well.

BMO Global Asset Management drops out of the list after selling its investment trust business to Columbia Threadneedle. Aberdeen Standard Investments (now rebranded as abrdn) has the largest number of trusts, slightly ahead of J.P. Morgan. The biggest firms typically launch and market their own trusts, as well as providing portfolio management and administrative functions, often centralising them. Smaller firms, by contrast, especially those managing specialist trusts, may only have one or more funds that they look after and will often sub-contract more services. ■

Vintage investment trusts

COMPANY NAME	AIC SECTOR	LAUNCH DATE	MARKET CAP (£M)	NET ASSETS (£M)
F&C Investment Trust	Global	19/03/1868	4,666	4,778
Alliance Trust	Global	21/04/1888	2,708	2,854
Investment Company	Flexible Investment	01/01/1868	13	16
Dunedin Income Growth	UK Equity Income	01/02/1873	391	395
Scottish American	Global Equity Income	31/03/1873	797	877
JPMorgan American	North America	18/06/1881	1,324	1,367
Mercantile	UK All Companies	08/12/1884	1,304	1,521
JPMorgan Global Growth & Income	Global Equity Income	21/04/1887	1,235	1,249
Henderson Smaller Companies	UK Smaller Companies	16/12/1887	530	616
Bankers	Global	13/04/1888	1,245	1,342
Global Smaller Companies Trust	Global Smaller Companies	15/02/1889	685	836
Merchants	UK Equity Income	16/02/1889	683	675
Edinburgh Investment	UK Equity Income	01/03/1889	936	1,046
AVI Global	Global	01/07/1889	880	979
Law Debenture Corporation	UK Equity Income	12/12/1889	854	890
City of London	UK Equity Income	01/01/1891	1,756	1,709
Aberdeen Diversified Income & Growth	Flexible Investment	05/01/1898	277	356
TR Property	Property Securities	05/05/1905	941	1,011
BlackRock Smaller Companies	UK Smaller Companies	02/05/1906	595	694
Baillie Gifford China Growth	China / Greater China	24/01/1907	156	177
Murray International	Global Equity Income	18/12/1907	1,465	1,548
Witan	Global	17/02/1909	1,461	1,596
Scottish Mortgage	Global	17/03/1909	11,173	12,741
Hansa Investment Company (A share)	Flexible Investment	01/01/1912	138	237

TICKER	YIELD %	% SPREAD	1YR AVG DISCOUNT / PREMIUM %	ONGOING CHARGE %	ONGOING CHARGE AS AT DATE
FCIT	1.5%	0.3%	-8.7%	0.54%	31/12/2021
ATST	2.6%	0.1%	-6.2%	0.60%	31/12/2021
INV	0.7%	0.0%	-12.3%	2.17%	30/06/2022
DIG	4.9%	0.8%	-0.6%	0.56%	31/01/2022
SAIN	2.9%	0.9%	-0.9%	0.62%	31/12/2021
JAM	1.0%	0.7%	-2.5%	0.38%	31/12/2021
MRC	4.2%	0.6%	-12.1%	0.45%	31/01/2022
JGGI	4.2%	0.4%	1.5%	0.53%	30/06/2021
HSL	3.4%	0.1%	-12.1%	0.42%	31/05/2022
BNKR	2.3%	0.8%	-4.9%	0.48%	31/10/2021
GSCT	1.5%	0.8%	-10.7%	0.75%	30/04/2022
MRCH	5.5%	0.9%	0.7%	0.55%	31/01/2022
EDIN	4.5%	0.5%	-7.9%	0.52%	31/03/2022
AGT	1.8%	0.1%	-9.1%	0.83%	30/09/2021
LWDB	4.3%	0.7%	0.6%	0.50%	31/12/2021
CTY	5.3%	0.4%	1.1%	0.37%	30/06/2022
ADIG	6.2%	2.7%	-17.1%	0.62%	30/09/2021
TRY	4.9%	31.5%	-3.7%	0.58%	31/03/2022
BRSC	2.9%	1.0%	-10.6%	0.70%	28/02/2022
BGCG	2.8%	0.4%	-5.0%	0.72%	31/01/2022
MYI	4.7%	0.2%	-4.8%	0.57%	31/12/2021
WTAN	2.6%	1.2%	-7.9%	0.71%	31/12/2021
SMT	0.5%	0.0%	-3.6%	0.32%	31/03/2022
HANA	1.8%	5.2%	-36.7%	1.10%	31/03/2022

COMPANY NAME	AIC SECTOR	LAUNCH DATE	MARKET CAP (£M)	NET ASSETS (£M)
Hansa Investment Company (Ord)	Flexible Investment	01/01/1912	73	119
Murray Income	UK Equity Income	07/06/1923	866	954
Finsbury Growth & Income	UK Equity Income	15/01/1926	1,729	1,811
Temple Bar	UK Equity Income	24/06/1926	641	677
Brunner	Global	01/01/1927	400	456
JPMorgan Japanese	Japan	02/08/1927	678	733
Monks	Global	06/02/1929	2,126	2,338
JPMorgan European Growth & Income	Europe	15/03/1929	326	381
Shires Income	UK Equity Income	31/03/1929	71	74
Canadian General Investments Unit	North America	15/01/1930	427	601
Henderson Far East Income	Asia Pacific Equity Income	30/05/1930	409	398
3i Group	Private Equity	01/04/1945	10,638	13,684
Henderson European Focus	Europe	01/01/1947	270	314
Keystone Positive Change	Global	19/11/1954	119	138
Caledonia	Flexible Investment	18/07/1960	1,727	2,754

Source: AIC/Morningstar, all figures to 30/09/22 unless otherwise stated

The first investment trust, F&C (FCIT), was formed in 1868 and continues in existence today. It celebrated its 150th anniversary in 2018. A number of other investment companies have also been around for many years. Seventeen can trace their histories back to the 19th century. This is a list of some of the oldest vintage trusts which are still in existence, although their names are rarely the same today as they were when launched.

A number of these trusts were started by wealthy families looking to invest their fortunes in a tax-efficient manner, but have since expanded to include outside investors as well. The first Scottish investment trust, Dunedin Income Growth (DIG), for example, was founded to provide a home for the savings of wealthy textile merchants in Dundee. Caledonia (CLDN) was founded by the Cayzer shipping dynasty and Brunner by one of the families whose chemical businesses combined to form ICI in 1926.

TICKER	YIELD %	% SPREAD	1YR AVG DISCOUNT / PREMIUM %	ONGOING CHARGE %	ONGOING CHARGE AS AT DATE
HAN	1.8%	6.6%	-36.4%	1.10%	31/03/2022
MUT	4.8%	0.3%	-6.4%	0.46%	30/06/2021
FGT	2.3%	1.4%	-5.2%	0.62%	30/09/2021
TMPL	4.1%	0.7%	-5.8%	0.48%	31/12/2021
BUT	2.3%	1.1%	-10.7%	0.63%	30/11/2021
JFJ	1.2%	1.1%	-5.7%	0.61%	30/09/2021
MNKS	0.2%	0.1%	-6.1%	0.40%	30/04/2022
JEGI	5.3%	5.1%	-11.8%	0.89%	31/03/2022
SHRS	6.0%	4.8%	-3.0%	0.98%	31/03/2022
CGI	3.1%	3.8%	-30.3%	1.37%	31/12/2021
HFEL	9.0%	0.8%	0.7%	1.09%	31/08/2021
III	4.3%	0.2%	2.0%	0.00%	00/01/1900
HEFT	2.6%	0.8%	-11.6%	0.80%	30/09/2021
KPC	5.8%	1.7%	-8.1%	0.51%	30/09/2021
CLDN	2.1%	1.3%	-25.1%	0.84%	31/03/2022

There is no obvious correlation between age and size or quality of trust, although the mere fact of having survived for so long indicates that a trust has at least successfully established a niche in the market. The wide range of average discounts illustrates the disparity in their liquidity, performance and popularity. Trusts with a founding family often take on third-party investors over time, surrendering their control in return for a broader asset base, but a long history is no guarantee that the trust will survive without new management.

A number of trusts have changed investment manager in recent years. In 2020 four of these trusts: Witan Pacific (Now BGCG), Edinburgh Investment Trust (EDIN), Temple Bar (TMPL) and Perpetual Income and Growth (PLI) moved from one management firm to another. Keystone (now KPC) did the same in 2021. The Scottish Investment Trust (SCIT) was absorbed into JPMorgan Global Growth & Income in 2022 and disappears from this list. ∎

Long-serving managers

COMPANY NAME	TICKER	AIC SECTOR	
Capital Gearing	CGT	Flexible Investment	
Lowland	LWI	UK Equity Income	
City of London	CTY	UK Equity Income	
Herald	HRI	Global Smaller Companies	
JPMorgan Emerging Markets	JMG	Global Emerging Markets	
abrdn Asia Focus	AAS	Asia Pacific Smaller Companies	
British & American	BAF	UK Equity Income	
Atlantis Japan Growth	AJG	Japanese Smaller Companies	
Atlantis Japan Growth	AJG	Japanese Smaller Companies	
CT UK Capital & Income	CTUK	UK Equity Income	
JPMorgan UK Smaller Companies	JMI	UK Smaller Companies	
JPMorgan European Discovery	JEDT	European Smaller Companies	
Chelverton UK Dividend	SDV	UK Equity Income	
CT Private Equity	CTPE	Private Equity	
BlackRock World Mining	BRWM	Commodities & Natural Resources	
Independent Investment Trust	IIT	UK All Companies	
European Opportunities	EOT	Europe	
Finsbury Growth & Income	FGT	UK Equity Income	
HgCapital	HGT	Private Equity	
Lindsell Train	LTI	Global	
International Biotechnology	IBT	Biotechnology & Healthcare	
Aberforth Smaller Companies	ASL	UK Smaller Companies	
JPMorgan Russian Securities	JRS	Country Specialist	
Impax Environmental Markets	IEM	Environmental	
Impax Environmental Markets	IEM	Environmental	
Henderson Smaller Companies	HSL	UK Smaller Companies	
Schroder UK Mid Cap	SCP	UK All Companies	
Artemis Alpha Trust	ATS	UK All Companies	
Law Debenture Corporation	LWDB	UK Equity Income	
Bankers	BNKR	Global	
abrdn UK Smaller Companies Growth	AUSC	UK Smaller Companies	
Global Opportunities	GOT	Global	
MIGO Opportunities	MIGO	Flexible Investment	
Murray International	MYI	Global Equity Income	
Schroder Real Estate	SREI	Property - UK Commercial	
BlackRock Greater Europe	BRGE	Europe	
Aberdeen New India	ANII	India	
Balanced Commercial Property	BCPT	Property - UK Commercial	
Biotech Growth	BIOG	Biotechnology & Healthcare	
JPEL Private Equity	JPEL	Private Equity	
JPEL Private Equity	JPEL	Private Equity	
JPMorgan China Growth & Income	JCGI	China / Greater China	
Global Smaller Companies Trust	GSCT	Global Smaller Companies	
JPMorgan European Growth & Income	JEGI	Europe	

MANAGER NAME	EFFECTIVE	YEARS IN SERVICE	10 YEAR NAV TOTAL RETURN % TO END JUN 22
Peter Spiller	05/04/1982	40 years 6 months	73.97
James H Henderson	01/01/1990	32 years 9 months	67.83
Job Curtis	01/07/1991	31 years 3 months	92.11
Katie Potts	16/02/1994	28 years 7 months	220.40
Austin Forey	01/06/1994	28 years 4 months	111.35
Hugh Young	19/10/1995	26 years 11 months	108.82
Jonathan Woolf	03/01/1996	26 years 9 months	133.43
Edwin C Merner	10/05/1996	26 years 4 months	152.56
Taeko Setaishi	10/05/1996	26 years 4 months	152.56
Julian Cane	01/03/1997	25 years 7 months	81.24
Georgina Brittain	02/01/1998	24 years 9 months	160.51
Francesco Conte	01/11/1998	23 years 11 months	200.33
David Horner	12/05/1999	23 years 4 months	120.07
Hamish Mair	01/02/2000	22 years 8 months	287.39
Evy Hambro	01/09/2000	22 years 1 months	49.38
Maxwell Ward	18/10/2000	21 years 11 months	123.81
Alexander Darwall	22/11/2000	21 years 10 months	141.67
Nick Train	11/12/2000	21 years 9 months	182.28
Nic Humphries	01/01/2001	21 years 9 months	406.95
Nick Train	22/01/2001	21 years 8 months	461.02
Kate Bingham	01/05/2001	21 years 5 months	271.40
Euan R MacDonald	14/05/2001	21 years 4 months	110.01
Oleg Biryulyov	09/01/2002	20 years 8 months	-88.00
Bruce Jenkyn-Jones	22/02/2002	20 years 7 months	266.79
Jon Forster	22/02/2002	20 years 7 months	266.79
Neil Hermon	01/11/2002	19 years 11 months	139.85
Andy Brough	30/04/2003	19 years 5 months	104.11
John Dodd	01/06/2003	19 years 4 months	9.03
James H Henderson	01/06/2003	19 years 4 months	133.65
Alex Crooke	01/07/2003	19 years 3 months	177.38
Harry Nimmo	01/09/2003	19 years 1 months	132.70
Sandy Nairn	15/12/2003	18 years 9 months	142.11
Nick Greenwood	06/04/2004	18 years 6 months	133.96
Bruce Stout	16/06/2004	18 years 3 months	104.63
Nick Montgomery	15/07/2004	18 years 2 months	154.50
Sam Vecht	20/09/2004	18 years 0 months	179.71
Kristy Fong	09/12/2004	17 years 9 months	193.05
Richard Kirby	17/03/2005	17 years 6 months	132.17
Geoffrey Hsu	19/05/2005	17 years 4 months	256.44
Troy Duncan	30/06/2005	17 years 3 months	58.56
Gregory Getschow	30/06/2005	17 years 3 months	58.56
Howard Wang	01/07/2005	17 years 3 months	175.04
Peter Ewins	31/07/2005	17 years 2 months	181.12
Alexander Fitzalan Howard	02/08/2005	17 years 2 months	151.15

COMPANY NAME	TICKER	AIC SECTOR	
Chelverton UK Dividend	SDV	UK Equity Income	
JPMorgan Indian	JII	India	
JPMorgan China Growth & Income	JCGI	China / Greater China	
JPMorgan Elect Managed Growth	JPE	Global	
JPMorgan Elect Managed Growth	JPE	Global	
Marwyn Value Investors	MVI	UK Smaller Companies	
Marwyn Value Investors	MVI	UK Smaller Companies	
Polar Capital Technology	PCT	Technology & Media	
Merchants	MRCH	UK Equity Income	
Macau Property Opportunities	MPO	Property - Rest of World	
Middlefield Canadian Income Trust	MCT	North America	
abrdn Property Income	API	Property - UK Commercial	
Murray Income	MUT	UK Equity Income	
International Biotechnology	IBT	Biotechnology & Healthcare	
abrdn Japan	AJIT	Japan	
Volta Finance	VTA	Debt - Structured Finance	
Henderson Opportunities	HOT	UK All Companies	
Henderson Far East Income	HFEL	Asia Pacific Equity Income	
Allianz Technology	ATT	Technology & Media	
UIL	UTL	Flexible Investment	
UIL	UTL	Flexible Investment	
Real Estate Credit Investments	RECI	Property - Debt	
Henderson Diversified Income	HDIV	Debt - Loans & Bonds	
Henderson Diversified Income	HDIV	Debt - Loans & Bonds	

Source: AIC/Morningstar, all figures to 30/09/22 unless otherwise stated

Some individual trusts are also notable for having long-serving managers who have been running the trust's investments for many years. In many cases the managers also have significant personal shareholdings in the trust. This is typically regarded as a good omen for other shareholders, since it should establish a close alignment of interest between the manager and the shareholders.

Because fund management is an extremely well-paid profession, the fact that a manager continues to manage a trust after many years in harness can be interpreted also as demonstrating exceptional commitment to the business. While some successful fund managers retire early to do other things, those who remain in post for decades are typically the enthusiasts who cannot think of anything more interesting or rewarding to do (look at Warren Buffett, still running Berkshire Hathaway in his 90s).

MANAGER NAME	EFFECTIVE	YEARS IN SERVICE	10 YEAR NAV TOTAL RETURN % TO END JUN 22
David Taylor	01/12/2005	16 years 10 months	120.07
Rajendra Nair	01/01/2006	16 years 9 months	147.75
Shumin Huang	02/01/2006	16 years 9 months	175.04
Katy Thorneycroft	01/02/2006	16 years 8 months	164.54
Katy Thorneycroft	01/02/2006	16 years 8 months	164.54
James Corsellis	22/02/2006	16 years 7 months	11.39
Mark Watts	22/02/2006	16 years 7 months	11.39
Ben Rogoff	01/05/2006	16 years 5 months	443.83
Simon Gergel	01/06/2006	16 years 4 months	117.31
Martin Tacon	05/06/2006	16 years 4 months	-22.17
Dean Orrico	06/07/2006	16 years 3 months	100.86
Jason Baggaley	13/09/2006	16 years 0 months	226.74
Charles Luke	03/10/2006	16 years 0 months	87.36
Ailsa Craig	01/11/2006	15 years 11 months	271.40
Chern-Yeh Kwok	10/11/2006	15 years 10 months	106.05
Alexandre Martin-Min	15/12/2006	15 years 9 months	131.76
James H Henderson	24/01/2007	15 years 8 months	128.03
Michael Kerley	02/02/2007	15 years 8 months	60.73
Walter Price	01/05/2007	15 years 5 months	606.17
Charles Jillings	20/06/2007	15 years 3 months	39.47
Duncan Saville	20/06/2007	15 years 3 months	39.47
Richard Lang	25/06/2007	15 years 3 months	135.03
John Pattullo	18/07/2007	15 years 2 months	41.51
Jenna Barnard	18/07/2007	15 years 2 months	41.51

Against that, sometimes situations arise where managers have such a large personal shareholding in a trust that they effectively control the running of the company, and as a result may not always make the interests of other shareholders as high a priority as they should. They are effectively being paid to look after their own money, often with a longer-term perspective that makes them worry less about short-term performance or the persistence of a wide discount.

Experience is a vital quality when it comes to choosing someone to manage your money, and many of these long-serving managers have strong performance records. From those included in this list a year ago, notable names who have announced retirements include James Anderson at Scottish Mortgage (SMT), Simon Knott at Rights and Issues (taken over by Jupiter) and Harry Nimmo at abrdn UK Smaller Companies. The longest serving manager still managing a trust now remains Peter Spiller at Capital Gearing Trust (CGT), who in 2022 celebrated 40 years of running the portfolio. ∎

Dividend heroes

COMPANY	AIC SECTOR	NUMBER OF CONSECUTIVE YEARS DIVIDEND INCREASED
City of London Investment Trust	UK Equity Income	56
Bankers Investment Trust	Global	55
Alliance Trust	Global	55
Caledonia Investments	Flexible Investment	55
Global Smaller Companies	Global Smaller Companies	52
F&C Investment Trust	Global	51
Brunner Investment Trust	Global	50
JPMorgan Claverhouse Investment Trust	UK Equity Income	49
Murray Income	UK Equity Income	49
Scottish American	Global Equity Income	48
Witan Investment Trust	Global	47
Merchants Trust	UK Equity Income	40
Scottish Mortgage Investment Trust	Global	40
Value and Indexed Property Income	Property - UK Commercial	35
CT UK Capital & Income	UK Equity Income	28
Schroder Income Growth	UK Equity Income	27
abrdn Equity Income	UK Equity Income	21

Source: AIC/Morningstar. Correct as at 30/09/2022

The AIC hit on an excellent marketing idea when it introduced its list of dividend heroes in 2009. To qualify for the list an investment trust has to have increased its annual dividend payout every year for at least 20 years. That is possible because the investment trust structure allows the boards of trusts to hold back up to 15% of the portfolio income each year as revenue reserves (effectively 'rainy day' money).

This policy means that the trust can usually call on its reserves during recessions (or indeed pandemics) to continue to pay a dividend. Only during really difficult periods will they be forced to cut the dividend below the previous year's figure. Qualifying as a dividend hero has proved particularly popular with shareholders since the global financial crisis and the subsequent decade of very low interest rates and minimal yields from cash and bonds.

Dividend hero status is not a guarantee that the income from a trust will persist indefinitely. Three trusts that featured on the list before the pandemic had to take an axe to their dividends and subsequently lost their place in the rankings. This year the Scottish Investment Trust fell out of the list following its absorption into the JPMorgan Global Growth & Income Trust.

It is also fair to say that some years trusts are only able to preserve their place on the list by making the tiniest of annual increases in the dividend. You occasionally also hear mutterings from fund managers that the need to preserve dividend hero status at almost any cost can have an inhibiting effect on their ability to maximise returns. Prioritising income obligations is not always optimal from a total return or taxation perspective.

Nevertheless, for many shareholders that does not seem to be much of a concern. Trusts such as the City of London, which heads the list, remain very popular despite not having the best long-term track record on other counts. As the table shows, 17 trusts can claim 20 or more years of consecutive dividend increases and 13 of them have been in that camp for 40 years or more.

Coming up behind them are another 28 trusts (see next page) which have between 10 and 19 years of consecutive dividend increases. One (Lowland) was in the original list but later demoted. You can be sure that not all of these will be able to maintain that feat for long enough to move up into the top tier, given the inevitability of another recession/bear market in due course.

As it stands, however, three more trusts will acquire Dividend Hero status in 2023. As at 30 September 2022, the average trailing 12-month yield on the 17 heroes was 3.5%, with a range from 7.2% (Value and Indexed Property) to 0.5% (Scottish Mortgage). What hero status does do very effectively is differentiates investment trusts from open-ended funds, which do not have the same dividend flexibility. ∎

Next generation dividend heroes

COMPANY	AIC SECTOR	NUMBER OF CONSECUTIVE YEARS DIVIDEND INCREASED
Athelney	UK Smaller Companies	19
BlackRock Smaller Companies	UK Smaller Companies	19
Henderson Smaller Companies	UK Smaller Companies	19
Artemis Alpha Trust	UK All Companies	18
Murray International	Global Equity Income	16
Henderson Far East Income	Asia Pacific Equity Income	15
BlackRock Greater Europe	Europe	15
Schroder Oriental Income	Asia Pacific Equity Income	15
CQS New City High Yield	Debt - Loans and Bonds	15
abrdn Asian Income	Asia Pacific Equity Income	13
International Public Partnerships	Infrastructure	13
Fidelity Special Values	UK All Companies	12
Lowland	UK Equity Income	12
Law Debenture Corporation	UK Equity Income	12
TR Property	Property Securities	12
Invesco Select Trust - Global Equity Income Shares	Global Equity Income	12
JPMorgan Elect Managed Income	UK Equity Income	12
Chelverton UK Dividend	UK Equity Income	11
Henderson Opportunities	UK All Companies	11
Dunedin Income Growth	UK Equity Income	11
Aberforth Smaller Companies	UK Smaller Companies	11
Fidelity European	Europe	11
North American Income	North America	11
Fidelity China Special Situations	China / Greater China	11
CT Global Managed Portfolio Income	Flexible Investment	11
Lindsell Train	Global	10
CT Private Equity	Private Equity	10
Mid Wynd International	Global	10

Source: AIC/Morningstar. Correct as at 30/09/2022

"QUALIFYING AS A DIVIDEND HERO HAS PROVED PARTICULARLY POPULAR WITH SHAREHOLDERS SINCE THE GLOBAL FINANCIAL CRISIS AND THE SUBSEQUENT DECADE OF VERY LOW INTEREST RATES AND MINIMAL YIELDS FROM CASH AND BONDS."

Largest/most liquid trusts

COMPANY NAME	AIC SECTOR	MANAGEMENT GROUP	SHARE TYPE	
Scottish Mortgage	Global	Baillie Gifford	Ordinary Share	
3i Group	Private Equity	3i Group	Ordinary Share	
Pershing Square Holdings	North America	Pershing Square Capital Management	Ordinary Share	
F&C Investment Trust	Global	Columbia Threadneedle	Ordinary Share	
Greencoat UK Wind	Renewable Energy Infrastructure	Greencoat Capital	Ordinary Share	
HICL Infrastructure	Infrastructure	InfraRed Capital Partners	Ordinary Share	
RIT Capital Partners	Flexible Investment	RIT Capital Partners	Ordinary Share	
Renewables Infrastructure Group	Renewable Energy Infrastructure	InfraRed Capital Partners	Ordinary Share	
International Public Partnerships	Infrastructure	Amber Infrastructure Group	Ordinary Share	
3i Infrastructure	Infrastructure	3i Investments	Ordinary Share	
Alliance Trust	Global	Willis Towers Watson	Ordinary Share	
Tritax Big Box REIT	Property – UK Logistics	Tritax Management	Ordinary Share	
Polar Capital Technology	Technology & Media	Polar Capital Holdings	Ordinary Share	
Worldwide Healthcare	Biotechnology & Healthcare	Frostrow Capital	Ordinary Share	
LXI REIT	Property – UK Commercial	LJ Capital	Ordinary Share	
Monks	Global	Baillie Gifford	Ordinary Share	

Source: AIC/Morningstar, data to 30/09/22

While a small minority of investment trusts are managed directly by the board of directors, the great majority delegate the management of their portfolios to specialist fund managers, employed on annual or multi-year management contracts with a mandate to meet the trust's investment objectives. Those objectives are set by the board of directors and need to be approved by shareholders before any significant changes can be made.

The investment trust with the greatest total assets, Scottish Mortgage (SMT), had an extraordinary year in 2020–21, making a return of more than 100% in 12 months, as the big technology stocks it has owned for years soared during the lockdown. At 30 September 2020 this one trust accounted for 12.5% of the industry total, compared to 7.5% a year earlier.

The 20 largest individual trusts on this measure accounted for just over 40% of total industry assets. In contrast, more than 100 trusts had less than £50m in assets, although this figure includes a large number of venture capital trusts, which are

TICKER	MARKET CAPITALISATION (M)	1MNTH DAILY AVG VALUE TRADED (M)	1YR DAILY AVG VALUE TRADED (M)	5YR DAILY AVG VALUE TRADED (M)	TRADED CURRENCY
SMT	11,173	23	35	25	GBX
III	10,638	22	26	22	GBX
PSH	5,835	2	2	3	USD
FCIT	4,666	13	4	3	GBX
UKW	3,488	9	7	4	GBX
HICL	3,283	9	6	5	GBX
RCP	3,253	4	4	3	GBX
TRIG	3,153	9	7	4	GBX
INPP	2,901	7	5	4	GBX
3IN	2,710	5	4	3	GBX
ATST	2,708	4	3	3	GBX
BBOX	2,538	15	16	10	GBX
PCT	2,476	5	5	4	GBX
WWH	2,134	4	4	3	GBX
LXI	2,126	10	7	2	GBX
MNKS	2,126	6	6	4	GBX

invariably much smaller on average. The largest trusts tend to have the best liquidity, meaning they are easier to buy and sell in size. The spread between bid and offer prices is typically well below 0.5%. Economies of scale also make it easier for the biggest trusts to accept reduced annual management fees, with Scottish Mortgage, boasting an OCF of just 0.36% again a prime example.

A majority of the largest trusts in the sector have been operating for many years, but newcomers can break in. Some of the largest newcomers, like Smithson (SSON) and Tritax Big Box REIT (BBOX), raised a lot of money but have dropped down the rankings this year.

At the same time there are regular departures from the investment trust universe, as funds either close down or return capital to shareholders, typically (though not invariably) as a result of indifferent performance, or where the trust has a predetermined wind-up date. Once again the diversity of the investment trust universe is well demonstrated in this table. ■

Best long-term performers

10 years

COMPANY NAME	TICKER	AIC SECTOR	MANAGEMENT GROUP	
3i Group	III	Private Equity	3i Group	
Allianz Technology	ATT	Technology & Media	Allianz Global Investors	
Scottish Mortgage	SMT	Global	Baillie Gifford	
CATCo Reinsurance Opportunities	CAT	Insurance & Reinsurance Strategies	Markel CATCo Investment Management	
VinaCapital Vietnam Opportunity	VOF	Country Specialist	VinaCapital Investment Management	
NB Private Equity Partners	NBPE	Private Equity	NB Alternatives Advisers	
Polar Capital Technology	PCT	Technology & Media	Polar Capital Holdings	
VietNam Holding	VNH	Country Specialist	Dynam Capital	
HarbourVest Global Private Equity	HVPE	Private Equity	HarbourVest Advisers L.P.	
HgCapital	HGT	Private Equity	Hg	
Oryx International Growth	OIG	UK Smaller Companies	Harwood Capital	
Impax Environmental Markets	IEM	Environmental	Impax Asset Management	
Mobeus Income & Growth 2 VCT	MIG	VCT Generalist	Gresham House	
Worldwide Healthcare	WWH	Biotechnology & Healthcare	Frostrow Capital	
Lindsell Train	LTI	Global	Lindsell Train	
JPMorgan American	JAM	North America	J.P. Morgan Asset Management	
Mobeus Income & Growth VCT	MIX	VCT Generalist	Gresham House	
Baillie Gifford Shin Nippon	BGS	Japanese Smaller Companies	Baillie Gifford	
Pacific Horizon	PHI	Asia Pacific	Baillie Gifford	
International Biotechnology	IBT	Biotechnology & Healthcare	SV Health Managers	
European Smaller Companies	ESCT	European Smaller Companies	Janus Henderson Investors	
CT Private Equity	CTPE	Private Equity	Columbia Threadneedle	
Baillie Gifford Japan	BGFD	Japan	Baillie Gifford	
JPMorgan US Smaller Companies	JUSC	North American Smaller Companies	J.P. Morgan Asset Management	
JPMorgan Global Growth & Income	JGGI	Global Equity Income	J.P. Morgan Asset Management	
India Capital Growth	IGC	India	Ocean Dial Asset Management	
Premier Miton Global Renewables	PMGR	Infrastructure Securities	Premier Miton	

£100 INITIAL INVESTMENT (SHARE PRICE TOTAL RETURN)	ANNUALISED %	£100 INITIAL INVESTMENT (NAV TOTAL RETURN)	ANNUALISED %	RANK LAST YEAR
614.0	21.7	702.8	23.2	2
601.9	21.5	607.2	21.6	3
512.7	19.9	530.3	20.2	1
446.9	18.5	432.0	18.2	New
433.5	18.2	340.2	16.0	21
411.9	17.7	359.9	16.5	28
386.6	17.1	441.2	18.4	6
381.2	17.0	379.0	17.0	9
355.2	16.4	474.9	19.1	27
348.4	16.2	407.0	17.6	29
341.2	16.0	356.2	16.4	4
330.9	15.7	271.5	14.0	13
325.2	15.6	190.6	11.3	26
323.1	15.5	326.5	15.6	19
318.9	15.4	465.2	18.9	5
315.2	15.3	341.8	16.0	33
314.8	15.3	251.1	13.4	New
305.8	15.0	320.0	15.4	7
303.6	15.0	279.7	14.3	11
294.7	14.7	271.6	14.0	14
283.3	14.4	265.0	13.8	18
275.5	14.2	287.4	14.5	New
274.1	14.1	261.5	13.7	25
272.1	14.0	279.5	14.3	23
262.9	13.8	242.7	13.1	New
260.3	13.7	189.3	11.2	New
258.9	13.6	203.1	11.7	New

COMPANY NAME	TICKER	AIC SECTOR	MANAGEMENT GROUP	
Fidelity China Special Situations	FCSS	China/Greater China	Fidelity	
F&C Investment Trust	FCIT	Global	Columbia Threadneedle	
abrdn Private Equity Opportunities	APEO	Private Equity	abrdn	
The Income & Growth VCT	IGV	VCT Generalist	Gresham House	
Biotech Growth	BIOG	Biotechnology & Healthcare	Frostrow Capital	
Oakley Capital Investments	OCI	Private Equity	Oakley Capital Investments	
Rights & Issues	RIII	UK Smaller Companies	Jupiter Unit Trust Managers	
3i Infrastructure	3IN	Infrastructure	3i Investments	
Monks	MNKS	Global	Baillie Gifford	
Mobeus Income & Growth 4 VCT	MIG4	VCT Generalist	Gresham House	
North Atlantic Smaller Companies	NAS	Global Smaller Companies	Harwood Capital	
Maven Income and Growth VCT 5	MIG5	VCT Generalist	Maven Capital Partners	
Edinburgh Worldwide	EWI	Global Smaller Companies	Baillie Gifford	

Although the turnover in surviving trusts from one year to the next is high, a good number of trusts have survived long enough to post 20- and 30-year track records. These tables list the best performing trusts over all these periods, as well as the past 10 years, measured as both the value of £100 invested and as a compound annualised rate of return, with dividends reinvested.

Of around 380 trusts whose data is recorded by the AIC, around a third have been launched in the last 10 years. Another third have compiled 20-year records and only a fifth have survived long enough to have a 30-year record. There is a Darwinian process at work in the sector, with the weakest trusts eventually being either liquidated, taken over and renamed, or absorbed into another investment trust.

Until this year, the average annualised rate of return achieved by the top trusts that have survived this long was higher over 10 years than over 20 or 30 years. Because of the magical effect of compounding, any trust that can grow at 10% every year will at least double in value every seven years and quadruple every 14. A 20% per annum compounder doubles its value in less than four years. The table toppers over 20 and 30 years are therefore the cream of the crop.

£100 INITIAL INVESTMENT (SHARE PRICE TOTAL RETURN)	ANNUALISED %	£100 INITIAL INVESTMENT (NAV TOTAL RETURN)	ANNUALISED %	RANK LAST YEAR
252.1	13.4	251.3	13.4	New
246.3	13.2	215.4	12.2	New
246.2	13.2	314.8	15.3	30
236.7	12.9	182.1	10.9	38
235.8	12.9	256.8	13.6	8
234.1	12.8	297.6	14.8	New
233.5	12.8	202.7	11.7	15
228.1	12.6	241.3	13.1	New
227.6	12.6	207.1	11.9	New
227.0	12.6	179.8	10.8	New
226.9	12.6	249.1	13.3	New
223.6	12.5	112.8	7.8	New
223.1	12.4	215.3	12.2	16

The longer the period, however, the harder it is to sustain a double-digit rate of return. The 30-year period for example includes two significant bear markets (2000–03 and 2007–09). The sell-off in equity markets in 2022 has brought the ten-year performance figures back down towards those of longer periods. It could be bringing to an end the long and impressive bull market which began in 2009 after the global financial crisis.

The 10th best performing trust over 10 years last year, BlackRock Throgmorton, had an annualised rate of return of 21.1%, 2.5% more than Edinburgh Worldwide, the tenth ranked trust in the 2021 edition. This year the trust with the tenth best performance record, HG Capital, has an annualised rate of return of just 16%. Some of the names at the top of the table have seen their 10-year compound rate of growth fall sharply: Scottish Mortgage (down by 8% per annum) and Allianz Technology are prime examples.

The top spot this year goes to 3i Group, the private equity trust whose continued growth reflects the extraordinary success of the Dutch retailer Action, its largest single holding. Private equity is also well represented and it is interesting to see the presence of two VCTs in the top 20 as well, helped by narrower reported discounts. Look out for more changes next year, however. ■

20 years

COMPANY NAME	TICKER	AIC SECTOR	
HgCapital	HGT	Private Equity	
Scottish Mortgage	SMT	Global	
Allianz Technology	ATT	Technology & Media	
Biotech Growth	BIOG	Biotechnology & Healthcare	
Polar Capital Technology	PCT	Technology & Media	
Pacific Horizon	PHI	Asia Pacific	
abrdn Asia Focus	AAS	Asia Pacific Smaller Companies	
JPMorgan Indian	JII	India	
Lindsell Train	LTI	Global	
International Biotechnology	IBT	Biotechnology & Healthcare	
BlackRock Smaller Companies	BRSC	UK Smaller Companies	
abrdn UK Smaller Companies Growth	AUSC	UK Smaller Companies	
European Smaller Companies	ESCT	European Smaller Companies	
JPMorgan European Discovery	JEDT	European Smaller Companies	
Montanaro European Smaller Companies	MTE	European Smaller Companies	
BlackRock Throgmorton Trust	THRG	UK Smaller Companies	
Scottish Oriental Smaller Companies	SST	Asia Pacific Smaller Companies	
Worldwide Healthcare	WWH	Biotechnology & Healthcare	
JPMorgan Emerging Markets	JMG	Global Emerging Markets	
Herald	HRI	Global Smaller Companies	
European Opportunities	EOT	Europe	
European Assets	EAT	European Smaller Companies	
British Smaller Companies VCT	BSV	VCT Generalist	
Global Smaller Companies Trust	GSCT	Global Smaller Companies	
Henderson Smaller Companies	HSL	UK Smaller Companies	
ProVen VCT	PVN	VCT Generalist	
Schroder UK Mid Cap	SCP	UK All Companies	
JPMorgan UK Smaller Companies	JMI	UK Smaller Companies	
Fidelity Asian Values	FAS	Asia Pacific Smaller Companies	
3i Group	III	Private Equity	

We have expanded the list of 20- and 30-year performers this year to show the number of trusts that have delivered double-digit annualised returns over two and three decades. Note for how many of these trusts the share price and NAV total returns are not that different. This is evidence of a general truth: over time the discount at which you buy the shares of a top performing trust matters less than you think. The return on invested capital of a well managed trust is far more important than the entry price, making a buy and hold strategy sensible for long-term investors.

MANAGEMENT GROUP	£100 INITIAL INVESTMENT (SHARE PRICE TOTAL RETURN)	ANNUALISED %	£100 INITIAL INVESTMENT (NAV TOTAL RETURN)	ANNUALISED %	RANK LAST YEAR
Hg	2,325.5	17.3	1,956.9	16.3	4
Baillie Gifford	2,070.8	16.6	1,769.7	15.8	2
Allianz Global Investors	2,070.7	16.6	1,775.6	15.8	21
Frostrow Capital	1,908.1	16.2	1,422.2	14.6	29
Polar Capital Holdings	1,906.3	16.2	1,654.3	15.4	20
Baillie Gifford	1,646.9	15.4	1,606.2	15.2	1
abrdn	1,577.8	15.1	1,514.6	14.9	3
J.P. Morgan Asset Management	1,563.7	15.1	1,580.9	15.2	15
Lindsell Train	1,543.2	15.0	1,539.8	15.0	8
SV Health Managers	1,516.9	14.9	903.9	12.2	New
BlackRock Investment Management (UK)	1,499.0	14.9	1,158.0	13.5	5
abrdn	1,462.7	14.7	940.9	12.4	26
Janus Henderson Investors	1,454.7	14.7	1,131.9	13.4	33
J.P. Morgan Asset Management	1,359.4	14.3	1,148.2	13.5	11
Montanaro Investment Managers	1,349.8	14.3	-	-	14
BlackRock Investment Management (UK)	1,313.5	14.2	935.6	12.4	7
First State Investments	1,290.5	14.1	1,295.0	14.1	9
Frostrow Capital	1,284.6	14.0	1,141.0	13.4	New
J.P. Morgan Asset Management	1,242.1	13.9	1,140.5	13.4	10
Herald Investment Management	1,182.0	13.6	1,036.0	12.9	38
Devon Equity Management	1,172.0	13.6	1,159.9	13.5	36
Columbia Threadneedle	1,162.3	13.5	756.3	11.3	30
YFM Private Equity	1,141.0	13.4	607.4	10.3	New
Columbia Threadneedle	1,130.5	13.4	932.3	12.4	37
Janus Henderson Investors	1,125.7	13.4	966.6	12.6	39
Beringea	1,119.3	13.3	397.4	8.4	New
Schroder Investment Management	1,102.8	13.2	-	-	New
J.P. Morgan Asset Management	1,100.0	13.2	949.4	12.5	16
Fidelity	1,086.9	13.2	989.0	12.7	25
3i Group	1,067.7	13.1	957.9	12.5	New

Over 20 years the story is not dissimilar, with many of the same names reappearing, but is notable for the stronger showing of Asia Pacific and smaller company trusts this year, including two UK trusts managed by BlackRock. The 10th ranked trust now has a 20-year annualised share price rate of return that is nearly 3% per annum lower than this time a year ago. Over 30 years the best performing trusts' annualised rates of return remain around the same as their long term average however, with only one niche trust, Rights and Issues, achieving more than a 15% per annum compound rate of return. ■

30 years

COMPANY NAME	TICKER	AIC SECTOR	
HgCapital	HGT	Private Equity	
Rights & Issues	RIII	UK Smaller Companies	
ICG Enterprise	ICGT	Private Equity	
TR Property	TRY	Property Securities	
Fidelity European	FEV	Europe	
European Smaller Companies	ESCT	European Smaller Companies	
JPMorgan European Discovery	JEDT	European Smaller Companies	
Scottish Mortgage	SMT	Global	
North Atlantic Smaller Companies	NAS	Global Smaller Companies	
Pacific Horizon	PHI	Asia Pacific	
Invesco Perpetual UK Smaller Companies	IPU	UK Smaller Companies	
RIT Capital Partners	RCP	Flexible Investment	
AVI Global	AGT	Global	
Henderson EuroTrust	HNE	Europe	
Canadian General Investments	CGI	North America	
JPMorgan UK Smaller Companies	JMI	UK Smaller Companies	
Henderson European Focus	HEFT	Europe	
JPMorgan American	JAM	North America	
BlackRock Smaller Companies	BRSC	UK Smaller Companies	
Dunedin Enterprise	DNE	Private Equity	
European Assets	EAT	European Smaller Companies	
Finsbury Growth & Income	FGT	UK Equity Income	
Pantheon International	PIN	Private Equity	
Mid Wynd International	MWY	Global	
Caledonia	CLDN	Flexible Investment	
BlackRock Throgmorton Trust	THRG	UK Smaller Companies	
Global Smaller Companies Trust	GSCT	Global Smaller Companies	
Aberforth Smaller Companies	ASL	UK Smaller Companies	
abrdn New Dawn	ABD	Asia Pacific	
Hansa Investment Company	HAN	Flexible Investment	

Source: AIC/Morningstar, data to 30/09/22

The 30-year period includes trusts from no fewer than 10 broadly different sectors, suggesting that these trusts do have something special about them, not just the good fortune of operating in the sectors that have performed particularly well. It is also a testament to the breadth and diversity of the investment company sector as a whole. Note however how the annualised rates of return come down the

MANAGEMENT GROUP	£100 INITIAL INVESTMENT (SHARE PRICE TOTAL RETURN)	ANNUALISED %	£100 INITIAL INVESTMENT (NAV TOTAL RETURN)	ANNUALISED %	RANK LAST YEAR
Hg	7,081.1	15.3	7,636.6	15.6	2
Jupiter Unit Trust Managers	6,613.2	15.1	7,938.4	15.8	1
Intermediate Capital Group	4,968.9	14.0	6,010.5	14.7	4
Columbia Threadneedle	4,634.0	13.7	2,629.0	11.7	14
Fidelity	4,365.2	13.5	4,285.4	13.4	New
Janus Henderson Investors	4,176.5	13.3	3,453.5	12.6	8
J.P. Morgan Asset Management	4,000.6	13.2	3,945.8	13.1	7
Baillie Gifford	3,998.8	13.2	3,374.4	12.6	3
Harwood Capital	3,957.0	13.1	4,011.3	13.2	5
Baillie Gifford	3,313.3	12.5	2,684.1	11.7	11
Invesco Asset Management	3,254.2	12.4	2,943.7	12.1	9
RIT Capital Partners	2,711.3	11.8	2,229.7	11.1	13
Asset Value Investors	2,705.8	11.8	2,446.8	11.4	19
Janus Henderson Investors	2,693.7	11.7	2,426.0	11.4	New
Morgan Meighen & Associates	2,684.3	11.7	2,234.1	11.1	6
J.P. Morgan Asset Management	2,640.2	11.7	2,425.9	11.4	16
Janus Henderson Investors	2,565.0	11.6	2,417.0	11.4	18
J.P. Morgan Asset Management	2,471.9	11.4	2,099.8	10.9	25
BlackRock Investment Management (UK)	2,413.0	11.4	2,261.3	11.1	12
Dunedin	2,368.6	11.3	1,307.7	9.2	29
Columbia Threadneedle	2,318.9	11.2	1,658.8	10.0	15
Frostrow Capital	2,309.7	11.2	1,987.2	10.7	30
Pantheon Ventures	2,240.7	11.1	3,325.5	12.5	10
Artemis Investment Management	2,234.8	11.1	1,715.6	10.2	26
Caledonia Investments	2,116.3	10.9	-	-	27
BlackRock Investment Management (UK)	2,091.4	10.8	1,502.0	9.7	17
Columbia Threadneedle	2,072.0	10.8	2,076.0	10.8	22
Aberforth Partners	2,068.1	10.8	2,621.1	11.6	21
abrdn	2,034.0	10.7	1,635.5	10.0	24
Hansa Capital Partners	2,004.7	10.7	2,149.7	10.9	31

longer you look back in time. The best performers are generally those that operate in growth sectors. Their returns are more volatile from one year to the next, but tend to come out on top in the end. While styles come in and out of fashion, as they have done this year, growth is usually the long-term winner for those who can tolerate the ups and downs along the way. ■

Z-scores

Z Scores

(current discount - average discount) / volatility of discount

1 year

Fund	Ticker	Discount Current	Average	Z Score
Capital Gearing	CGT	-1.3	2.2	**-8.0**
Alternative Income REIT	AIRE	-32.2	-13.7	**-5.2**
Aquila European Renewables Income	AERS	-13.2	-2.4	**-4.4**
Target Healthcare REIT	THRL	-19.8	0.8	**-4.1**
Round Hill Music Royalty	RHM	-28.4	-5.8	**-4.1**
Life Science REIT	LABS	-29.2	-2.3	**-4.1**
Value & Indexed Property Income	VIP	-32.1	-14.1	**-4.1**
SDCL Energy Efficiency Income Trust	SEIT	-4.1	13.8	**-4.1**
Gore Street Energy Storage	GSF	2.0	12.4	**-4.1**
Supermarket Income REIT	SUPR	-7.8	11.2	**-4.0**
GCP Asset Backed Income	GABI	-14.8	-2.4	**-4.0**
Unite Group	UTG	-8.7	22.2	**-4.0**
Aquila European Renewables Income	AERI	-11.2	-1.7	**-3.9**
Digital 9 Infrastructure	DGI9	-9.9	5.1	**-3.9**
Atrato Onsite Energy	ROOF	2.7	10.9	**-3.9**

Fund	Ticker	Discount Current	Average	Z Score
Chelverton UK Dividend	SDV	12.4	-5.3	**4.5**
F&C IT	FCIT	-2.6	-8.7	**3.3**
DP Aircraft	DPA	-76.1	-86.3	**3.0**
North American Income	NAIT	-3.2	-8.7	**2.8**
Fundsmith Emerging Equities	FEET	-3.7	-11.6	**2.5**
Athelney Trust	ATY	-2.0	-15.9	**2.4**
Macau Property Opportunities	MPO	-57.4	-68.1	**2.4**
Trian Investors 1	TI1	-7.5	-25.4	**2.4**
Aberdeen Asian Income	AAIF	-9.9	-12.2	**2.3**
Independent IT	IIT	-3.5	-12.9	**2.2**
Securities Trust of Scotland	STS	1.9	-1.0	**2.2**
Doric Nimrod Air One	DNA	4.6	-39.3	**2.1**
CT Global Managed Portfolio Income	CMPI	4.6	0.9	**2.1**
Middlefield Canadian Income	MCT	-7.9	-13.1	**2.0**
Aurora	ARR	-1.8	-6.6	**2.0**

Source: Numis Securities. As at 30 September 2022

Z-scores measure mathematically how far a trust's current discount or premium has diverged from its average over some previous period (days, months or even a year can be used). Brokers and other professional investors calculate the figures regularly in order to look for trading opportunities or good entry/exit points. A minus figure for a z-score suggests that a trust looks 'cheap' relative to its past discount history; and a positive figure the reverse.

There may, however, be a good reason for the change in sentiment towards a particular trust, so they are a blunt instrument without specialist knowledge and should never be relied on by inexperienced investors. If you already have a specific investment trust on your watchlist and are looking for a good moment to buy, then checking the z-scores can be useful in timing your purchase. Bear in mind however that discounts widen for a reason; if the z-score is looking attractive, it is often because there is some negative story or headline out there.

By the same token, if you are thinking of selling part or all of your holding in a trust, then at the margin it makes most sense to do so when the trust's shares are showing up as 'dear' in the z-score rankings. Since most investors tend to hold the trusts they own for a number of years, these opportunities do not arise very often in practice.

The table that is shown opposite is for illustration only. The data was current at 30 September 2022, but remember that z-scores tend to be volatile. Trusts in the upper part of the table, which look 'cheap' at that point, can easily appear in the 'dear' section of the table a few weeks later, having gained in price and seen the discount narrow in the interim. Only two trusts in the list this year (Aquila European Renewables Income and Macau Property Opportunities) were also in the table a year ago, one 'cheap' and one 'dear'. Neither has performed well in the last 12 months.

Investment trusts are best held for the longer term. A consistent 15% return over 20 years, if you are smart enough to find such a thing, will be worth far more at the end of the period (nearly 19 times your original investment) than anything bought in the hope of gaining from a short-term z-score movement. Nevertheless they can help at the margin. ∎

New issuance

Number of investment company IPOs by year since 2000

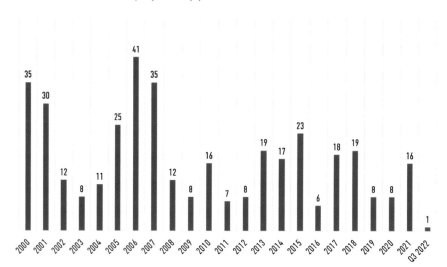

Whereas buybacks and tender offers reduce the amount of capital invested in the trust sector, in any year they will be offset by a combination of new and secondary issues by other trusts. New trusts are commonly launched through an IPO (initial public offering), although it is also possible to list a trust on the stock market without raising any new capital.

The IPO process runs to an irregular cycle. Some periods are characterised by a spurt of new issues in a particular segment of the market. Property trusts and hedge funds, for example, were hugely popular in the run up to the financial crisis in 2008. Income-generating trusts operating with alternative assets, notably infrastructure, renewable energy and specialist property sectors, have been particularly popular since then.

At any one time, there are always potential IPOs being worked on by brokers, of which only a handful will make it to the starting line. After two good years for IPOs in 2017 and 2018, the next two years were relatively disappointing with just seven new launches successfully completed in 2019 and eight in 2020. There were 16 in 2021, but in the first 10 months of 2022 that figure shrunk to just one (raising a miniscule £1.5m). In other words the new issue market has effectively been closed; according to broker Numis Securities, it has been the worst year for IPOs since they started recording the data in 2000.

To have a realistic chance of succeeding, new trusts these days need more than just a manager or an investment approach with a good track record. They have to be sufficiently differentiated in some way from existing trusts and comparable open-ended funds to attract attention. The successful IPOs in 2021 largely met that criterion. This year we have seen three new IPOs announced, in farmland, social housing and Chinese private equity; an eclectic bunch. All three were withdrawn or postponed because of the difficult market conditions.

The analysts at Numis Securities summed up as follows: "The bar remains high to get IPOs over the line, with investors requiring ever increasing timescales for due diligence processes and many investors preferring to avoid execution risk by waiting to back funds once (if) they succeed. In addition, recent trends have shown that me too products in crowded sectors may struggle to get away". ■

Secondary issuance

Secondary fundraising (£m)

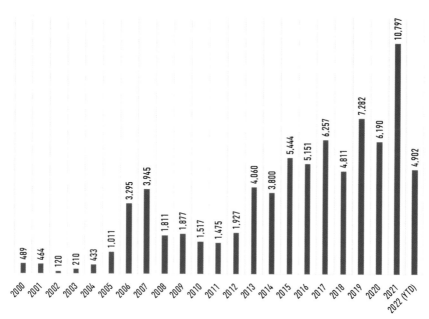

COMPANY NAME	SECONDARY FUNDRAISING 2022 YTD (£M)
International Public Partnerships	326
Capital Gearing	325
Supermarket Income REIT	307
Renewables Infrastructure Group	277
Home REIT	263
LXI REIT	250
Ruffer Investment Company	241
SDCL Energy Efficiency Income	235
Greencoat Renewables	235
Cordiant Digital Infrastructure	200
BH Macro	172
Personal Assets	165
HICL Infrastructure	160
Digital 9 Infrastructure	155
Gore Street Energy Storage	150
Bluefield Solar Income Fund	150
Gresham House Energy Storage	150
VH Global Sustainable Energy Opportunities	122

COMPANY NAME	SECONDARY FUNDRAISING 2022 YTD (£M)
Smithson	93
Polar Capital Global Financials	88
City of London	78
Impact Healthcare REIT	62
JLEN Environmental Assets Group	61
JPMorgan Global Growth & Income	58
Merchants	54
Downing Renewables & Infrastructure	53
Foresight Sustainable Forestry	45
abrdn European Logistics Income	38
Impax Environmental Markets	34
Law Debenture Corporation	30
Fidelity Special Values	29
Ecofin Global Utilities and Infrastructure	25
Mid Wynd International	25

Secondary issuance is how investment trusts that have already succeeded in obtaining a listing can continue to grow their capital base. As the chart shows, 2021 was a record year for investment companies raising money through secondary share issues. The going in 2022 has been harder.

The seeds for secondary fundraising were sown two decades ago when it became possible for trusts that were proving popular with investors to issue additional shares more easily, without the need to produce an expensive legal prospectus in every case. The new regime is still nothing like as simple as the daily process by which open-ended funds can issue or cancel units in their funds, but it does enable trusts to tap into additional demand on a regular basis.

Secondary issues can take a number of different forms. The most common are placings of new shares and so-called 'C-share issues'. These two mechanisms, which are less cumbersome and time-consuming than a new issue, both have the effect of allowing an existing trust to expand its capital base by growing the number of shares in issue.

A C-share issue is typically used when it may take some time for the capital raised to be invested. The shares are then traded separately until the investment process is largely complete and the two shares classes are consolidated into one. Placings are more common and are used when a trust has already identified where it wants to invest the money and can complete the transactions in quick order.

Boards that have bought back their own shares also have the option of reissuing shares that they have not yet cancelled. A number of well-known trusts whose performance or style of investing have become popular in recent years have been able to issue a steady stream of new shares at a premium to NAV. Issuing shares at a higher price than the current NAV per share enables the trust to grow without penalising existing shareholders.

By convention investment trusts only issue new shares if they can do so at a premium to the latest net asset value. The widespread derating that has dragged down share prices in Q3 2022 means that the opportunity to fund new investments will remain limited until more favourable conditions return. Some trusts may find life difficult if they have committed to investments that they can no longer fund with equity, only with debt. ■

Return of capital

Return of capital in 9M 2022 (£m)

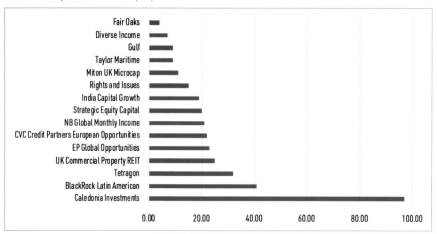

Source: Numis Securities, October 2022. Excludes companies that liquidated in their entirety in 2022. Excludes buybacks

Summary of return of capital by fund in 9M 2022 (£m)

FUND	CORPORATE ACTION	BUY-BACKS	RETURN OF CAPITAL	DELISTING / WIND UP DISTRIBUTION	TOTAL
Monks	Buybacks to support discount	183	-	-	183
Scottish Mortgage	Buybacks to support discount	150	-	-	150
Alliance Trust	Buybacks to support discount	132	-	-	132
Witan	Buybacks to support discount	105	-	-	105
Caledonia Investments	Special dividend following realisations	2	95	-	97
Pershing Square	Buybacks to support discount	97	-	-	97
Polar Capital Tech	Buybacks to support discount	88	-	-	88
Vietnam Enterprise	Buybacks to support discount	47	-	-	47
F&C IT	Buybacks to support discount	65	-	-	65
Finsbury Growth & Income	Buybacks to support discount	65	-	-	65
Jupiter Em. & Frontier Inc	Liquidation of fund	-	-	61	61
Balanced Commercial Property	Buybacks to support discount	53	-	-	53
Smithson	Buybacks to support discount	44	-	-	44
CATCo Reinsurance Opp	Markel CatCo buys out exposure	-	-	81	81
ScotGems	Liquidation of fund	-	-	42	42
SME Credit Realisation	Distributions as part of wind up	-	-	42	42
BlackRock Latin American	Tender offer for 25% share capital	-	41	-	41
CIP Merchant Capital	Delisting following mandatory offer from CFE	-	-	39	39
Worldwide Healthcare	Buybacks to support discount	38	-	-	38
Third Point Investors	Buybacks to support discount	36	-	-	36
Herald	Buybacks to support discount	34	-	-	34
Tetragon	Tender offer for up to $50m share capital	-	32	-	32
Strategic Equity Capital	Tender offer for 10% of share capital	10	20	-	30
SLF Realisation	Distributions as part of wind up	-	-	30	30
Aberforth SmCos	Buybacks to support discount	29	-	-	29
Other		833	164	53	1050
Total		**2011**	**352**	**348**	**2711**

Source: Numis Securities, to 11 October 2022

Summary of delistings

FUND	DATE	NET ASSETS (£M)	DETAILS
Electra	Jan-22	222	Demerger into Unbound; declassified as an IC
Raven Property Group	Mar-22	437	Shares suspended following Russia's invasion of Ukraine
JPM Emerging & Frontier Income	Jun-22	61	Fund liquidated following shareholder vote
CIP Merchant	Jun-22	39	87% of share capital acquired by CFE
ScotGems	Sep-22	42	Fund liquidated following shareholder vote

There can be a number of reasons why a trust decides to return capital to its shareholders. One is to try and limit the discount at which the shares in the trust are trading. Another is because a trust's board of directors has decided to liquidate or offer an exit to shareholders, typically after a run of poor performance. In some other cases a trust may decide to make a distribution of capital because of the sale of a significant asset that it owns.

Around 50 investment companies now have measures in place with which they attempt to control the discount and/or reduce discount volatility – see the list on page 258. Some trusts give a specific discount target, a level at which they promise to take remedial action. Others content themselves with a more modest statement of intent to keep the discount in mind.

These measures include buying back shares in the market, making tender offers at periodic intervals (enabling those who wish to sell a chance to tender at least a proportion of their shares at a price close to NAV) and agreeing to hold a continuation vote at some date in the future. It is fairly routine these days for investment companies to adopt the power to buy back their own shares. This requires shareholder approval at a general meeting and more than two-thirds of the companies in the sector have obtained this approval.

In 1999 it became possible for investment companies to hold shares they have bought back 'in treasury', meaning they can be retained without being cancelled and so can be reissued later if and when demand for the shares has grown again. Buybacks have been running at an average rate of around £1.2bn a year over the past 20 years, but the trend has picked up in 2022 as discounts generally have widened, with four trusts buying back £120m or more of their shares.

The alternative approach of offering shareholders the chance to tender their prices back to the company is less common. The biggest tender saw around a third of shareholders in the £1bn-plus Genesis Emerging Markets Trust tendering their shares after the board switched the mandate to Fidelity. Proposed corporate/management changes were also what triggered the other tenders in the table. ∎

"'SKIN IN THE GAME' MATTERS. OTHER THINGS BEING EQUAL, IT IS COMFORTING TO KNOW THAT THOSE OVERSEEING THE COMPANY AND MANAGING ITS INVESTMENTS STAND TO GAIN OR LOSE IN THE SAME WAY AS THOSE PROVIDING THE CAPITAL FOR THE BUSINESS."

Skin in the game

Why it matters

T HE EXTENT TO which the interests of the directors and managers of a company are aligned with the interests of the shareholders is an important factor for investors. Other things being equal, it is comforting to know that those overseeing the company and managing its investments stand to gain or lose in the same way as those providing the capital for the business (which is what shareholders effectively do). 'Skin in the game' matters.

Directors of investment trusts are required to disclose at least once a year in the company's annual report and accounts the extent of their holdings in the trusts on whose boards they serve. It is also a stock exchange listing requirement that they notify the market within 24 hours of any further dealings in their trust's shares. All significant shareholders must also notify the market if they own more than 3% of the share capital in any trust.

While directors' interests are always publicly available, it is less easy to discover how much the portfolio managers have invested in their trusts. They only have to disclose their shareholding if it exceeds 3% of the total issued share capital of the trust. Some choose to do so voluntarily and more probably should.

Alan Brierley, an investment trust analyst at Investec, periodically compiles a summary of the shareholdings of directors and managers (where the latter can be ascertained). His latest research on this topic, based on analysing 298 trusts, was published in June 2021. Earlier reports appeared in 2019, 2018, 2017, 2014, 2012 and 2010, making it easy to spot some of the most striking trends in board composition.

Some headline findings

- The total investment by boards and managers in the 2021 report was £4.8bn. While changes in the number of trusts make comparisons of limited value, this was materially higher than the total of £3.4bn in 2019, £1bn in 2014 and £687m in 2012. It represents about 2% of the total value of the universe.

- 51 chairmen/directors had an individual investment in their trusts of more than £1m, and 78 managers or management teams a personal investment of at least that amount. 39 investment trusts had boards where all the directors on a board can claim the same.

- On the other hand 8% of directors had no investment at all in their trusts (vs 14% in 2018 and 16% in 2014), while 44 chairmen with more than five years sitting on the board have shareholdings worth less than their annual fees.

- 95% of boards can be deemed to be independent in corporate governance terms, meaning they have no business or close personal relationship with the fund manager of the trust. This is a big change from the past when boards were often very 'chummy', with many directors facing conflicts of interest that potentially inhibited their ability to act solely in the interests of shareholders.

No further report has been issued since June 2021. Because share prices have moved so much in 2022, several managers on the list opposite will have experienced declines in the market value of their shareholdings. Although precise figures are hard to come by, it is generally believed to be the case that managers of investment trusts typically have bigger shareholdings than their stakes in open-ended funds.

Progress on diversity

A notable trend is that there has been a sharp increase in the percentage of women directors on boards, Mr Brierley reported. As the chart indicates, women represented 34.5% of all investment company directorships, compared to just 8.0% in his first 'Skin in the Game' report back in 2010.

Significant growth in women's representation on investment company boards (% of total board positions)

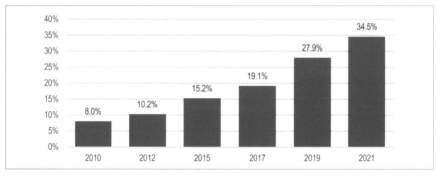

Source: Investec Securities analysis

The number of women on trust boards in 2021 for the first time bore comparison with the (voluntary) 33% target for UK listed companies set by the Hampton-Alexander corporate governance report. 23 trusts without female representation remained, while 95, around third of the total, had one woman only on the board. There are no all-male boards left in the FTSE 350 index.

Managers with a personal investment in excess of £1m at COB 1 June 2021

COMPANY	MANAGER	INVESTMENT VALUE (£'000)
Pershing Square Holdings	Bill Ackman, Nicholas Botta & Management team	1,315,016
Tetragon Financial Group	Reade Griffith/Paddy Dear & Management team	243,467
Apax Global Alpha	Management team	236,711
Scottish Mortgage	Management team	200,000
North Atlantic Smaller Companies	Christopher Mills	167,022
Manchester & London	Mark Sheppard/Richard Morgan	132,010
Third Point Offshore	Management team	104,873
Boussard & Gavaudan	Management team	63,100
Utilico Emerging Markets	Management team	60,842
New Star	John Duffield	55,444
Smithson Investment Trust	Management team	53,203
HgCapital Trust	Management team	46,500
Lindsell Train	Michael Lindsell/Nick Train/team	34,151
Finsbury Growth & Income	Nick Train/Alastair Smith	31,745
Jupiter European Opportunities	Alex Darwall	28,090
Warehouse REIT	Management team	24,690
JZ Capital Partners	Jay Jordan/David Zalaznick	24,688
Value and Indexed Property Income Trust	Matthew Oakeshott	24,557
Capital Gearing	Peter Spiller/team	21,948
Mobius Investment Trust	Mark Mobius/Carlos Hardenberg	21,234
Montanaro UK Smaller Companies	Management team	19,722
Tritax Big Box	Management team	19,261
Gresham House Energy Storage	Ben Guest/Bozkurt Aydinoglu	18,878
Montanaro European Smaller Companies	Management team	18,031
Mid Wynd International	Simon Edelsten	17,799
Riverstone Energy	Management team	14,373
International Public Partnerships	Management team	13,844
Odyssean Investment Trust	Management team	13,440
Artemis Alpha Trust	John Dodd/Kartik Kumar	13,190
VinaCapital Vietnam Opportunity Fund	Management team	11,799
Fundsmith Emerging Equities	Terry Smith/Mike O'Brien	11,630
Honeycomb Investment Trust	Management team	10,635

Source: Investec Securities analysis

Discount control policies

INVESTMENT TRUST	TARGET DISCOUNT	PRINCIPAL METHOD
JGC Jupiter Green	0.0%	B
MAVT Momentum Multi-Asset Value	0.0%	B
IVPG Invesco Perp. Select	0.0%	B
GMP Gabelli Merger Plus	0.0%	U
STS Securities Trust of Scotland	0.0%	B
MNP Martin Currie Global Portfolio	0.0%	B
CGT Capital Gearing	0.0%	B
NBMI NB Global Monthly Income	2.0%	T
TIGT Troy Income & Growth	2.0%	B
MWY Mid Wynd International	2.0%	B
PNL Personal Assets	2.0%	B
ATS Artemis Alpha	3.0%	T
ALAI Aberdeen Latin American Income	5.0%	B
CMPI CT Global Managed Portfolio Income	5.0%	B
CHI CT UK High Income	5.0%	B
CMPG CT Global Managed Portfolio Growth	5.0%	B
RNEW Ecofin US Renewables Infrastructure	5.0%	B
BRLA BlackRock Latin American	5.0%	T
MMIT Mobius IT	5.0%	B
AJOT AVI Japan Opportunity	5.0%	B
SMIF TwentyFour Select Monthly Income	5.0%	T
FAIR Fair Oaks Income	5.0%	U
JUSC JPMorgan US Smaller Cos	5.0%	B
EAT European Assets	5.0%	B
AAIF Aberdeen Asian Income	5.0%	B
JEMI JPMorgan Global Emerging Markets Income	5.0%	U
JCH JPMorgan Claverhouse	5.0%	B
NAIT North American Income	5.0%	U
ATR Schroder Asian Total Return	5.0%	U
GSEO VH Global Sustainable Energy Opps	5.0%	B
UEM Utilico Emerging Markets	5.0%	T
PCFT Polar Capital Global Financials	5.0%	B
PINT Pantheon Infrastructure	5.0%	B
BCPT Balanced Commercial Property	5.0%	B
TFIF TwentyFour Income	5.0%	B
SOI Schroder Oriental Income	5.0%	B
GSCT Global Smaller Companies	5.0%	B
SEIT SDCL Energy Efficiency Income Trust	5.0%	B
JGGI JPMorgan Global Growth & Income	5.0%	B
FGT Finsbury Growth & Income	5.0%	B
ATST Alliance Trust	5.0%	B
BPCP BioPharma Credit	5%-10%	B
BIOG Biotech Growth Trust	6.0%	U
WWH Worldwide Healthcare	6.0%	U
ATT Allianz Technology	7.0%	U
TPOU Third Point Investors	7.5%	T
SHED Urban Logistics REIT	7.5%	B
BHMU BH Macro	8.0%	U
HEIT Harmony Energy Income	8.0%	B

INVESTMENT TRUST	TARGET DISCOUNT	PRINCIPAL METHOD
AUSC abrdn UK Smaller Companies Growth	8.0%	T
JPMorgan Asia Growth & Income	8%-10%	B
JMG JPMorgan Emerging Markets	8%-10%	U
SSIF Secured Income Fund	10.0%	C
AJIT Aberdeen Japan	10.0%	C
FJV Fidelity Japan	10.0%	U
MTE Montanaro European Smaller Cos	10.0%	B
IAT Invesco Asia	10.0%	T
SHIP Tufton Oceanic Assets	10.0%	B
RHM Round Hill Music Royalty	10.0%	B
JEGI JPMorgan European	10.0%	B
SDP Schroder AsiaPacific	10.0%	B
FSV Fidelity Special Values	10.0%	U
DGI9 Digital 9 Infrastructure	10.0%	B
FCSS Fidelity China Special Situations	10.0%	U
IEM Impax Environmental	10.0%	B
ABD Aberdeen New Dawn	15.0%	L
FAS Fidelity Asian Values	15.0%	U

Source: *Money Makers*, from broker and other sources

Key to abbreviations
B=buybacks; T=tender offer; C=continuation vote; L=liquidation; U=unspecified

As mentioned earlier, a significant minority of investment trusts have formally adopted discount control policies designed to reassure shareholders that they will not allow the discount on the trust's shares to widen beyond a certain threshold. The targets vary from zero to 15%; and while some are firm commitments, others are more loosely worded to give boards some discretion to do nothing in 'abnormal' market conditions.

This table, a new one in the *Handbook*, lists the most important trusts with discount controls. The most common commitment is to buy back shares when discounts breach the target. A commitment to make a tender offer allowing shareholders to sell shares close to net asset value at a certain date is another method. Some boards agree to offer shareholders the chance to vote on whether a trust should continue or be wound up if performance falls below a certain target.

For shareholders, the knowledge that discounts will not be allowed to become too wide can be an important positive factor in deciding whether to invest. It is worth looking for details of any such policy when researching a possible investment. This year's derating will put the strength of a number of boards' commitments under the spotlight.

Enhanced income trusts

COMPANY	AIC SECTOR	DIVIDEND YIELD (%)
International Biotechnology	Biotechnology & healthcare	4.78
Invesco Perpetual UK Smaller Companies	UK smaller companies	5.67
Invesco Asia	Asia Pacific equity income	4.66
Montanaro UK Smaller Companies	UK smaller companies	6.64
CT Private Equity	Private equity	5.42
JPMorgan European Growth & Income	Europe	5.16
European Assets	European smaller companies	10.92
JPMorgan China Growth & Income	China/Greater China	7.28
JPMorgan Japan Small Cap Growth & Income	Japanese smaller companies	6.19
JPMorgan Asia Growth & Income	Asia Pacific equity income	4.78
JPMorgan Global Growth & Income	Global equity income	4.07
BlackRock Latin America	Latin America	5.02
Atlantis Japan Growth	Japanese smaller companies	6.25
Princess Private Equity Holding	Private equity	7.24
BBGI Global Infrastructure S.A.	Infrastructure	4.68
Blackstone Loan Financing	Debt – structured finance	11.43
Chenavari Toro Income	Debt – structured finance	13.98

A small number of investment trusts have adopted a policy known as 'enhanced income' in recent years. In essence this means that they aim to pay out a fixed percentage of their net asset value each year as a dividend, whatever the NAV turns out to be. Typically this figure is around 4%. J.P.Morgan Asset Management is the fund management company most closely associated with this policy. Five of the 13 trusts it manages have a policy of this kind.

The origins of this practice date back to 2012, when it was decided to give investment trusts the flexibility to pay dividends out of any retained capital profits, not just from current year income and revenue reserves. To do this, a trust's articles of association need to be amended to give the directors power to make such distributions, with at least 75% approval in a shareholder vote.

Some very well-known trusts, like Personal Assets and RIT Capital Partners, have gone down this route. However, a number of trusts have taken this idea a little further by embracing what is called the enhanced income concept. Rather than just using capital profits to support a progressive dividend policy, they try to appeal to income-seeking investors by saying they will pay a fixed percentage of their net asset value each year.

This means shareholders get the reassurance of knowing what the next year's annual payout rate will be, even if the amount of the dividend itself is not known, as that will depend on what the NAV turns out to be. With the rates on savings

5YR DIVIDEND GROWTH (%) P.A.	DIVIDEND COVER	DIVIDEND FREQUENCY	TRADED CURRENCY
6.42	N/A	Semi-annually	GBX
5.92	0.09	Quarterly	GBX
28.90	0.14	Semi-annually	GBX
25.12	0.04	Quarterly	GBX
9.72	1.91	Four times a year	GBX
0.27	0.79	Quarterly	GBX
4.04	0.00	Quarterly	GBX
70.12	0.00	Quarterly	GBX
N/A	N/A	Quarterly	GBX
3.49	0.00	Quarterly	GBX
20.77	0.00	Quarterly	GBX
10.95	0.48	Four times a year	GBX
N/A	N/A	Quarterly	GBX
4.41	N/A	Semi-annually	EUR
3.24	0.00	Semi-annually	GBX
-2.33	0.00	Quarterly	EUR
2.01	0.00	Quarterly	EUR

accounts having been pitiful for a long time now, an enhanced income policy can broaden the appeal of a trust to income-focused investors while the extra demand for its shares can help narrow its discount.

The table lists those trusts which have adopted a fixed rate for determining their future dividend payments. These 17 trusts have around £8bn in assets, or about 3% of assets in the investment trust sector, but there are some sizeable trusts in the list. JPMorgan Global Growth & Income (ticker: JGGI) is the largest, followed by Bellevue Healthcare (BBH). It is a mixed bag, drawn from a wide range of sectors.

Few of these companies adopted this approach before 2016, so there was no rush towards it when the rules were relaxed in 2012. European Assets has had such a policy since 1999. It used to be a Dutch company, where different rules applied relating to distributions, and only migrated to the UK in 2019. BB Healthcare is the only trust on the list that adopted the enhanced dividend approach when it was first listed.

Almost all these trusts were trading at discounts above 10% when they adopted the policy, clearly hoping the enhanced income approach would allow them to stand out from their peer group. In the majority of cases, the discount has narrowed since the initial announcement, although that could be for several reasons. Some of these trusts still trade on a double-digit discount, so it's certainly not a magic bullet.

* As explained in an article about enhanced income on the *Money Makers* website.

Investment trusts vs open-ended funds

SECTOR	NAV TOTAL RETURNS (ANNUALISED)			NAV TOTAL RETURNS (ANNUALISED)			
	OE funds			ICs			
	1 yr	5 yr	10 yr	1 yr	5 yr	10 yr	
UK – equity income	-8.7	0.7	5.7	-7.8	2.1	6.9	
UK – all companies	-15.4	0.6	5.7	-21	0	6.8	
UK – smaller companies	-32.4	0.6	8.2	-34.8	-0.2	8.5	
US – equity	-2.4	11.4	14	-9.4	12.3	11.7	
US – smaller companies	-10.7	9.2	13	-6.3	8.9	11.6	
Global – equity	-9.1	7.2	10	-23.4	11	13.5	
Global – equity income	-0.5	6	9.1	5.6	7.1	9.4	
Europe – equity	-16	2	8.2	-19.9	4	9.7	
Europe – smaller companies	-28.9	0.3	8.9	-31.3	1.5	11.8	
Asia Pacific – equity	-10.5	4.1	7.5	-12	6.8	10.1	
Japan – equity	-15.8	2.9	9.1	-25.4	3.6	11.1	
Japan – smaller companies	-15.6	3.4	12	-25.3	2.4	12.4	
Emerging – global	-15.5	1.1	4.5	-16.9	2.6	5.4	
Technology	-21	12.4	14.8	-20.4	14.3	16.8	

Note: Data to 30 September 2022. Blue shading indicates outperformance by ICs relative to open-ended funds
Source: Morningstar, Numis Securities Research

It is not uncommon for the investment managers of trusts to manage other funds outside the investment trust sector at the same time. In fact, a number of fund managers start their careers managing different kinds of fund (typically unit trusts and OEICs, though also hedge funds) and if successful are encouraged to take over or start an investment trust with a broadly similar investment objective.

Adding an investment trust to their responsibilities gives successful fund managers the opportunity to take advantage of the benefits of the investment trust structure, including the use of gearing and freedom from unhelpful forced selling as a result of fund flows. They can also use derivative securities such as futures and options for investment purposes.

These advantages show up regularly in comparisons between the long-term performance of investment trusts and that of open-ended funds with either the same manager or the same investment objective. Where trusts and similar funds can be directly compared in this way, trusts typically show up with superior performance records. Where a trust and an open-ended fund with the same mandate are managed by the same individual, it is rare for the trust not to do better over the longer term.

	PRICE		
		ICs	
1 yr	5 yr	10 yr	
-9.3	2.2	6.5	
0	-0.4	7.4	
-38.4	0	9.1	
-25.5	12.1	11.3	
-10.5	6.7	9.4	
-29.9	8.9	13.6	
-4.2	5	8	
-10.7	3.1	9.6	
-31.7	-0.2	12	
-31	6.2	10.5	
-19.4	2.6	11.9	
-28.4	0.7	12	
16.8	1.9	4.8	
-7	11.2	15.6	

The degree to which comparable trusts outperform does vary markedly however from sector to sector and is not true every year (2019 being an example when the effect was less marked). The table summarises the difference in the performance of directly comparable trust and open-ended equivalent sectors as at 30 June 2022. The blue-shaded cells show the periods over which trusts in each sector have outperformed.

For the first time in many years, the general trend of outperformance has failed to hold over the past 12 months, although investment companies still hold the advantage over three- and five-year periods. It is fair to point out that such simple comparisons can be criticised by statisticians on the grounds that the two samples are very different in size and also may display what is called survivorship bias. In 2018 academics at Cass Business School in London reported that a detailed analysis of investment trust returns between 2000 and 2016 appeared to support their superior performance. However, the study has now been abandoned because of 'data issues', principally the sample size and survivorship bias problems. ∎

Who owns investment trusts?

Age profile of investment trust investors

Source: Warhorse Partners Dianomi survey 2022

Typical private investor portfolios

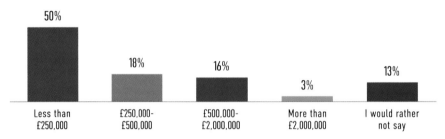

Source: Warhorse Partners Dianomi survey 2022

TYPE OF INVESTOR	END 2021%	END 2013%	CHANGE %
Hargreaves Lansdown (EO)	8.7	2.2	6.5
Interactive Investor (EO)	5.6	1.0	4.6
Rathbones	5.3	5.4	-0.1
Brewin Dolphin	3.5	5.5	-2.0
Investec Wealth	3.2	4.1	-0.9
BlackRock	2.9	2.5	0.4
Charles Stanley	2.7	2.5	0.2
AJ Bell (EO)	2.2	0.3	2.0
City of London IM	2.0	2.1	-0.1
Smith & Williamson	1.9	1.5	0.4
Legal & General IM	1.9	3.2	-1.3
Quilter Cheviot IM	1.7	1.8	-0.1
HSDL (EO)	1.6	1.8	-0.3
abrdn	1.5	2.8	-1.3
Lazard Asset Management	1.4	2.2	-0.7
Fidelity (platform)	1.3	1.0	0.4
Wells Capital Management	1.2	0.4	0.7
JM Finn	1.2	1.0	0.1
Canaccord Genuity Wealth	1.1	0.7	0.4
Vanguard Group	1.0	0.1	0.9

Source: Richard Davies IR, Warhorse Partners

Private investors are becoming an ever more important market for investment trusts. Research by two specialist share register analysis and marketing firms (Richard Davies IR and Warhorse Partners) shows how the proportion of shares in investment trusts held by private investors has been rising over the past decade, thanks in part to the big platforms such as Hargreaves Lansdown, Interactive Investor and A.J.Bell. The trend is slow but steady rather than dramatic, but evident nonetheless.

It is strongest in the traditional equity sectors of the universe, where few big institutions such as pension funds and insurance companies remain shareholders. They mostly now manage their investment portfolios directly themselves or by hiring the services of specialist fund managers on bespoke terms. The trend is somewhat less marked in the alternative asset classes.

The wealth management industry, traditionally the biggest buyer of investment trusts since the institutions departed, has meanwhile been consolidating and for a variety of reasons are no longer relying on investment trusts as mainstays of their client portfolios as much as they did.

Another survey by Warhorse and Dianomi in May 2022 revealed more about the private investor market for investment trusts. Investment trusts are predominantly owned by older investors; 80% are aged 51 or older. This group has the time to conduct research before investing and typically carefully research and review their investments.

They use a wide range of online and traditional sources of information, tuned to their individual preferences and needs. Half of investors use online platforms, such as Interactive Investor and Hargreaves Lansdown. Around 40% also use third-party websites, such as Trustnet and Morningstar, and read coverage in the national press, for example, the *Telegraph*, *The Times* and the *Mail on Sunday*. Older investors are typically less reliant on social media than younger investors.

Holdings vary significantly among investors. Half of investors have investment holdings valued at less than £250,000. However, over 30% have holdings between £250,000 and £2m. Most investors have multiple holdings of investment trusts. A quarter have 11 or more. Investment diversification is clearly a consideration in decision-making. ∎

Fees

COMPANY NAME	AIC SECTOR	TICKER	
British & American	UK Equity Income	BAF	
Blue Planet Investment Trust	Global	BLP	
Worsley Investors	UK Smaller Companies	WINV	
Rockwood Strategic	UK Smaller Companies	RKW	
Chelverton Growth Trust	UK Smaller Companies	CGW	
Sure Ventures	Technology & Media	SURE	
JZ Capital Partners	Flexible Investment	JZCP	
Riverstone Energy	Commodities & Natural Resources	RSE	
Pershing Square Holdings	North America	PSH	
Geiger Counter	Commodities & Natural Resources	GCL	
SVM UK Emerging Fund	UK Smaller Companies	SVM	
VietNam Holding	Country Specialist	VNH	
Athelney	UK Smaller Companies	ATY	
Marwyn Value Investors	UK Smaller Companies	MVI	
UIL	Flexible Investment	UTL	
Investment Company	Flexible Investment	INV	
Baker Steel Resources	Commodities & Natural Resources	BSRT	
Crystal Amber	UK Smaller Companies	CRS	
Chelverton UK Dividend	UK Equity Income	SDV	
abrdn Latin American Income	Latin America	ALAI	
Golden Prospect Precious Metals	Commodities & Natural Resources	GPM	
Vietnam Enterprise Investments	Country Specialist	VEIL	
CQS Natural Resources Growth & Income	Commodities & Natural Resources	CYN	
Menhaden Resource Efficiency	Environmental	MHN	
Weiss Korea Opportunity	Country Specialist	WKOF	
RTW Venture	Biotechnology & Healthcare	RTW	
Downing Strategic Micro-Cap	UK Smaller Companies	DSM	
Tetragon Financial Group	Flexible Investment	TFG	
Augmentum Fintech	Technology & Media	AUGM	
Gulf Investment	Global Emerging Markets	GIF	
Bailiwick Investments	Flexible Investment	BAIL	
Momentum Multi-Asset Value	Flexible Investment	MAVT	
Premier Miton Global Renewables	Infrastructure Securities	PMGR	
Atlantis Japan Growth	Japanese Smaller Companies	AJG	
VinaCapital Vietnam Opportunity	Country Specialist	VOF	
Barings Emerging EMEA Opportunities	Global Emerging Markets	BEMO	
Jupiter Green	Environmental	JGC	
Mobius Investment	Global Emerging Markets	MMIT	
Oryx International Growth	UK Smaller Companies	OIG	
AVI Japan Opportunity	Japanese Smaller Companies	AJOT	

SHARE TYPE	ONGOING CHARGE %	ONGOING CHARGE DATE	MARKET CAP (£M)
Ordinary Share	11.94%	31/12/2021	4
Ordinary Share	5.20%	30/04/2022	5
Ordinary Share	4.71%	31/03/2022	8
Ordinary Share	4.36%	31/03/2022	36
Ordinary Share	4.26%	31/08/2021	2
Ordinary Share	4.23%	31/03/2022	7
Ordinary Share	3.31%	28/02/2022	133
Ordinary Share	2.70%	31/12/2021	326
Ordinary Share	2.70%	31/12/2021	5,835
Ordinary Share	2.67%	30/09/2021	63
Ordinary Share	2.64%	31/03/2022	4
Ordinary Share	2.52%	30/06/2021	88
Ordinary Share	2.38%	31/12/2021	4
Ordinary Share	2.37%	31/12/2021	56
Ordinary Share	2.20%	30/06/2022	158
Ordinary Share	2.17%	30/06/2022	13
Ordinary Share	2.13%	31/12/2021	57
Ordinary Share	2.07%	30/06/2021	92
Ordinary Share	2.03%	30/04/2022	34
Ordinary Share	2.00%	31/08/2021	31
Ordinary Share	1.90%	31/12/2021	28
Ordinary Share	1.89%	31/12/2021	1,315
Ordinary Share	1.80%	30/06/2021	119
Ordinary Share	1.80%	31/12/2021	76
Ordinary Share	1.80%	31/12/2021	119
Ordinary Share	1.78%	31/12/2021	242
Ordinary Share	1.75%	28/02/2022	26
Ordinary Share	1.70%	31/12/2021	843
Ordinary Share	1.70%	31/03/2022	164
Ordinary Share	1.67%	30/06/2022	88
Ordinary Share	1.67%	31/12/2018	
Ordinary Share	1.66%	30/04/2022	44
Ordinary Share	1.65%	31/12/2021	31
Ordinary Share	1.65%	30/04/2022	69
Ordinary Share	1.64%	30/06/2021	767
Ordinary Share	1.62%	30/09/2021	65
Ordinary Share	1.57%	31/03/2022	41
Ordinary Share	1.50%	30/11/2021	134
Ordinary Share	1.45%	31/03/2022	158
Ordinary Share	1.45%	31/12/2020	150

COMPANY NAME	AIC SECTOR	TICKER	
Odyssean Investment Trust	UK Smaller Companies	OIT	
Ecofin Global Utilities and Infrastructure	Infrastructure Securities	EGL	
Miton UK Microcap	UK Smaller Companies	MINI	
Utilico Emerging Markets	Global Emerging Markets	UEM	
Canadian General Investments	North America	CGI	
Nippon Active Value	Japanese Smaller Companies	NAVF	
BlackRock Frontiers	Global Emerging Markets	BRFI	
JPMorgan Global Core Real Assets	Flexible Investment	JARA	
MIGO Opportunities	Flexible Investment	MIGO	
Fundsmith Emerging Equities	Global Emerging Markets	FEET	
River & Mercantile UK Micro Cap	UK Smaller Companies	RMMC	
Majedie	Global Equity Income	MAJE	
Middlefield Canadian Income Trust	North America	MCT	
BlackRock Income & Growth	UK Equity Income	BRIG	
BlackRock Energy and Resources Income	Commodities & Natural Resources	BERI	
JPMorgan Russian Securities	Country Specialist	JRS	
International Biotechnology	Biotechnology & Healthcare	IBT	
Aberforth Split Level Income	UK Smaller Companies	ASIT	
abrdn Smaller Companies Income	UK Smaller Companies	ASCI	
BlackRock Latin American	Latin America	BRLA	

Source: AIC/Morningstar, data to 30/09/22

The costs that investors have to pay for the privilege of having their investments managed by an investment company is a surprisingly important factor in determining the returns that they obtain. It is standard practice for a fund management firm to charge an annual management fee that is expressed as a percentage, typically somewhere between 0.3% and 2.0%, of the amount of the money they look after.

As a result, other things being equal, the larger the trust, the greater a fee the firm will earn, creating an incentive for the management firm to grow the size of the trust. In a rising market, the management firm also benefits from rising fee income even if they fail to outperform the fund's benchmark.

Deceptively modest percentage fees can quickly become big business; a trust with £500m of assets paying a management fee of 0.6% per annum will earn the manager £3m every year for its services, in addition to other administrative expenses, such as accountancy and legal fees. Some fund

SHARE TYPE	ONGOING CHARGE %	ONGOING CHARGE DATE	MARKET CAP (£M)
Ordinary Share	1.45%	31/03/2022	156
Ordinary Share	1.43%	30/09/2021	244
Ordinary Share	1.41%	30/04/2022	58
Ordinary Share	1.40%	31/03/2022	435
Ordinary Share	1.37%	31/12/2021	621
Ordinary Share	1.37%	31/12/2020	130
Ordinary Share	1.36%	30/09/2021	242
Ordinary Share	1.35%	28/02/2022	228
Ordinary Share	1.30%	30/04/2022	84
Ordinary Share	1.30%	31/12/2021	352
Ordinary Share	1.29%	30/09/2021	48
Ordinary Share	1.25%	30/09/2021	87
Ordinary Share	1.24%	31/12/2021	128
Ordinary Share	1.21%	31/10/2021	38
Ordinary Share	1.21%	30/11/2021	158
Ordinary Share	1.21%	31/10/2021	30
Ordinary Share	1.20%	31/08/2021	270
Ordinary Share	1.20%	30/06/2022	107
Ordinary Share	1.16%	31/12/2021	51
Ordinary Share	1.14%	31/12/2021	111

managers also charge a performance fee, an extra fee that is only paid if the trust beats a given target.

Given that only a minority of fund managers can consistently outperform a benchmark or passive fund equivalent, and the best rarely beat either by 2% per annum over time, the overall annual cost of owning any kind of investment fund can make a huge difference in determining whether they offer value for money. Regulators have expended a huge amount of time and effort in trying to develop a standardised measure that will allow investors to compare the cost of competing funds.

The standard measure today is an 'ongoing charge ratio', expressed as a percentage. It is an imperfect measure, but can at least give shareholders a first indication of whether a trust is worth paying for or not. Many firms these days charge tiered fees, meaning the percentage annual management fee declines once the size of a trust reaches a threshold.

The table lists trusts with the highest ongoing charge ratios. ∎

Platform costs

PLATFORM	£5,000	£15,000
AJ Bell Youinvest	1.05%	0.47%
Barclays	1.44%	0.48%
Bestinvest	1.00%	0.60%
Charles Stanley Direct	1.40%	0.66%
Close Brothers A.M. Self Directed Service	0.97%	0.49%
Fidelity Personal Investing	1.70%	0.57%
Halifax Share Dealing	1.48%	0.49%
Hargreaves Lansdown	1.41%	0.62%
iDealing	1.19%	0.40%
IG	2.56%	0.85%
Interactive Investor (Investor Product)	2.40%	0.80%
iWeb	2.40%	0.80%
Sharedeal	1.76%	0.59%
Willis Owen	1.00%	0.60%
X-O	0.48%	0.16%

Source: AIC/the Lang Cat consultancy, data as at 18/07/22

How much does it cost to hold shares in investment trusts on a private investor platform? The table gives an illustrative estimate for most of the largest platforms. The costs are shown as an annual percentage of the value of your portfolio, based on the amount you have invested. The data is collected by the Lang Cat consultancy and published on the AIC website. It is a valuable source of information, albeit with some important caveats.

It is important to note that your investment is assumed to be within an ISA tax wrapper. The figures shown only include ongoing platform fees, additional wrapper charges (if any) and trading charges (where applicable). Other charges, for example the management charges of the investment companies themselves,

£25,000	£50,000	£100,000	£250,000	£500,000	£1,000,000
0.28%	0.14%	0.07%	0.03%	0.01%	0.01%
0.29%	0.15%	0.12%	0.11%	0.10%	0.10%
0.52%	0.46%	0.43%	0.41%	0.31%	0.25%
0.53%	0.44%	0.29%	0.11%	0.06%	0.03%
0.39%	0.32%	0.29%	0.26%	0.26%	0.23%
0.34%	0.17%	0.09%	0.03%	0.02%	0.01%
0.30%	0.15%	0.07%	0.03%	0.01%	0.01%
0.37%	0.19%	0.09%	0.04%	0.02%	0.01%
0.24%	0.12%	0.06%	0.02%	0.01%	0.01%
0.51%	0.26%	0.13%	0.05%	0.03%	0.01%
0.48%	0.24%	0.12%	0.05%	0.02%	0.01%
0.48%	0.24%	0.12%	0.05%	0.02%	0.01%
0.35%	0.18%	0.09%	0.04%	0.02%	0.01%
0.52%	0.46%	0.38%	0.27%	0.21%	0.18%
0.10%	0.05%	0.02%	0.01%	0.00%	0.00%

are excluded. The data is based on publicly available charging structure information, with some details verified in conversations with platforms.

This table assumes you only hold investment trusts on the platform. A separate table on the website shows how the figure varies if you also hold open-ended funds on the platform. Their platform charges are generally higher, though only for larger portfolios (£50,000 or more). Bear in mind however that charges are not the sole, or even the most important, criterion for choosing a platform. The quality of the service – the range of options, the quality of the research and how smoothly and efficiently the platform works – are every bit as relevant. ∎

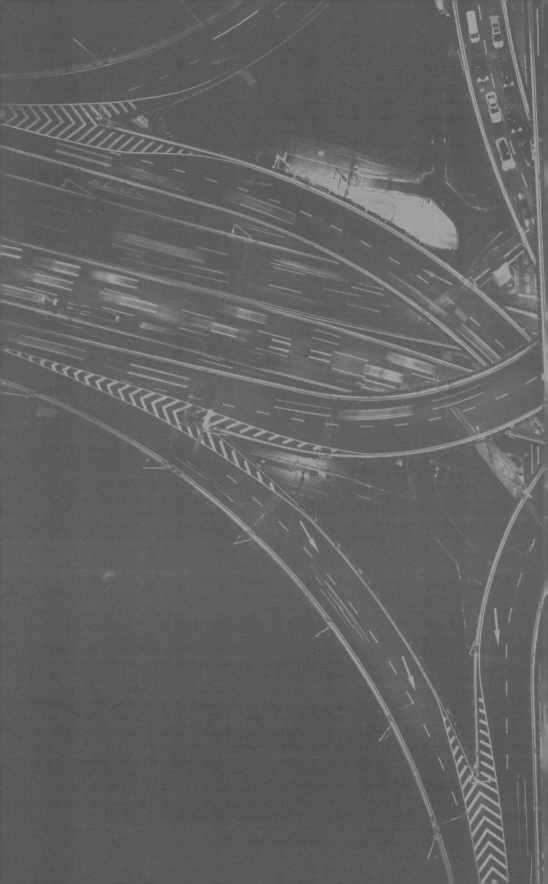

PARTNERS

About abrdn

- abrdn is a global investment company that helps clients and customers plan, save and invest for their future.

- abrdn manages and administers £508bn of assets for clients, and has over 1 million shareholders. (Figures as at 30 June 2022.)

- Enabling our clients to be better investors drives everything we do. Our business is structured around three vectors – Investments, Adviser and Personal – focused on their changing needs.

- Our investments solutions are built on the strength of our insight – generated from wide-ranging research, worldwide investment expertise and local market knowledge.

- Our teams collaborate across regions, asset classes and specialisms, connecting diverse perspectives, working with clients to identify investment opportunities that suit their needs.

- Our Investments vector manages £386bn on behalf of our clients (as at 30 June 2022) with support and expertise from 800 investment professionals across 30 locations.

For more information on the range of investment trusts we offer:

invtrusts.co.uk

abrdn.com

The value of investments and the income from them can go down as well as up and investors may get back less than the amount invested.

Investing for Generations

Established in 1888, the Company's purpose is to grow shareholders' wealth by investing in global equities.

We aim to outperform our benchmark over the long term, while increasing dividends every year.

To achieve this investment objective, we use a multi-manager approach that blends the highest conviction ideas of a team of complementary stock-pickers.

The stock-pickers are chosen by our investment manager, Willis Towers Watson (WTW), a leading global investment firm specialising in advising and managing money for some of the world's largest institutional investors, such as pension funds and sovereign wealth funds.

WTW instructs their top-rated stock-pickers to select 10–20 of their highest-conviction ideas from across global equity markets that offer the best return potential.

The outcome of this investment process is a portfolio of around 200 stocks that is:

- differentiated from the benchmark to increase its outperformance potential,
- diversified by manager, sector, country and investment style to reduce risk and volatility.

Our Philosophy: Returns Driven by Stock Selection, Not Market Timing

We believe balancing return and risk in this way makes Alliance Trust an ideal core global equity holding for investors' portfolios.

The investment strategy's performance is designed to be driven by stock selection, not country, industry, or style biases. We believe that growth in the fundamentals of businesses, such as sales revenues, profit margins and cash flows, drive share prices in the long run.

Why Invest in Alliance Trust?

1. High-conviction stock-picking to maximize potential returns.

2. Multi-manager approach to control risk.

3. Exclusive access to best-in-class managers' customized stock selections.

4. Fifty-five-year track record of dividend growth.

5. Responsibly managed, integrating ESG considerations into manager and stock-selection processes to help manage risk and deliver better returns.

6. Competitive costs – ongoing charges ratio of 0.60% in 2021.

About Allianz Global Investors

Allianz Global Investors is one of the world's leading active investment managers. Understanding our clients' needs in order to act to their best advantage is embedded in our business, using our insightfulness to partner with clients and to drive performance.

Allianz Global Investors works for many clients around the world. From pension funds, large and small, to blue-chip multinationals; from charitable foundations to families, individuals and their advisers. We have created a business that enables us to meet the demands of our clients on a local basis and that empowers our investment managers to focus on achieving strong and consistent investment results.

Allianz Global Investors and its predecessors have been managing investment trusts since 1889, providing investors with access to investment opportunities around the world. Each trust is a company listed and traded on the London Stock Exchange that has its own independent board of directors whose duty it is to look after your interests as an investor.

Established in 1889, The Merchants Trust PLC has, throughout its history, provided shareholders with an opportunity to benefit from investment in a diversified portfolio of leading companies with strong balance sheets and the potential to pay attractive dividends. Merchants aims to provide its investors with an efficient, competitive and cost-effective way to achieve an above average level of income and income growth together with long-term capital growth through a policy of investing mainly in higher yielding large UK companies.

The Brunner Investment Trust PLC aims to provide growth in capital and dividends over the long term by seeking out the world's most exciting growth opportunities. We believe that it's the quality of the company that matters, not its location – so through Brunner, investors can access a spread of high-quality growth companies operating in different sectors and countries in a single portfolio. The Trust favours large, well-financed businesses with global reach, pricing power and brand strength.

Allianz Technology Trust invests in a diversified, but focused, portfolio of companies that use technology in an innovative way to gain a competitive advantage. Particular emphasis is placed on companies that are addressing major growth trends with innovation that replaces existing technology or radically changes products and services and the way in which they are supplied to customers. The Manager aims to invest in the most attractive technology shares globally, seeking to identify the leading companies in emerging technology growth sub-sectors.

Independent Global Investment Managers

Baillie Gifford is privately and wholly owned by its partners. This is the crucial underpinning of our approach: we have no short-term commercial imperatives and no outside shareholders to distract us. We can simply do what's right for clients, and that's what has sustained our business since 1908.

We are the largest manager of investment trusts in the UK with a range of 13 trusts. We have an extensive range of OEIC sub-funds and manage investments globally for pension funds, institutions and charities.

Some see the collective failure of active management as an argument to embrace passive. We see it as an opportunity to redefine our original purpose of deploying clients' capital into tangible, returns-generating activities. And we believe that redefinition is "actual investment".

Actual investment is not easy in our world of 24-hour news, where complexity and noise is confused with rational judgement. It requires the resolve to focus only on what really matters, to think independently and to maintain a long-term perspective. It requires a willingness to be different, to accept uncertainty and the possibility of being wrong. Most of all, it requires a rejection of the now conventional wisdom that has led our industry astray: investment management is not about processing power, trading and speed. It is about imagination and creativity, and working constructively on behalf of our clients with inspiring individuals and companies who have greater ideas than our own.

The best investment ideas spring from thinking about future possibilities, not short-term probabilities. Our research covers the globe and we set no barriers to the imagination of our investors, encouraging fresh perspectives and the use of diverse sources of information.

We believe our approach to investing not only best delivers good outcomes for clients, but it also helps to develop great companies that provide for the needs and wants of people, thereby benefiting society as a whole. Investing responsibly for the long term is not counter to outperforming for clients, it's intrinsic to it.

All investment strategies have the potential for profit and loss, your or your clients' capital may be at risk. Past performance is not a guide to future returns.

BlackRock.

About BlackRock

BlackRock's purpose is to help more and more people experience financial well-being. As a fiduciary to investors and a leading provider of financial technology, we help millions of people build savings that serve them throughout their lives by making investing easier and more affordable. We can help you chart a path to financial health through a range of products, including Investment Trusts.

So, whether you're looking for income, growth or both, our experienced team has a range of nine investment trusts to suit your needs.

About BlackRock World Mining Trust plc

Capital at risk. The value of investments and the income from them can fall as well as rise and are not guaranteed. Investors may not get back the amount originally invested.

Energy and natural resources are crucial elements in economic growth across the world. This creates long-term structural drivers for the world mining sector. It is also dynamic, with the shift towards de-carbonisation bringing new opportunities, including demand for infrastructure in both emerging and developed economies.

The BlackRock World Mining Trust (BRWM) is a concentrated high conviction portfolio, providing targeted exposure to mining and metals companies globally. BRWM is a 'one-stop shop' for investors looking for exposure to the sector. The trust is actively managed across commodities, regions and themes, and will include exposure to base metals, precious metals and bulk commodities such as iron ore.

The trust is managed by BlackRock's specialist team, led by Evy Hambro, alongside Olivia Markham, as co-manager. It is one of the most experienced teams operating within the sector. BlackRock's Sectors and Thematics team is one of the largest investors in natural resources. The team has the resources to undertake extensive, proprietary, on-the-ground research to get to know the management of the companies in which they invest.

In addition to the long-term structural drivers for the sector, mining and metals groups have exercised strong discipline on their cost structure and capital expenditure programmes in recent years. Constrained supply and structural demand created by the energy transition, the growth of economic super-powers such as China and India, plus ongoing demand from resource intensive economies such as the US, has pushed commodity prices higher. This has resulted in improved corporate balance sheets, profitability and dividend pay-outs.

This means BRWM also has appeal for investors seeking an income from their portfolio. It offers an attractive dividend yield and draws income from a number of royalty and debenture investments. This helps diversify and stabilise the long-term payouts to investors.

 For more information visit
blackrock.com/uk/brwm

Risk Warnings

Capital at risk: *The value of investments and the income from them can fall as well as rise and are not guaranteed. Investors may not get back the amount originally invested.*

Past performance is not a reliable indicator of current or future results and should not be the sole factor of consideration when selecting a product or strategy.

Changes in the rates of exchange between currencies may cause the value of investments to diminish or increase. Fluctuation may be particularly marked in the case of a higher volatility fund and the value of an investment may fall suddenly and substantially. Levels and basis of taxation may change from time to time.

BlackRock World Mining Trust plc

Exchange rate risk: *The return of your investment may increase or decrease as a result of currency fluctuations.*

Emerging markets risk: *Emerging market investments are usually associated with higher investment risk than developed market investments. Therefore, the value of these investments may be unpredictable and subject to greater variation.*

Gold/mining risk: *Mining shares typically experience above average volatility when compared to other investments. Trends which occur within the general equity market may not be mirrored within mining securities.*

Gearing risk: *Investment strategies, such as borrowing, used by the Trust can result in even larger losses suffered when the value of the underlying investments fall.*

Important Information

About Fidelity International

Fidelity International provides world-class investment solutions and retirement expertise to institutions, individuals and their advisers – to help our clients build better futures for themselves and generations to come.

As a private company we think generationally and invest for the long term. Helping clients to save for retirement and other long-term investing objectives has been at the core of our business for over 50 years.

We are responsible for total client assets of £499.3bn from over 2.8 million clients across the UK, Continental Europe and Asia Pacific.

Our UK Investment Trust Business

Fidelity has over 28 years' experience managing investment companies, and manages over £4.9bn in assets across six investment trusts. These are all focused on equity growth strategies.

As a major platform distributor, Fidelity is able to offer its own investment trusts and those managed by third parties to professional investors and retail investors alike through a range of different product wrappers. Fidelity also promotes its range of trusts directly to institutions and wealth managers through its highly experienced in-house sales teams.

We offer our own investment solutions and access to those of others, and deliver services relating to investing; for individual investors and their advisers we provide guidance to help them invest in a simple and cost-effective way.

For institutions including pension funds, banks and insurance companies we offer tailored investment solutions and full-service asset management outsourcing. And for employers we provide workplace pension administration services on top, or independently, of investment management.

Source for all data: FIL International, 30 June 2022

Schroders

About Us

As a global asset and wealth manager, Schroders delivers a broad range of investments designed to meet the diverse needs of institutions, intermediaries and individuals.

For over 200 years we have built principled partnerships with our clients, putting them at the centre of everything we do. They trust us to deliver sustainable returns through times of economic prosperity and of uncertainty.

We are a global business, managed locally. Our international presence supports us in understanding the needs of our clients and delivering them the right expertise from across the business.

As an active investment manager we believe that we have an important role to play in driving better outcomes for our clients and society as a whole. We bring together people and data to identify the trends that will shape the prosperity of individuals, businesses and future generations.

Schroders Investment Trusts

Schroders has been managing investment trusts since 1924 and has established a strong reputation. Our specialist teams draw on Schroders' extensive investment resources, combining global insights with local market knowledge.

We offer a range of investment trusts, focusing on the UK, Asia, Real Estate and Private Equity. With clearly defined investment strategies, they help investors meet different financial objectives.

Find out more: **www.schroders.com/investmenttrusts**

Please remember that the value of investments and the income from them may go down as well as up and investors may not get back the amounts originally invested.

Issued by Schroder Unit Trusts Limited, 1 London Wall Place, London EC2Y 5AU. Registered Number 4191730 England. Authorised and regulated by the Financial Conduct Authority.